WEST GERMANY

The Politics of Democratic Corporatism

M. DONALD HANCOCK

Vanderbilt University

CHATHAM HOUSE PUBLISHERS, INC.
Chatham, New Jersey

WEST GERMANY
The Politics of Democratic Corporatism

CHATHAM HOUSE PUBLISHERS, INC.
Post Office Box One
Chatham, New Jersey 07928

PUBLISHER: Edward Artinian
ILLUSTRATIONS: Adrienne Shubert
COVER DESIGN: Antler & Baldwin
COMPOSITION: Chatham Composer
PRINTING AND BINDING: Color-Art, Inc.

LIBRARY OF CONGRESS CATALOGING-IN-PUBLICATION DATA

Hancock, M. Donald
    West Germany : the politics of democratic corporatism / M. Donald
    Hancock.
       p. cm.
    Bibliography: p.
    Includes index.
    ISBN 0-934540-30-6 : $12.95
    1. Germany (West)--Politics and government. 2. Corporate state-
-Germany (West)   I. Title
    DD258.75.H36 1989
    320.943--dc 19   88-13833
                                                               CIP

Manufactured in the United States of America
10   9   8   7   6   5   4   3   2   1

Contents

Preface

This study of German politics is a product of a long-term personal and professional encounter with the requisites and prospects of German democracy. In the course of research, lectures, seminars, and extensive conversations with friends in both Europe and North America, I have sought to comprehend Germany's turbulent past, its ever-changing present, and its uncertain future. My ultimate conclusion is that the Bonn regime constitutes both continuity and a discernible break with historical political tendencies. Therein lies the qualified promise of West Germany as a model of relatively stable political, economic, and social change.

I am grateful to a number of friends and colleagues for their intellectual stimulation, insights, and encouragement. Among them are Dankwart Rustow, Karl Dietrich Bracher, Hans-Helmuth Knütter, Peter H. Merkl, Erhard and Heidrun Kehlen, Dietmar and Ingrid Geest, Manfred and Heike Schreiner, Lucian and Ingrid Kern, Heribert and Marianne Schatz, Gerd and Elisabeth Fork, Gisela and Klaus Siebel, Walter Wetzel, Gaines Post, Russell Dalton, Rudolf Wildenmann, Hans-Adolf Jacobsen, Dena A. Gustafsson, Robert D. King, Charles Delzell, Erwin Scheuch, and the late Otto Kirchheimer and Peter Christian Ludz. I am especially thankful to members of my family—Kay, Erik, and Kendra—for their support and patience.

Thanks, too, to the German Academic Exchange Service (DAAD), the Vanderbilt University Research Council, the Earhart Foundation, the German Information Center, the Bundespresseamt, and colleagues and students at Vanderbilt University, The University of Texas at Austin, Columbia University, Bielefeld, Mannheim, and Regensburg.

For my daughter
KENDRA

Introduction: West Germany in Comparative Perspective

For both domestic and comparative reasons, Germany is a compelling study of political change. Since the middle of the nineteenth century, Germany has experienced two abortive popular revolutions and four sweeping transformations initiated from above. Twice, German regimes have launched imperialistic wars, thereby profoundly altering the course of twentieth-century European and world affairs. Sharply contrasting leadership groups have exercised executive power during Germany's recurrent political upheavals. They have ranged from Prussian aristocrats during the Imperial period to the *Vernunftrepublikaner* (republicans of rational convenience rather than conviction) of the Weimar Republic, Nazi totalitarians in the 1930s and 1940s, Communist officials in the postwar German Democratic Republic in the East, and constitutional democrats in the Federal Republic in the West. Germany's historical discontinuities and political-military excesses amply justify continuing interest among scholars, journalists, and citizens in the perennial "German question."[1]

At the same time, postwar West Germany has experienced a marked transformation in comparison with previous German regimes. Politically, the Federal Republic is a far more stable system than its democratic Weimar antecedent. From the founding of the Federal Republic in 1949 through the mid-1980s, extremist movements on the left and right all but disappeared as three political parties—the Christian Democrats, the Social Democrats, and the Free Democrats—succeeded in establishing themselves as West Germany's dominant political forces. The simplification of the party system facilitated in turn both executive coherence and the orderly transfer of government power at regular intervals comparable to the long-established practice of democratic governance in the United States, Canada, and the United Kingdom. Even the entrance of the pro-environmentalist, antinuclear Greens into the West German parliament following the March 1983 election testifies more to the "health and vitality of the postwar democratic order"[2] than to an incipient erosion of public support for fundamental constitutional-political principles, as explained in chapters to come.

West Germany's economic performance has proven to be of equal significance. The much acclaimed "economic miracle" of the 1950s and 1960s has given way to erratic performance patterns in more recent years. Since the mid-1970s, Germany has experienced consequences of successive oil price "shocks" of 1973-74 and 1979-80 similar to those in other industrial nations: sluggish growth, increased inflation, high unemployment, and recurrent budgetary deficits. Yet, in international comparison, the Federal Republic has fared better on most of these counts than other advanced democracies. Between 1970 and 1980, West Germany's average annual rate of economic growth of 2.6 percent was less than that of both the United States and Canada (3.0 percent and 3.9 percent, respectively) but higher than that of the United Kingdom (1.9 percent) and Sweden (1.7 percent). Its average annual rate of inflation of 5.3 percent during the same period was significantly lower than the average of 9.4 percent among the 25 member nations of the Organization for Economic Cooperation and Development (OECD). With a per capita income of over $14,600 in 1986, West Germany ranked alongside the United States, Canada, and the Scandinavian countries—and ahead of France and Britain—as one of the world's wealthiest industrial democracies. Only with respect to unemployment levels did Germany fail to sustain its exemplary standards of the 1960s and 1970s. In contrast to the 1.2 annual average rate of unemployed workers from 1959 through 1978, the unemployment level in the Federal Republic gradually inched upward to more than 9 percent by the mid-1980s.

The combination of postwar political stability and relative economic success has earned for the Federal Republic international recognition as "the German Model" (*das Modell Deutschland*) of advanced industrial society. Celebrated by the Social Democrats during the 1976 parliamentary campaign and alternately praised and criticized by domestic and foreign scholars in the interim,[3] the concept of a "German model" of industrial democracy stands in marked contrast to other system abstractions—including the "Swedish model" of advanced welfare society, the "English sickness" (characterized by laggard economic performance compounded by recurrent labor unrest), and "Japan as Number One."

The purpose of this volume is to assess three fundamental aspects of the German model: (1) the underlying causes of West Germany's departure from the nation's historical record of political extremism and discontinuity; (2) the group, institutional, and cultural factors that account for contemporary patterns of policy making and system performance in the Federal Republic; and (3) the effects of domestic policy outcomes on West German society and its citizens. My thesis argument is that the institutional and performance characteristics of the German model constitute a distinctive form of postwar "democratic corporatism."

Corporatism is admittedly an ambiguous and controversial concept. Originally employed to describe decision-making linkages among autonomous "corporations" in late medieval Europe, the term was coopted by twentieth-century fascist rulers such as Italy's Benito Mussolini to justify all-encompassing policy coordination and societal domination by a single authoritarian party. In more recent decades, American and European scholars have applied the concept to assess various modes of interest group "intermediation" and/or participation in the policy-making process in the advanced industrial democracies of Western Europe and elsewhere.[4] Critics have responded by characterizing postwar corporatist policy-making arrangements as nefarious forms of interest group and government control of rank-and-file workers and other citizens.[5]

Corporatism has thus assumed both authoritarian and nonauthoritarian forms in diverse historical and contemporary settings. In this volume, I utilize "democratic corporatism" to mean the approximate equivalent of Gerhard Lehmbruch's notion of "liberal corporatism,"[6] an institutionalized arrangement whereby government officials, employer groups, organized labor, and other socioeconomic associations voluntarily participate in making (and in some cases implementing) economic and social policies. Democratic corporatist policy-making arrangements exist in a number of West European countries, notably Austria, Sweden, Norway, and Denmark. Democratic corporatism is distinctive in the Federal Republic primarily for two reasons: (1) The national government, rather than organized interest groups (as in Scandinavia), plays the central role in initiating major policy decisions; and (2) corporatist linkages have varied over time with respect to their degree of formality versus informality in the national decision-making process.

Knowledge about Germany's historical discontinuities and its postwar institutional and policy-making transformation is essential for understanding the Federal Republic's present-day role as one of the Atlantic Community's most important political and economic partners. West Germany is not only one of the world's most prosperous nations; it is also, with France and the United Kingdom, one of the principal actors within the European Community (the Common Market). West Germany's efficient and well-equipped Bundeswehr is the strongest European component of the North Atlantic Treaty Organization (NATO) and thereby constitutes a major factor in the strategic balance of forces between West and East.

For multiple political, economic, and foreign policy reasons, then, the Federal Republic of Germany commands serious attention by students of comparative politics, enlightened citizens, and national policy makers. It is indeed crucial to know why *Bonn ist doch nicht Weimar* (Bonn is not Weimar after all)[7] and to acknowledge the strengths and weaknesses of the current political regime.

Notes

1. A classical liberal view of the "German question" is presented in Ralf Dahrendorf, *Society and Democracy in Germany* (Garden City, N.Y.: Doubleday, 1967).

2. David P. Conradt, "Changing German Political Culture," in *The Civic Culture Revisited*, ed. Gabriel A. Almond and Sidney Verba (Boston: Little, Brown, 1980), 265.

3. Various American and West German scholars assess facets of the "German model" in Andrei S. Markovits, ed., *The Political Economy of West Germany: Modell Deutschland* (New York: Praeger, 1982).

4. Excellent collections of original and reprinted essays on postwar variants of corporatism can be found in Philippe C. Schmitter and Gerhard Lehmbruch, eds., *Trends toward Corporatist Intermediation* (Beverly Hills, Calif.: Sage, 1979); Lehmbruch and Schmitter, eds., *Patterns of Corporatist Policy-Making* (Beverly Hills, Calif.: Sage, 1982); and Ulrich von Alemann and Rolf G. Heinze, eds., *Verbände und Staat: Vom Pluralismus zum Korporatismus: Analysen, Positionen, Dokumente* (Opladen: Westdeutscher Verlag, 1979). Another good overview of the corporatist literature is Reginald J. Harrison, *Pluralism and Corporatism: The Political Evolution of Modern Democracies* (London: Allen & Unwin, 1980).

5. Leo Panitch, "Recent Theorizations of Corporatism: Reflections on a Growth Industry," *British Journal of Sociology* 31, no. 2 (1980): 161-87.

6. In distinguishing between "liberal" and "authoritarian" corporatism, Lehmbruch emphasizes that the " 'new corporatism' of Western and Northern Europe has remained embedded in a system of liberal constitutional democracy, comprising institutional rules such as freedom of association." Lehmbruch, "Liberal Corporatism and Party Government," *Comparative Political Studies* 10 (1977): 91-126. Reprinted in Schmitter and Lehmbruch, *Trends toward Corporatist Intermediation*.

7. The originator of the concept "Bonn is not Weimar" is presumably Fritz Rene Allemann, author of *Bonn ist nicht Weimar* (Cologne: Kipenheuer & Witsch, 1956). More recently, Charles Maier has emphasized historical continuities between the two systems in his chapter, *"Bonn ist doch Weimar:* Informal Reflections on the Historical Legacy of the Federal Republic," in Markovits, *Political Economy of Germany,* 188-98. Even Maier, however, concedes that fundamental contrasts exist between the two regimes. That is my contention as well.

1. Modernity Gone Awry: Political Discontinuity and National Division

From the perspective of the late twentieth century, 7 May 1945 stands out as modern Germany's most important historical watershed. On that date the High Command of the German Wehrmacht unconditionally surrendered to the Western Allies in a spartan ceremony at Rheims, France.[1] Thus the totalitarian regime of Adolf Hitler's "Thousand Year Reich" came to an ignominious end, its war machine shattered on both the Eastern and Western fronts and its cities in rubble. With the Reich's capitulation and the death or arrest of most of its former leaders, the military forces of the United States, Great Britain, France, and the Soviet Union moved into their respective zones of occupation to begin their joint administration of the prostrate nation.

The capitulation by no means meant, as the British historian A.J.P. Taylor initially prophesized, that "German history had run its course."[2] Germany remained at the geographical crossroads of Central Europe, its material resources and remaining industry still with extraordinary economic potential. Despite staggering wartime losses, Germany retained a population of over 70 million citizens. Most adult Germans were highly literate, disciplined, and technologically skilled—thereby possessing the requisite qualities of economic and social modernity.

Nevertheless, the piercing silence of defeat—following 12 tumultuous years of Nazi dictatorship and a massive war effort—signaled the abrupt beginning of an uncertain political future for the Germans. A few political activists dared to hope that the end of hostilities would mark the emergence of a peaceful and democratic Germany. Many feared a vengeful occupation in retaliation for Hitler's brutal aggression. Most seemed too dazed to care.

How had it happened? Not only Hitler's rise to power in 1933 and his barbarization, first of Germany, and later of much of Europe—but also the historical pattern of instability in German politics that had preceded National Socialism? Equally important, what lessons would the occupation powers and the Germans themselves draw from such historical queries in seeking to prevent the future resurgence of German militarism and imperialism? These questions were hardly academic in the formative months after May 1945, for contrasting responses to them proved decisive in determining the postwar course of German political development.

The Quest for National Unity

Unlike the English and the French, the Germans had failed to establish a unified national kingdom prior to the emergence of political liberalism and the first stirrings of industrialization. This historical omission was rooted in the inability of the titular emperors of the Holy Roman Empire (established in A.D. 962) to fashion a cohesive secular state through the centralization of executive authority at the expense of regional and local princes. The result was that political power remained highly decentralized among the rulers of hundreds of small kingdoms, principalities, duchies, and city-states.

The Reformation, symbolically proclaimed by Martin Luther in 1517, further accentuated Germany's political and territorial fragmentation. In part out of a genuine desire to reform religious practices associated with the Catholic church, and in part to advance their own political ambitions, a number of north German princes severed their ties with Rome. Recurrent conflict between defenders of the two faiths, culminating in the Thirty Years War of 1618-48, brought not only the physical destruction of much of Germany but also permanently sealed a north-south division between Protestants and Catholics.

Only with the rise of Prussia during the eighteenth century did Germany begin its hesitant march toward national unity under recognized central authority. Lacking national frontiers and possessing only two cities of note (Berlin in the center of Brandenburg Province and Königsberg on the Baltic coast), Prussia was a formless, largely Protestant kingdom that encompassed extensive forests, numerous lakes, and fertile agricultural tracts. Controlling most of its economic and political resources were the Junkers—aristocratic heirs of thirteenth-century Order of Teutonic Knights whose self-proclaimed task had been the colonization of east-central Europe. Imbued in most instances with a stern mixture of Protestant asceticism and feudal values of fealty and personal honor, the Junkers constituted a cohesive social class that governed paternalistically over Prussia's more numerous agricultural workers.

A succession of strong-willed rulers forged out of Prussia's limited resources one of Europe's most powerful states. Frederick William and his son, Frederick I—who was crowned the first king of Prussia in 1701—initiated far-reaching bureaucratic and military reforms in their efforts to increase Prussian security. Building on these measures to establish a well-equipped standing army led by a new professional officer corps, the second Prussian king, Frederick the Great

6

(1740-86), launched successful military campaigns against Austria and Poland. The result was that Prussia more than doubled its size by the end of the eighteenth century and emerged alongside Austria, Britain, France, and Russia as a major European power.

The French Revolution of 1789 and Napoleon's rise to power a decade later profoundly affected subsequent German political development. Following his defeat of Prussia and Austria, Napoleon dissolved the Holy Roman Empire in 1806 and created the Confederation of the Rhine as a buffer between France and the two largest German states. The Confederation did not survive Napoleon's own defeat in 1814, but French efforts to redraw political boundaries in west-central Europe were partially sanctioned when delegates to the Congress of Vienna (1814-15) agreed to reduce the number of German states to 38. At the same time, they created a loosely united German Confederation under Austrian leadership to replace the defunct Holy Roman Empire.

An important indirect consequence of the revolutionary events of 1789-1814 was the rise of a liberal movement in Germany. Its adherents were primarily youthful intellectuals inspired by French ideals of constitutionalism and nationalism to criticize traditional forms of political authority and the absence of national unity. The number of liberal dissidents steadily increased as a politically conscious middle class emerged out of Germany's incipient industrialization, urbanization, and expansion of secondary and higher education. Tension between the liberal reformers and the nation's autocratic ruling classes sparked revolutionary upheaval in 1848. The various German rulers hastily agreed to elections to a national constituent assembly.

Tragically, the liberals failed in their efforts to achieve German unity. By the time members of the National Assembly in Frankfurt decided to exclude Austria from the proposed federal Reich, Germany's monarchists had regained their courage. The Prussian king contemptuously rejected an offer from the National Assembly to assume the crown of a German Empire and ordered his troops to suppress liberal supporters of a national constitution. The result was a paralyzing blow to German liberalism from which it never fully recovered.

Following the liberals' defeat, Prussia reverted at first to a policy of unrelieved traditionalism. Continuing processes of industrialization and social mobilization gradually yielded a liberal majority in the Prussian parliament, but the absence of constitutional provisions for executive accountability effectively insulated the Prussian ruling class from democratizing inroads. Nonetheless, a conservative counterelite began to emerge during the 1850s whose spokesmen rejected the change-resistant rigidity of the Prussian establishment. Hardly liberal democrats, they nevertheless borrowed from the revolutionaries of 1848 the vision of a unified German Reich under Prussian leadership.

Perfectly exemplifying the new "national" conservative was a nonconformist Junker, born in modest family circumstances in 1815, named Otto von Bismarck. A friend of the king's brother, Wilhelm (prince of Prussia), Bismarck studied law in Berlin and Göttingen. Even as a student, Bismarck displayed the personality traits that were later to characterize his political career—stubborn determination, unpredictability, aloofness, and—when pressed by circumstances —brilliant performance.

As Prussian representative to the German Confederation from 1851 to 1859, Bismarck acquired an intense contempt for "Austria's airs as 'the presiding power' " and resolved to assert his full diplomatic powers to promote "the aggrandizement of Prussia" at Austria's expense.[3] This policy terrified many traditional Prussian conservatives, who maintained a romantic deference to Austria's executive role within the Confederation. Accordingly, Prince Wilhelm, who became regent in 1858, reassigned Bismarck as Prussian ambassador to Russia. But Wilhelm recognized in Bismarck a determined and skillful leader, and after his coronation as Prussian king in 1861 Wilhelm repeatedly summoned the rebellious Junker to Berlin for policy consultations. In 1862, in an effort to deal with a recalcitrant liberal majority in the Prussian parliament, Wilhelm appointed Bismarck minister-president and foreign minister.

Bismarck utilized his dual assignment, first, to resolve the parliamentary conflict with the liberals in favor of the monarchy, and, second, to launch an activist foreign policy. In the first of a series of bold diplomatic and military moves, he invited Austria in 1863 to join Prussia in a joint campaign against Denmark to force the Danes to relinquish sovereignty over the north German duchies of Schleswig and Holstein. Following Denmark's defeat and Prussian-Austrian occupation of the two duchies, Bismarck surreptitiously goaded the Austrians into war in 1866. He declared the German Confederation dissolved and, following Austria's decisive defeat, established a Prussian-dominated North German Confederation in its place. Only the kingdom of Bavaria and the duchies of Baden and Württemberg remained outside the new union.

Prussia's spectacular military successes of 1864 and 1866 not only dazzled Bismarck's domestic opponents but also provoked the deepening antipathy of neighboring France, governed since 1848 by Napoleon III. Fearful that the growth of Prussian power would diminish French influence in Europe, Napoleon declared war on Prussia in July 1870. The French move completed Bismarck's unification strategy. Immediately, the three south German kingdoms allied themselves with Prussia, and together their armies carried the battle through the heart of France to Paris itself. The Prussians and their German allies resoundingly defeated the French and surrounded the French capital. When the city's radical republican defenders capitulated in January 1871, Bismarck prevailed on the Bavarian king to urge Wilhelm to accept the crown of a unified German Reich. Somewhat reluctantly, Wilhelm agreed, and on 18 January 1871 he was crowned German emperor in the glittering halls of the former residence of French kings at Versailles.

The Imperial Reich

With the proclamation of the Imperial Reich, Germany achieved formal political unity under recognized national authority. As Dankwart Rustow notes, both of these conditions are essential for successful political modernization: the former "to lay the foundation for a secure sense of nationality," the latter to facilitate cooperation among citizens and the provision of essential public services.[4] Yet, for a combination of reasons, the Imperial system lacked the capacity to attain effective political modernity comparable to that in Britain or (after the turn of the century) the Scandinavian countries. As a result, Imperial Germany ultimately proved only a transitional regime.

A basic flaw of the new constitutional order was its highly authoritarian character. This feature was most clearly evident in the structure of executive authority. Bismarck rejected the concept of parliamentarism as it had evolved by then in Britain in favor of a dual executive that was wholly independent of representative institutions. Central political authority was vested in the German emperor (the kaiser), who possessed sweeping powers to appoint Cabinet officials, command the armed forces, make alliances, and declare war. In his dual role as king of Prussia, Kaiser Wilhelm simultaneously governed over internal Prussian affairs. The imperial chancellor and chancellor of Prussia (Bismarck), meanwhile, was responsible for the day-to-day supervision of domestic and foreign affairs. In both roles, the chancellor was appointed by the kaiser and was accountable to him alone. Together, the kaiser and the imperial chancellor thus easily dominated national politics.

Augmenting Imperial Germany's executive authoritarianism was Prussia's preponderant power in relation to the various smaller kingdoms, grand duchies, duchies, principalities, and "free cities" that made up the German Reich. Each of these units was represented on the basis of population in an upper house designated the Bundesrat. Membership in the Bundesrat varied from 1 seat allocated the smallest principalities to 17 seats for Prussia. This formula easily allowed Prussia the dominant voice in Imperial Germany's legislative process, as the consent of the Bundesrat was required for the passage of all bills.

Alongside the Bundesrat, an outwardly democratic legislative body existed in the form of a popularly elected lower house, the Reichstag, whose members were chosen on the basis of manhood suffrage. But the Reichstag's legal competence was severely restricted. Deputies were empowered to vote on tax bills and appropriations, but they were explicitly excluded from control over all-important issues of foreign policy and military affairs.

The sum of these institutional arrangements was a concentration of political power in the hands of Germany's new breed of conservative modernizers. Like their stoic forebears who had settled the agricultural plains and forests east of the Elbe River, members of the empire's political elite fervently believed in feudal virtues of service, loyalty, and paternalism. Moreover, they considered themselves a natural governing class. Accordingly, they rejected liberal demands for constitutional government on the British model, thereby denying political equality and participatory rights to the mass of Germany's citizens.

The institutionalized contradiction between a governing autocratic elite and Germany's powerless middle and lower classes was the principal factor preventing the Reich's transition to stable modernity. Economically and socially, Imperial Germany experienced rapid development. Workers employed in agriculture, forestry, and fishing still made up the largest occupational category in the early 1880s, but by 1907 industry had become the dominant economic sector. In combination with improved sanitation facilities and better health care, industrialization encouraged an increase in population from 41 million in 1871 to nearly 63 million by 1910. Industrialization and population growth were accompanied by continuing urbanization, with the percentage of Germans residing in metropolitan areas jumping from a minuscule 5.5 percent in 1871 to 23 percent by the turn of the century.

Politically, however, Imperial Germany became increasingly beset by domestic and external conflicts. A key measure of impending political discord was growing popular support for three opposition political parties: the Progressive Liberals, whose leaders criticized the autocratic structure of the Reich in the name of classical liberal demands for constitutionalism and individual freedom; the Center party, which was founded in 1870 to defend the social and political interests of the country's Catholic minority; and the Social Democratic party (SPD), which was established in 1875 to represent industrial workers.[5] Because all three parties espoused fundamental ideological alternatives to the Imperial system, Bismarck strove throughout his tenure as imperial chancellor to restrict their influence. He coerced, first, the Catholic Center party, and, later, the Social Democrats. At the same time, he introduced legislation during the 1880s to establish state-sponsored insurance programs for illness, industrial accidents, and retirement in a cunning but ultimately fruitless attempt to wean rank-and-file workers from the Social Democratic movement.

Despite these stick-and-carrot measures, antiregime forces continued to gain in popular support. As a group, the Progressives, the Center, and the Social

Democrats increased their combined popular support from 38 percent in 1871 to an absolute majority in 1881. By 1912, the Social Democrats alone amassed nearly 35 percent of the popular vote to become Germany's largest political party.

As long as Bismarck remained chancellor, his personal prestige and skillful conduct of public policy enabled him to contain the inherent contradictions within the Imperial political system. But after the death of Kaiser Wilhelm and the coronation of his grandson, Wilhelm II, in 1888, Bismarck's status became precarious. He and the young and headstrong new emperor repeatedly clashed over policy issues, resulting finally in Bismarck's dismissal in 1890. Well-meaning but lesser men followed him in office, thereby helping provoke international tensions that ultimately brought about the demise of the empire.

World War I and the First Republic

With the ascension to power of Wilhelm II, Imperial Germany entered a new phase of foreign policy belligerence. Romantically impressed by the earlier valor and colorful precision of the Prussian army, the new kaiser adopted a strident stance toward other European powers that personified a growing spirit of German militarism. Thus he abandoned what had been a defensive foreign policy under Bismarck in favor of a "new course" that aimed at securing Germany's status as a major world power. To that end, Wilhelm II encouraged the expansion of Germany's modest colonial empire to encompass far-flung African and Pacific possessions. The empire's imperialist aspirations led to an ambitious program of naval armament that greatly alarmed the British — until then, the supreme naval power in Europe — and thereby encouraged the formation of an anti-German coalition made up of Britain, France, and Russia.

Growing tension among the European powers erupted in World War I in August 1914. The war actually involved two struggles in one: (1) an Austrian attack against Serbia (now part of Yugoslavia) in retaliation for the assassination in Sarajevo of the Austrian crown prince by Serbian nationalists; (2) an effort by German nationalists to defeat France and Russia as a means to establish Imperial Germany as the dominant power in central Europe and thereby shore up its tenuous domestic status.[6] Hopes for an early victory were dashed as the Western campaign ground to a halt in northeastern France in a bitter war of attrition, stretching on for more than four dismal years of senseless bloodshed and grim acrimony on both sides.

As the conflict dragged on, a growing minority of Social Democrats began to oppose the war effort. By 1916, the SPD openly split over the issue. A group of radical dissidents who were expelled from the party for their refusal to support further war credits established the Independent Social Democratic party

(USPD) to denounce the war and demand domestic socialist reforms. The Left Socialist rebellion marked the beginning of a revolutionary upheaval against the Imperial Reich. Antiwar sentiment began to spread among members of parliament and the public at large. Opposition intensified following the resumption of unrestricted submarine warfare in February 1917 (a move that provoked the United States to enter the conflict on the side of Britain and France). Revolution in March 1917 in Russia and the Bolshevik coup d'etat in November exerted an electrifying effect among both critics and supporters of the war effort. Radicals took heart that Germany, too, was ripe for revolutionary change, while conservatives were stricken with terror at that very prospect.

Ironically, Germany's Military High Command proved the final catalyst prompting the regime's demise. When the arrival of American troops caused the collapse of a final offensive campaign on the Western Front during the summer of 1918, the commanding generals concluded that Germany could no longer win the war. Consequently they urged the kaiser to introduce a parliamentary form of government as a prelude to negotiating an armistice with the Anglo-American powers and France. As military conditions continued to worsen, the High Command then strongly intimated that Wilhelm II should abdicate. He did so on 9 November, and Friedrich Ebert, a prominent Social Democrat, became head of a new provisional government.

The news of the kaiser's abdication and a pending armistice with the Western powers triggered violently conflicting emotions among the Germans. Conservatives and moderates reacted with stunned disbelief, unable to comprehend the reality of Germany's military defeat, while left radicals (including members of a revolutionary faction known as the Spartacists) immediately launched plans to declare a socialist republic on the Soviet model. In a desperate gamble to wrest the political initiative from the would-be revolutionaries, the Social Democrats hastily proclaimed a republic. Two days later, on 11 November, Germany signed an armistice. World War I was over.

From Weimar to the Third Reich

Amid overwhelming centrifugal forces, the reform parties of the Imperial era strove valiantly to establish an effective democratic order. The conflict of 1914-18 had not only exposed the Imperial regime's fundamental contradiction between political autocracy and aspirations for democratic reform; it had also generated new ideological cleavages. Foremost among them was the appearance of new militant parties and action groups on the two extremes of the political spectrum. On the left, the Spartacists organized themselves in early January 1919 as the Communist party of Germany (KPD) and proclaimed their determination to overthrow the new republic in favor of a Soviet system. On the right, a number of nationalist antidemocratic groups appeared to denounce Germany's military defeat. Their spokesmen—among them, Adolf Hitler, a demagogic Austrian corporal who had served in the Bavarian army during World War I—attributed the empire's collapse variously to republican efforts to "stab Germany in the back" and an alleged Jewish conspiracy against the German state.

One of the first actions by the provisional government was to convene elections to a constituent assembly to draw up a new constitution. The results on 19 January 1919 revealed a dramatic electoral shift to the left. The Social Democrats emerged as the decisive victor with nearly 40 percent of the popular vote, the Independent Social Democrats won nearly 8 percent, and the Center and the Progressive Liberals (now called the Democrats) each scored nearly a fifth. In contrast, the former dominant parties during the Imperial era—the Conservatives (rechristened the National German People's party) and the National Liberals (renamed the German People's party)—received only 10 and 5 percent, respectively. None of the extremist parties won any seats.

To avoid the turmoil of continuing revolutionary ferment in Berlin, the constituent assembly met from early February through the end of July 1919 in the Saxon city of Weimar, which was the symbolic center of Germany's humanistic countertradition to Prussian militarism. The delegates elected Chancellor Ebert president of the new republic and entrusted day-to-day government operations to a coalition made up of the SPD, the Center, and the Democrats.

During their deliberations, assembly delegates confronted two issues of pressing importance: peace terms dictated by the Western Allies and the future institutional arrangements of the German state. The Allies presented their demands in May. They included the restoration of French sovereignty over Alsace-Lorraine, the temporary detachment of the industrialized Saar on Germany's western border with France, the transfer of portions of Prussia to the newly reconstituted state of Poland, a reduction in the size of the German army to 100,000 men, and Germany's obligation to provide an indeterminate sum in reparation payments to France, Belgium, and Britain. Nearly all delegates to the Weimar assembly denounced the Versailles *Diktat* as excessive, but in the face of an Allied threat to resume hostilities if the Germans did not sign the treaty, a majority reluctantly voted to accept its terms.

The new constitutional order proved significantly easier to resolve. In place of the former confederation of semisovereign states that had characterized the Imperial regime, the Weimar assembly approved a more centralized federal system based on the principle of popular sovereignty. Most legislative authority was vested in the Reichstag, whose members were elected on the dual basis of the right of both men and women to vote and proportional representation.

Executive authority was divided between a popularly elected Reich president and an appointed chancellor. The president was accorded the right to govern by emergency decree under Article 48 of the constitution if Germany's domestic order and security were threatened. He could also dissolve the Reichstag, call new elections, and appoint and dismiss the chancellor and other members of the Cabinet. Under normal circumstances, however, the government was to serve at the behest of a majority of the members of the Reichstag in accordance with prevailing principles of parliamentary government in Britain, France, and Scandinavia. Only in the absence of a working majority in the Reichstag could the president designate a chancellor at his own discretion.

The constitution was endorsed by an overwhelming majority of the members of the Weimar assembly and went into effect in mid-August when President Ebert, members of the three-party "Weimar coalition," and assembly delegates returned to Berlin to assume the affairs of government. As events proved, however, no amount of constitutional engineering could fully resolve Germany's massive political fragmentation. Admittedly the constitution seemed to enhance basic modernizing conditions of national unity, authority, and citizen equality. Nonetheless, the new political order was undermined from its inception by two fundamentally debilitating circumstances: (1) the absence of elite and mass allegiance to the Weimar system, and (2) successive domestic and foreign policy crises.

That extremists refused to accept the legitimacy of the Republic was painfully apparent during the initial stage of institutional consolidation. Even though the Social Democrats had emerged as the major beneficiary of the 1918 revolution, the SPD lacked sufficient popular support to undertake fundamental economic and social reforms. Moreover, the Social Democrats and their coalition partners were forced to rely on the German army to maintain public order. As a result, the SPD confronted simultaneous opposition from socialist purists on the left and both unrepentant monarchists and the new racist, antidemocratic parties on the right.

Political activists on the two extremes sought repeatedly to overthrow the Republic during its early years: the Communists staged armed uprisings in a number of states, rightists undertook an abortive military coup against the government in Berlin in 1920, and in 1923 Hitler—by then the leader of a small but vocal nationalist splinter group known as the National Socialist German Workers party (NSDAP)—attempted a similar *Putsch* against the Bavarian government in Munich. In each instance, government officials were able to reassert their authority with the help of the army and civil servants, but the successive attacks on established authority clearly revealed widespread ideological hostility to the new regime.

Compounding the Weimar coalition's difficulties with ideological extremists was a succession of foreign and domestic policy crises. In 1921, the Western powers submitted their bill for reparations, which amounted to a then-staggering sum equivalent to $32 billion. To pay the initial installments on this sum, the German government resorted to heavy borrowing and increased circulation of paper money. These measures triggered in turn a devastating inflationary spiral. Private savings were wiped out, and earned incomes became practically worthless as the value of the German currency plummeted from an exchange rate of 4 marks to an American dollar to 25 *billion to one* by the beginning of 1923. The result was financial ruin for countless households.

Because runaway inflation disrupted Germany's reparation schedule, the French and Belgian governments ordered their troops to occupy the industrial Ruhr as a guarantee against future payments. This action brought Germany's joint economic and foreign policy crises to an abrupt head. Gustav Stresemann, one of the founding members of the German People's party, assumed the chancellorship as head of a broadly based coalition government. With Stresemann's rise to power, national politics shifted to the moderate right.

Stresemann proved a capable leader. He acted swiftly to curtail inflation and negotiated both a French-Belgian withdrawal from the Ruhr and a more equitable reparations repayment schedule. The result was economic stabilization by the end of 1924 and the beginning of an unprecedented period of prosperity.

Despite Stresemann's impressive policy achievements, Germany remained as politically divided as ever. National elections from June 1920 through the remainder of the decade revealed a continuing tendency toward polarization. After the SPD and the Independent Socialists reunited in 1924, the Communists increased their electoral strength to over 12 percent. Simultaneously, Hitler's NSDAP gained its first parliamentary mandates with 6 percent of the vote in the 1924 election, while conservative strength rebounded to more than 20 percent. Germany's shift toward the right was further underscored when Field Marshal Paul von Hindenburg was elected president in 1925.

The Weimar Republic's potential for political instability became suddenly pronounced when economic crisis once again swept the country—this time in the form of the international depression that began with the collapse of the New York stock market in late October 1929. The immediate result in Germany, as elsewhere, was a sharp jump in unemployment. By March 1930, more than 2.2 million persons were out of work. Two years later, the number had increased to over 6 million. Government failures to cope with the massive economic and social consequences of the depression brought about a political crisis from which the Republic never recovered.

The demise of the Weimar Republic began with the fall of an SPD-led coalition government in March 1930. President Hindenburg subsequently appointed a series of "presidential chancellors," whom he authorized to use emergency powers to implement antideflationary economic policies and maintain domestic order. Moreover, he ordered three special elections between 1930 and late 1932 in a fruitless effort to achieve Germany's recovery from the prevailing crisis. The results proved disastrous. The electoral strength of the NSDAP jumped from a minuscule 2.6 percent in 1928 to 18 percent in 1930 and 37 percent in 1932. Communist support likewise grew from nearly 11 percent in 1928 to 14 percent in 1932. With the exception of the Catholic-based Center party, all the traditional parties—including the Social Democrats, the Liberals, and the Conservatives—lost support to political extremes on the left and right.

In the light of Germany's growing electoral polarization and resulting political stalemate, President Hindenburg wearily agreed to a proposal by Conservative politicians to appoint a NSDAP-Conservative coalition in the hopes of restoring political stability. Thus, on 30 January 1933, Adolf Hitler assumed the reins of government. With this fateful step, the Weimar Republic gave way to the Third Reich, and Germany embarked on its dark passage to domestic tyranny and another world war.

Nazi Totalitarianism

The NSDAP's rise to power was a consequence of both Germany's tortured political-cultural history and Hitler's charismatic qualities.[7] The movement was born out of the anguish of military defeat in 1918 and sought to mobilize Germans from all socioeconomic backgrounds in a disciplined effort to transcend their historical dualisms in a new unity of state, nation, and race. Hitler brought to the original party nucleus a messianic determination to destroy the postwar democratic order. He exploited the so-called shame of Versailles, German fears of revolutionary socialism, the recurrent economic crises of the 1920s, and traitional forms of religious and cultural anti-Semitism to advance the National Socialists' claim to power. He promised the Germans everything the Weimar Republic allegedly failed to provide: decisive political leadership, the restoration of German honor, sustained economic growth, full employment, low interest rates, stable prices, domestic law and order, and above all national unity. Means to these ends included the creation of a "strong central power in the Reich," the transformation of Germany into a racially homogeneous "people's community," and the repudiation of the Versailles treaty.

Hitler's success in forging a powerful mass movement based on these principles lay in his unusual ability to command intense personal loyalty. His charisma was characterized by hypnotic intensity, carefully planned theatrics, flattery if appropriate, and threats when necessary. These qualities enabled him to allay the doubts of skeptical critics and, in time, to arouse the loyalty of millions of enthusiastic followers.

Nothing in the Nazis' ideology, leadership, or electoral support preordained their triumph in 1933. Undeniably, defensive class interests played a role in Hitler's successful bid for the chancellorship. Frightened lower-middle-class voters (including many farmers and urban dwellers who felt abandoned by the liberal and conservative parties) contributed most of the groundswell in NSDAP support from July 1930 onward. During this period Hitler also attracted considerable financial contributions from apprehensive Ruhr industrialists who saw in him a tactical ally in their struggle to contain Communist influence. Yet the very rapidity of the Nazi electoral advance between 1928 and 1932 (as well as an abrupt decline in their support in a special election held in November 1932) indicates that the movement was basically ephemeral. In short, the growth of Nazi strength was the product of Germany's economic crisis and the absence of sufficient political resolve and imagination on the part of the Weimar Republic's governing elite. Hitler and his party might well have suffered the historical irrelevance of their racist-nationalist counterparts in Britain and Scandinavia if republican leaders had been able to devise an effective program to combat the domestic effects of the depression or, failing that, at least to unite in defense of the Weimar system. They did neither, and consequently the NSDAP's vision of a national revolution became increasingly plausible to nationalist conspirators and a cynical electorate alike.

Once in office, Hitler consolidated power in the hands of his party through a comprehensive program of political, economic, and finally ethnic *Gleichschaltung* (literally, "coordination"). He dissolved the Reichstag and ordered new elections in March 1933. Through a massive propaganda effort and the forceful intimidation of the Communist and Social Democratic parties, the NSDAP succeeded in increasing its share of the popular vote to nearly 44 percent. Claiming a technical parliamentary majority after banning the KPD for allegedly engaging an arsonist to burn down the Reichstag building in the heart of Berlin, Hitler petitioned parliament for a grant of extraordinary authority to deal with Germany's "national emergency." A majority meekly complied, with only the Social Democrats voting against the so-called Enabling Act of 23 March. By transferring all legislative powers to the Cabinet, this measure in effect made Hitler dictator. A year later Hitler achieved the ultimate concentration of personal power when Hindenburg's death enabled him to unite the offices of the chancellorship and the presidency to become Germany's all-powerful Führer (leader).

The National Socialists rapidly institutionalized a totalitarian regime. By the end of 1933, they had dissolved all political parties except for the NSDAP and had proclaimed the "insoluble" merger of party and state. Simultaneously, Hitler neutralized the meager influence of the conservatives in his Cabinet, eventually replacing them with trusted party aides. Accompanying these steps were the replacement of previously elected and appointed state officials with loyal Nazis and the subordination of the various states to central Reich authority.

Parallel processes of economic and social *Gleichschaltung* included the dissolution of trade unions, the subordination of private capital to central state planning, and the extension of National Socialist controls over the mass media and the educational system. Discriminatory racial policies began with the promulgation of the infamous "Nürnberg laws" of September 1935, which stripped Jews of their legal and political rights. A gradual escalation of official harassment against the 500,000 Jews in Germany (who made up less than 1 percent of the population) erupted in a violent pogrom during the night of 9-10 November 1938 in which numerous synagogues were destroyed and 91 people were murdered. Henceforth, the regime implemented an increasingly blatant policy of official anti-Semitism that culminated in the notorious wartime "final solution." Ultimately, some 6 million European Jews and regime opponents died, either through illness or execution, in Nazi-administered concentration camps.

The domestic effects of the Nazi takeover were highly mixed. Politically, Germany became "united" as never before under clearly recognized national authority. Yet citizen equality was negated through the Nazis' suppression of parliamentarism, political parties, and individual rights. Socially, Nazi efforts to eliminate all sources of potential opposition had the important consequence of destroying the institutionalized power of the traditional aristocracy. Henceforth, Germany's monarchists and heirs to the Junker tradition of paternalistic rule were never again to play a decisive role in national affairs.[8] In terms of its social performance, the Third Reich maintained previously attained levels of mass literacy and technical competence. But public education and intellectual life suffered seriously. The number of secondary and university students declined in comparison with the Weimar period, and the quality of higher education, research, and culture suffered dramatically as a result of the party's imposition of narrow standards of ideological orthodoxy and the emigration or arrest of most leading intellectuals.

The National Socialists achieved their greatest success in the economic sphere. Within three years after Hitler's rise to power, Germany had recovered from the ravaging effects of the depression. Restored productivity brought an end to mass unemployment and falling prices for industrial goods and farm products. Without question, Germany's economic recovery was attributed in part to global factors, including the gradual resumption of international trade from the mid-1930s onward. Recovery was also stimulated by the central government's expanded powers to direct manpower allocation, investments, prices, and incomes.

World War II and the Occupation

With the attainment of totalitarian political and social controls and renewed economic growth, Hitler turned his sights to foreign policy. In quick order, he implemented a calculated effort to extend Nazi Germany's external influence and boundaries. The Saar rejoined the Reich in 1935. A year later, Hitler remilitarized the Rhineland in flagrant violation of the Versailles treaty. Simultaneously, he proclaimed a "natural alliance" between Germany and fascist Italy against the Western democracies. In 1938, Germany annexed Austria and, with British and French acquiesence, absorbed most of Czechoslovakia. Encouraged by Hitler's success, the National Socialists promptly launched a new propaganda campaign aimed at the recovery of the strip of territory (the Polish Corridor) between West and East Prussia that had been detached from Germany after World War I. This time, however, Britain and France balked at the Nazi demand.

Determined to restore Germany's eastern boundary by whatever means, Hitler stunned the Western world by negotiating a 10-year neutrality and nonaggression pact with the Soviet Union in August 1939. This agreement, which contained a secret protocol providing for the division of Poland between Germany and Russia, opened the way to military conflict in Europe. Hitler knew that the British and the French would respond to a German attack on Poland with a declaration of war, but there was little that either country could do to assist the Poles in the face of Stalin's pledge to refrain from war with the Third Reich. Thus, Hitler ordered his troops to cross the German-Polish border on 1 September.

The resulting six years of total war, aerial bombardments of civilian populations, and mass exterminations belong to the most tragic in human history. The course of the war included Germany's and Russia's joint subjugation of Poland, a separate Russian attack on Finland, and Germany's breathtaking occupation of most of Western Europe in 1940. In June 1941 Hitler revealed the full extent of his imperialist ambitions when he launched a full-scale invasion of the Soviet Union. In response, the Soviets forged a military alliance with Britain and the United States. After two years of Nazi military advances into Eastern Europe, the Red Army dramatically turned the tide on the Eastern Front by halting the German offensive in January 1943 at Stalingrad. Simultaneously, the Anglo-American powers launched a massive counteroffensive against the Axis states in North Africa and Italy. In June 1944, Anglo-American troops staged the largest amphibious operation in history by crossing the English Channel to establish an Allied bridgehead on the northern coast of occupied France. Henceforth, it was only a matter of time until Germany would fall before the joint advance of American, British, French, and Russian forces.

The escalation of Germany's demand for living space into a global war transformed the historical "German question" into an international issue with high political, military, and economic stakes for all the major powers. No longer were the Germans free to pursue their historical quest for modernity on their own terms. Instead, Germany became increasingly an object of international politics. As a result, the underlying causes of German political instability and external aggression became of direct relevance for the wartime Allies. Their joint task from 1943 onward was to devise a suitable strategy to ensure that Germany would never again threaten world peace.

As the Allied armies began to press toward the German heartland, their civilian leaders initiated high-level consultations concerning a postwar political settlement in Europe. International security was uppermost in the policy calculations of American President Franklin Roosevelt, British Prime Minister Winston Churchill, and Soviet Premier Josef Stalin. Following a meeting with Churchill in January 1943, President Roosevelt announced that the Allies would seek Germany's unconditional surrender. When Roosevelt, Churchill, and Stalin met for the first time at a conference in Teheran in November 1943, the Allies agreed to the political and economic decentralization of Germany and the transfer of German territory east of the Oder River to the Soviet Union and Poland.

At a second Big Three summit meeting, which was held at Yalta in the Soviet Union in February 1945, the wartime leaders concurred on including France as a fourth occupation power. The principal objectives of the joint Allied occupation would include demilitarization, denazification, political and economic decentralization, and partial territorial dismemberment. Supervising the implementation of these measures would be a four-power Allied Control Council, which would be composed of the supreme military commanders of the various occupation zones and would be located in Berlin. The former German capital, located deep in the heart of the zone assigned the Soviet Union, would similarly be divided into four sectors for occupation purposes.

The Potsdam Conference: Consensus and Dissent

Following Hitler's suicide in a bunker beneath the rubble of the Reich Chancellery on 30 April 1945 and the High Command's capitulation a week later, the victorious Allies assumed sovereignty over the devastated Reich. To codify terms of the occupation regime, as well as consult about broader issues of war and peace, the new American President, Harry S. Truman, traveled to Germany in mid-July to confer with Soviet and British leaders. The Allied heads of government and their advisers convened on 17 July in the former garrison town of Potsdam on the western outskirts of Berlin in what proved to be the final Big Three summit conference.

When the wartime Allies affixed their signatures to the official communiqué summarizing the results of the Potsdam Conference on 2 August, they seemed to have reached a basic consensus on means to prevent future German aggression. Their joint response to Germany's historical record of external aggression and the rise of National Socialism involved a combination of punitive measures and positive reconstruction. In the former category, the Allies agreed to the following specific objectives of the occupation:

1. Beyond immediate steps to achieve German disarmament and demilitarization, "the elimination or control of all German industry that could be used for military production."

2. The destruction of the NSDAP "and its affiliated and supervised organizations. . . ."

3. The abolition of all "nazi laws which provided the basis of the Hitler regime or established discrimination on grounds of race, creed, or political opinion."

4. The punishment of war criminals "and those who have participated in planning or carrying out Nazi enterprises involving or resulting in atrocities or war crimes."

5. Control of German education in order "completely to eliminate Nazi militarist doctrines and to make possible the successful development of democratic ideas."

6. The reorganization of the judicial system "in accordance with the principles of democracy, of justice under law, and of equal rights for all citizens without distinction of race, nationality, or religion."[9]

In addition, the Potsdam communiqué called for (1) the elimination or control of Germany's economic war potential, and (2) the decentralization of the economic system through the elimination of "cartels, syndicates, trusts and other monopolistic arrangements. . . ."

At the same time, the Allies explicitly affirmed democratization as a positive strategy to enable the Germans to resolve their historical struggles over political authority and the rights of citizenship. As specific steps toward the piecemeal revival of German political activity, the Potsdam accord stipulated:

1. Local self-government shall be restored throughout Germany on democratic principles and in particular through elective councils as rapidly as is consistent with military security and the purposes of the military occupation.

2. All democratic parties with rights of assembly and of public discussion shall be allowed and encouraged throughout Germany.

3. Representative and elective principles shall be introduced into regional, provincial, and state (Land) administration as rapidly as may be justified by the successful application of these principles in local self-government.

Although the wartime Allies did not sanction the immediate creation of a central German government, they did concur that "certain essential German administrative departments, headed by State Secretaries, shall be established, particularly in the fields of finance, transport, communications, foreign trade and industry. Such departments will act under the direction of the Control Council (in Berlin)." They further confirmed that Germany would be treated as a single economic unit during the period of occupation and that occupation officials would pursue common economic policies within their respective zones.

Undermining the apparent East-West consensus on basic political and economic objectives of the occupation was intense disagreement concerning important security and economic issues affecting the Allies themselves: Germany's future eastern boundary and its postwar reparation obligations. In order to compensate Poland for the Soviet annexation of territory to the east, Stalin sought to draw Poland's new boundary with Germany as far west as possible, namely, along the Oder and Neisse rivers. Churchill objected that such a move was excessive and proposed instead that the boundary should be drawn along the length of the Oder River. For his part, President Truman declared that he was sympathetic to Polish claims to territorial compensation but that he opposed any unilateral reduction in German boundaries without prior consultation with the Western Allies.

Nearly as controversial was Stalin's simultaneous demand that Germany pay $10 billion in reparations to the Soviet Union. Of this amount, he suggested that 50 percent should be extracted within 2 years "by removal of national wealth" from Germany as a whole. The remainder would be paid in the form of annual deliveries in kind over a 10-year period. The United States responded that the Soviet plan was impractical.

Impatient to resolve both issues and conclude the conference, the American delegation suggested that the Polish boundary and reparation questions be considered jointly. After an intense exchange between Stalin and British officials about the legal status of the eastern territories, the three heads of government finally agreed to the maximum Polish claim to the entire region east of the Oder and Neisse rivers. President Truman and the British prime minister did so on the explicit condition that the transfer of German territory should be considered only temporary and that the final demarcation of the German-Polish border should await an eventual peace treaty. A parallel agreement on reparations marked an apparent retreat from the original Soviet position. Stalin declared that the Soviet Union would accept an American suggestion that reparation payments should be calculated in terms of a "statement of percentages" rather than a fixed dollar sum and that Russia could extract the bulk of reparations from its own zone of occupation.

Both decisions proved fateful for the future course of postwar German political development. British and American acceptance of the Oder-Neisse boundary accorded ex post facto sanction to unilateral action within the Soviet Union's sphere of military presence. In turn, Stalin's endorsement of the American formula for extracting reparations on a zonal basis marked a significant retreat from the formal Allied commitment to treat Germany as a single economic unit.

The Beginning of Divergence

The Potsdam Conference proved the final benchmark in international collaboration among the three major powers. Initially, the military commanders acted swiftly within the Allied Control Council in Berlin to establish central administrative procedures to plan and oversee quadripartite occupation measures. These included the liquidation of Nazi organizations and laws, demilitarization, the trial and punishment of prominent Nazi war criminals, the dismantling of industries for reparation purposes, and the reorganization of the German judicial and educational systems.

In addition, the occupation powers undertook a major move in July toward the construction of a posttotalitarian political system when they authorized the restoration of semiautonomous states (Länder) based on Germany's historical state boundaries. Soviet officials established 5 states in the east, while the Western Allies initially created 12. Most of the latter were based on earlier kingdoms and city-states such as Bavaria, Lower Saxony, Bremen, and Hamburg. Two, however, were new constructs, both carved out of former Prussian territory: North Rhine-Westphalia, a large populous state encompassing the Ruhr industrial base; and Rhineland-Pfalz, a more agrarian Land located on the west bank of the Rhine.

In a parallel but less coordinated step to restore political life, the four Allies sanctioned the revival of political parties, trade unions, and other voluntary associations. The Soviet Union acted first by licensing four "antifascist" parties in June 1945. They included the resurrected Communist party of Germany (KPD), the Social Democrats, a new Liberal Democratic party (LPD), and a new Christian Democratic Union (CDU). All four parties were subsequently established on a regional level in the three western zones as well, although at a somewhat erratic pace. A similar pattern characterized the revival of trade union and other group activities. Soviet officials sanctioned the forthright establishment of the Free German Federation of Trade Unions (FDGB) and a farmers' cooperative organization. In contrast, the Western Allies permitted workers, farmers, business associations, and professionals to organize in their own zones only on a decentralized and gradualist basis.

Despite initial Allied success in coordinating key elements of their occupation policies, zonal autonomy proved to be the fatal flaw in the Potsdam agreement. France was the first to thwart the accord. Apprehensive that the restoration of a national government could lead to the eventual resurgence of German military strength, French officials vetoed American efforts late in 1945 to establish central administrative departments. Similarly, the French military commander blocked other Allied proposals to permit the restoration of national political parties and trade unions. In each case, French officials justified their refusal on the grounds that the Allies should seek prior agreement on measures to prevent future German aggression. Among them were the detachment of the Ruhr and the incorporation of the Saar into the French economy.

These omissions proved of critical significance in the light of divergent Soviet and Western interpretations of the political and economic provisions of the Potsdam agreement. Pursuing a Marxist-inspired strategy to eliminate the economic basis of historical German authoritarianism, Soviet military administrators had authorized the expropriation of all banks within their zone and the establishment of new municipally owned ones as early as August 1945. The following month, the Saxon state government implemented a massive land reform in which 2 million hectares of land that had formerly belonged to the Junkers and other large landowners were distributed among 333,000 farmers. Under the authority of the Potsdam agreement to punish war criminals, the Soviet Military Administration then nationalized heavy industry, mines, and all property of the Reich government, the Prussian state, and the National Socialist party. These measures were endorsed in a popular referendum held in Saxony in June 1946 that subsequently served as the ideological justification for expropriating virtually all privately owned enterprises throughout the Soviet zone. To ensure that domestic political control over the new collective economic resources would remain safely in the hands of the orthodox Marxist-Leninists, the Soviets forced the merger of the east zonal KPD and SPD in April

1946 into a single Socialist Unity party (SED) under firm Communist domination.

In contrast to the sweeping economic and political reforms sponsored by Soviet occupation officials, the Western Allies pursued far less revolutionary objectives. Similar to the Soviets, they utilized the Potsdam accord as the legal basis for prosecuting Nazi war criminals and dismantling heavy and light industry that had been utilized for wartime production. In like manner, they recruited reliable nonfascist leaders to assume leadership positions in political parties, trade unions, industry, and state administrations. Beyond denazification, demilitarization, and economic and political decentralization, however, the Western occupation powers stopped short of sweeping industrial or land reform. Instead, their occupation policies were designed to eliminate Germany's economic war potential and maximize sociopolitical conditions of libertarian democracy.

The absence of common reform policies and central German administrative agencies accentuated the development of fundamental differences between the Soviet zone of occupation and the three western zones. As cold-war tensions deepened in response to multiple factors of East-West rivalry, sessions at the Allied Control Council in Berlin became more and more acrimonious. The Soviets renewed their wartime claim to $10 billion in reparation payments from Germany as a whole, which the United States promptly rejected, while the French continued to press their demands to detach the Ruhr and integrate the Saar into their own national economy.

When a four-power foreign ministers' conference held in 1946 in Paris failed to reconcile these policy differences, American officials concluded that the basic difficulty confronting the Allies was the absence of German economic unity. Accordingly, the United States offered to merge its zone of occupation with that of any of the other three. Both France and the Soviet Union balked, but Britain cautiously accepted the American offer in late July. Thus the stage was set for a series of policy moves that would mean the final repudiation of the Potsdam facade of four-power government.

The Founding of Separate Republics

The United States and Britain proceeded to negotiate a series of agreements during the fall of 1946 to establish bizonal agencies governing finance, agriculture, transportation, and communication. These arrangements were made in close consultation with German administrative officials in both zones and were formalized in a two-power agreement signed in December establishing "Bizonia."

The formation of Bizonia coincided with the revival of German political life throughout the divided nation. Statewide elections were held in June 1946 in the American zone to choose delegates to draft new state constitutions. French, British, and Soviet officials conducted local elections in September, and statewide elections followed in the Soviet zone in October. In each case new local and state government bodies were formed and assumed limited legislative and administrative powers. Hence, the Anglo-American move to merge occupation zones inevitably pointed toward the eventual transfer of political authority back to the Germans. The central question that confounded Allied policy councils at the beginning of 1947, then, was whether France and the Soviet Union would join in the restoration of German political unity or whether either or both would continue to withhold their cooperation.

A significant shift in American foreign policy during 1947 settled the issue. George C. Marshall, who became U.S. secretary of state in January, declared at a foreign ministers' meeting in Moscow that the United States intended to push toward "economic self-sufficiency (within Bizonia), no matter what the political and economic costs."[10] In a move obviously designed to mobilize French support for Anglo-American policies in Germany, Marshall simultaneously announced that the United States would endorse French claims to economic union with the Saar and would seek to establish international controls over coal and steel production in the Ruhr.

Underlying Marshall's simultaneous emphasis on German economic recovery and appeasement of France was the American realization that international cooperation with the Soviet Union was no longer possible under conditions of the escalating cold war. Accordingly, President Truman and his key foreign policy advisers had decided by the beginning of 1947 to promote general European recovery as a deterrent against perceived Soviet military and ideological threats to the North Atlantic region. To achieve this objective, American officials concluded that German productivity must be restored as quickly as possible. But for that to be feasible, the United States would have to secure French cooperation. This, then, was the reason for Secretary Marshall's conciliatory gestures toward France—as well as his dramatic invitation at Harvard University in June 1947 to extend American economic assistance to Europe to facilitate its postwar reconstruction. Through these multiple foreign policy initiatives, Marshall signaled American determination to promote the rehabilitation of Germany within a broader context of European recovery and cooperation.

The proclamation of the Marshall Aid program was accompanied by further measures to encourage German economic self-sufficiency. American and British officials authorized the creation of an Economic Council and an Executive Committee in Bizonia. In July 1947 the Anglo-American powers agreed to increase Bizonia's steel and coal production to the level that had prevailed in 1936. These moves encouraged the French to modify their own German policies, in part because the prospect of American economic assistance drastically diminished the necessity for France to exploit German resources for rebuilding its own economy. In addition, Anglo-American determination to strengthen Bizonia imposed perceptible limits on France's capacity to influence economic and political developments in Germany unless it agreed to coordinate policies with London and Washington.

In a secret meeting with the British and American foreign ministers in December 1947, the French foreign minister indicated that his government was willing to consider merging its zone with Bizonia. Subsequently, France was invited to participate in a tripartite conference on Germany the following month in London. The purpose of the meeting was to allow the three Western Allies an opportunity to discuss the full scope of German and European recovery. "It was in this indirect way," Roy Willis notes, "that the British, American, and French governments decided to hold what proved to be the most important conference on the future of Germany since the end of the war."[11]

In the significant absence of the Soviet Union, the Western powers conferred about Germany's fate with representatives of Belgium, the Netherlands, and Luxembourg from late February through early June 1948. Three crucial decisions emerged from the sessions that sealed Germany's division and, as an unexpected consequence, prepared the way for eventual economic integration within Western Europe:

1. The Western Allies agreed to the formation of a federal West German state that would encompass the American, British, and French zones. The three Western military commanders were thereby instructed to convene, in agreement with the ministers-president of the various states in the western zones, a constituent assembly whose mandate would be to draw up a written constitution for a "free and democratic" political system.

2. The occupation regime would be replaced by an Occupation Statute that would govern arrangements for achieving a trizonal fusion and would codify continued Allied restrictions on West German sovereignty.

3. The Allies would establish, in concert with the West Germans and the Benelux countries, an International Authority of the Ruhr to govern coal and industrial production in that region.

The military governors transmitted the instructions contained in the London Agreements to the ministers-president of the 12 West German states at the beginning of June 1948. Subsequently, a Parliamentary Council, made up of delegates elected by the various Land parliaments, convened on 1 September in Bonn to draw up a constitution for the new federal republic. In the crucial preliminary session, the delegates elected Konrad Adenauer—leader of the western branch of the postwar Christian Democratic Union (CDU)—to serve as the council's chairman.

The Allied initatives, coupled with countermoves by the Soviet Union, resulted in a rapid escalation of tension between East and West. On 20 March 1948 the Soviet military governor walked out of the Allied Control Council in Berlin, thereby bringing to an end the remaining semblance of four-power government in Germany. On 18 June the Western powers implemented a long-overdue currency reform in their zones to stimulate economic growth. The Soviet Union reacted by introducing a new "east mark" in their own zone that they sought to extend to all of Berlin. When the Western Allies introduced the west mark into their sectors of West Berlin, Soviet military officials imposed a blockade on access to the city by highway, train, and canal. The West, led by the United States, responded with an airlift of foodstuffs and essential supplies to maintain the Allied garrisons and the city's beleaguered population.

Soviet intentions in implementing the Berlin blockade were apparently aimed at blocking the establishment of a separate West German state. Through a combination of official denunciations of Western policy and the convocation of a "German People's Congress" in October 1948 in East Berlin to draft a social-ist-inspired constitution for a unified German state, Russian officials sought to advance their substitute vision of a centralized all-German government based on the economic and political principles of the Soviet zone. They finally aban-doned their efforts in the face of Allied determination to remain in the divided city and progress within the Parliamentary Council in Bonn toward drafting a constitution for the western zones. On 5 May 1949 the Soviet Union agreed to lift the blockade. Three days later, on 8 May, the Parliamentary Council formally adopted the Basic Law, or provisional constitution, establishing the legal-institutional framework for the Federal Republic of Germany.

Similar to the constitution of the Weimar Republic, the Basic Law provid-ed for a capitalist-libertarian system based on the dual principles of popular sovereignty and states' rights. Legislative power was vested in a popularly elected Bundestag and an appointive upper house designated the Bundesrat whose task was to represent the financial, territorial, and administrative interests of the various West German states. Highly conscious of the constitutional weaknesses of Germany's first experiment with parliamentary democracy, the framers of the Basic Law provided for a weak, indirectly elected federal president. They concentrated most executive authority in the hands of a federal chancellor who was to be elected by a majority vote of the Bundestag. They also drew heavily from the American precedent to establish an independent Federal Constitutional Court with sweeping powers of constitutional review.

After the Basic Law had won the approval of the Western Allies and the endorsement of all the West German Länder except Bavaria,[12] the Parliamentary Council proclaimed its official ratification on 23 May. West German national elections followed on 14 August, resulting in a narrow Christian Democratic plurality. Konrad Adenauer was elected federal chancellor in early September by a single-vote majority in the newly constituted Bundestag. He proceeded to form a coalition government with the Free Democrats and a smaller regional party. On 21 September Adenauer presented his Cabinet to the three Allied high commissioners, who, on the same day, succeeded the military governors as the highest representatives of the Western powers in Germany. By receiving Adenauer and his Cabinet, the American, British, and French commissioners formally recognized the establishment of the Federal Republic as the successor government to the former German Reich.

Soviet authorities responded with the proclamation of the (East) German Democratic Republic (*Deutsche Demokratische Republik,* or DDR) in their zone in October. The German People's Council reconstituted itself as a provisional People's Chamber (*Volkskammer*), and elected an East German president and a Cabinet. Ministerial positions were distributed among leaders of the various East German political parties, although de facto leadership was vested in the Communist-dominated Socialist Unity party.

Thus, through their parallel actions to interpret and even thwart the Potsdam agreement in the light of divergent national security interests and ideological values, the Western powers and the Soviet Union engineered Germany's division into separate libertarian and Communist regimes. In the process they fundamentally altered the requisites of political modernity in Germany. By dismembering and dividing the former Reich, the wartime Allies undid Bismarck's success of 1871 in achieving German unity. At the same time, their efforts to demilitarize and democratize Germany resulted in a profound transformation of authority relations and fundamental rights of citizenship in the two parts of the occupied nation. The result in the DDR was a decisive break with Germany's economic and political past. There, radical occupation reforms and SED dominance resulted in the introduction of a Soviet model of centralized state socialism. The founding of the West German Federal Republic, in contrast, offered democratic German leaders an opportunity to achieve what had eluded their ideological forebears of 1848 and 1919, namely, a working constitutional order that would command the voluntary allegiance of its citizens, sustain domestic political stability, and live in peace with its European neighbors.

Notes

1. A second, "official," capitulation was signed the following day between the German military and Soviet officials in Berlin.

2. A.J.P. Taylor, *The Course of German History* (New York: Capricorn Books, 1946), 225.

3. A.J.P. Taylor, *Bismarck: The Man and the Statesman* (New York: Knopf, 1955), 33, 35.

4. Dankwart A. Rustow, *A World of Nations* (Washington, D.C.: Brookings Institution, 1967), 35-36.

5. The SPD was established as an amalgamation of the General German Workers Association, which was founded by Ferdinand Lassalle in Leipzig in 1863, and the Marxist-oriented Social Democratic Workers party, which was established by August Bebel and Wilhelm Liebknecht in 1869.

6. V.R. Berghahn, *Germany and the Approach of War in 1914* (New York: Macmillan, 1973).

7. The literature on Hitler and the National Socialist movement is voluminous. Standard references include Karl Dietrich Bracher, *The German Dictatorship* (New York: Praeger, 1970); Alan Bullock, *Hitler: A Study in Tyranny* (New York: Harper & Row, 1964); Carl J. Friedrich and Zbigniew Brzezinski, *Totalitarian Dictatorship and Autocracy,* 2d ed. rev. (Cambridge, Mass.: Harvard University Press, 1965); Hitler's own *Mein Kampf* (Boston: Hougton Mifflin, 1943); Franz Neumann, *Behemoth. The Structure and Practice of National Socialism* (New York: Free Press, 1942); and John Toland, *Adolf Hitler* (Garden City, N.Y.: Doubleday, 1976). A particularly compelling acccount of Hitler's hypnotic effect on others can be found in Albert Speer's memoirs, *Inside the Third Reich* (New York: Macmillan, 1970), 15-16.

8. For a discussion of the Nazi displacement of the aristocracy as a social class, see Ralf Dahrendorf, *Society and Democracy in Germany* (Garden City, N.Y.: Doubleday, 1967).

9. U.S. Department of State, *Foreign Relations of the United States. Diplomatic Papers. The Conference of Berlin (The Potsdam Conference),* 1945, vol. 2 (Washington, D.C.: Government Printing Office, 1960), 1504.

10. John Gimbel, *The American Occupation of Germany* (Stanford: Stanford University Press, 1968), 167.

11. F. Roy Willis, *The French in Germany 1945-1949* (Stanford: Stanford University Press, 1962), 51.

12. A majority of the members of the Bavarian state parliament voted against the Basic Law because it provided for a more centralized form of government than they would have wished. Nonetheless, the Barvarian Landtag endorsed the Basic Law as binding on the state. An excellent account of the Bavarian debate can be found in Peter H. Merkl, *The Origin of the West German Republic* (New York: Oxford University Press, 1963), 148-61.

2. Consolidation and Legitimation: The Federal Republic's Formative Years

With the formal promulgation of the Federal Republic on 21 September 1949, the West Germans once again became international actors in their own right. Admittedly, the Occupation Statute sharply circumscribed the legal competence of the new government. Under terms of the statute, the United States, Britain, and France retained the authority to enforce disarmament, demilitarization, decartelization, economic decentralization, and reparation payments and to control coal and steel production in the Ruhr. In addition, they were responsible for the conduct of West German foreign affairs, the protection of the Allied occupation forces, and "respect for the Basic Law and the Land (state) constitutions."

The Allies also reserved the right "to resume in whole or in part the exercise of full authority if they consider that to do so is essential to security or to preserve democratic government in Germany or in pursuance of the international obligations of their Governments." Within these broad legal constraints, however, the federal and state governments of the new West German republic were accorded "full legislative, executive, and judicial powers in accordance with the Basic Law and with their respective constitutions."[1]

West German officials confronted a multitude of pressing domestic and international issues as they assumed office under the new constitution. The institutions of the Federal Republic had been the object of intense partisan controversy during Parliamentary Council sessions in 1948-49, and it was by no means certain how they would function in practice. Despite the stimulative effects of the 1948 currency reform, industrial production in September 1949 had attained only 90 percent of the 1936 level. Unemployment stood at 11 percent. More than 8 million expellees and refugees from Czechoslovakia, the territories east of the Oder-Neisse rivers, and the Soviet zone of occupation crowded temporary camps in the countryside or substandard quarters in the still-devastated cities. Many of them were out of work and encountered deep resentment among native residents. Their presence aggravated a severe housing shortage that afflicted all of Germany.

Unresolved territorial issues and public apprehension about the consequences of the nation's forced division were additional causes of grave political concern. As a result of the otherwise abortive Moscow Foreign Ministers Conference in November 1947, the Saar had been tentatively detached from Germany and economically joined with France. Its ultimate fate awaited future negotiations between the Western Allies and the Federal Republic. The new government in Bonn had yet to negotiate the right to disburse Marshall Aid funds or to join the International Authority of the Ruhr, the Organization for European Economic Cooperation, and other regional associations. To the east, Berlin remained isolated within the DDR and was therefore politically vulnerable to the surrounding Soviet military presence. Convinced that most East Germans opposed Communism, a majority of West Germans steadfastly affirmed their desire for national reunification under conditions of libertarian democracy; yet they were pessimistic that it could be achieved. Most were simultaneously ambivalent about the course of postwar political development, expressing little genuine interest in the Basic Law and viewing the Federal Republic as at best a provisional arrangement. Many Germans were convinced that another European conflict would occur within the foreseeable future.[2]

Thus, under exceptionally difficult circumstances, West German political leaders assumed the arduous task of consolidating and legitimizing the new socioeconomic and political order sanctioned by the Basic Law. Their immediate tasks were threefold: (1) to establish a functioning national political system, (2) to implement adequate policy measures to encourage economic growth and achieve West Germany's physical reconstruction, and (3) to defend German national interests against diverse territorial and security claims on the part of the Western Allies.

Electoral Choices and Institutional Consolidation

The Basic Law prescribed the institutional framework of the Federal Republic, but electoral outcomes and individual personalities defined its substance. From the outset of the occupation regime, three distinct ideological movements had emerged as the dominant forces shaping Germany's political rehabilitation in the western zones. They were the Christian Democrats, the Social Democrats, and the Liberal (Free) Democrats. These movements — along with the Communists — had been the first political parties to be licensed by Allied military authorities during the summer and fall of 1945. Consequently, they were able to establish an early record of administrative expertise and a near-monopoly of popular support before nationalists and other splinter groups were permitted to organize and compete for votes. Among the latter, only one proved of long-term significance during the formative years of the Federal Republic: the German party (DP), a conservative organization established on the regional and ideological basis of an earlier states' rights movement in Lower Saxony.

Shared ideological characteristics significantly enhanced the electoral status of the three dominant parties. In contrast to the belief of Communist leaders in political action to achieve a predefined model of state socialism, the principal West German parties jointly endorsed a constitutional political system based on individual civil liberties and free competition among different groups and ideas. Their affirmation of libertarian-democratic values and their hostility to orthodox Marxism-Leninism as practiced by the SED in the DDR reflected the political preferences of an overwhelming majority of the West German and Berlin electorate. Together, the Christian Democrats, the Social Democrats, and the Liberals amassed upward from 70 percent of the vote in local elections in the French zone in September 1946 and 72 percent in local balloting that same month in the British zone to 90 percent in constitutional assembly elections held in the American zone. In citywide elections to the Berlin Assembly in October 1946, the same three parties received 80.2 percent. The Communists, in contrast, obtained 7.6 percent in the American zone, 5.3 percent in the British zone, and 6.5 percent in the French zone in elections held between June and October. Only in the Soviet sector of Berlin and eastern zone of occupation did the SED achieve an appreciably greater share of the vote, thanks in varying degrees to popular endorsement of the SED's programs of nationalization and land reform and indirect support provided by Soviet military authorities. In free elections held in September and October 1946 in Berlin and the Soviet zone, SED strength ranged from 19.7 percent to 57 percent, respectively.

Among the three dominant parties in the west, only the Social Democrats (SPD) claimed an unbroken legacy from Germany's pre-Nazi past. Founded in 1875, the SPD had survived both the republican-era split with the KPD and Nazi suppression to reappear in 1945 under new national leadership but with much of its prewar program and its membership intact. Kurt Schumacher, an outspoken, frequently sarcastic party militant who had risen to the rank of SPD Reichstag deputy during the final years of the Weimar Republic, successfully defied the authority of the party's Central Committee in Berlin to establish himself as party leader in the western zones in October 1945.[3] From this position, Schumacher, who was a survivor of 12 years of imprisonment in Nazi concentration camps, thwarted Soviet efforts to extend the 1946 merger of the SPD and the KPD in the eastern zone to the rest of Germany. Schumacher was elected chairman of the truncated West German Social Democratic party in May 1946 and subsequently devoted his considerable political energies to the reconstruction of party and state. His most pressing objective was to mobilize Germany's industrial working class and other social groups in support of Social Democrat demands for selective nationalization and national economic planning. Not surprisingly, the SPD attracted most of its electoral strength in the working-class districts of the Ruhr, Hesse, and Germany's major metropolitan areas.

In contrast to the SPD, the Christian Democrats were strictly a postwar phenomenon. The movement actually comprised two party organizations — the Christian Democratic Union (CDU) in northern and southwestern Germany, and the Christian Social Union (CSU) in Bavaria. Drawing heavily on personnel and ideological concepts of the pre-Nazi Catholic Center party, the CDU was founded in Berlin during the summer of 1945. The CDU and the CSU were distinguished from the earlier Center party, however, in that both were "supraconfessional" — that is, their leaders sought to unite Protestants and Catholics in a common struggle to achieve economic and political reform based on progressive Christian social values. In the initial postwar years, this effort took the form of proposals advanced by Christian Democratic officials in Berlin, Frankfurt, and Cologne to nationalize industry in the name of "Christian Socialism." Gradually, however, conservative elements within the movement began to assert themselves in behalf of a more diluted program of limited economic planning and social reform. The CDU's shift to the right became apparent after the formation of the Economic Council in Bizonia in June 1947 when party leaders openly embraced a free-market concept of competitive capitalism. With the adoption of their Düsseldorf program of 1949, the Christian Democrats formally repudiated their earlier prescriptions for economic planning in favor of the indirect exercise of government influence over the economy through active fiscal and monetary policies, import regulations, and the provision of comprehensive welfare services.

Like the Social Democrats, the Christian Democrats were dominated during the early postwar years by a single personality — Konrad Adenauer, a venerable (born in 1876) former member of the Center party and mayor of Cologne. Adenauer was suspended from public office by the National Socialists in 1933 and temporarily imprisoned. After spending the years of the Third Reich in forced retirement at his home in a small village south of Bonn, Adenauer resumed political activity in May 1945 when the Americans reappointed him mayor of Cologne. The British fired him in October, ostensibly because of political insubordination, but permitted him to reenter political life by the end of the year. In January 1946 Adenauer became the self-proclaimed leader of the CDU in the British zone.

Supremely self-confident and a superb tactician, Adenauer utilized his extensive administrative and political expertise to outmanuever a number of early rivals in establishing himself as chairman by June 1948. The Bavarian-based

CSU retained its own structure, program, and chairmanship but entered into what became a largely permanent alliance with the CDU when the two parties forged a unified parliamentary group within the Parliamentary Council in September 1948. At the same time, Adenauer was elected president of the council, thereby enhancing his national visibility as an acknowledged legislative leader and practitioner of the elusive art of political compromise.[4]

Significantly smaller than either the SPD or the CDU/CSU, West Germany's liberal movement also commanded a hetereogeneous clientele and a decentralized party structure. Like the other major parties, the Liberal Democrats were initially licensed by Soviet authorities in Berlin in June 1945 and quickly formed local and later statewide party organizations in the other occupation zones. In each instance, the postwar liberal movement encompassed many former leaders and supporters of traditional bourgeois parties — among them the Democrats, the German People's party, and to a lesser extent the Conservatives. Ideologically, the Liberals advocated the creation of a centralized political system, limited government intervention in the economy, and a clear separation between state and religion (especially with respect to religious instruction in the schools).

Initially, the Liberals organized themselves under different party labels in the various Länder. These ranged from the Liberal Democratic party in the Soviet zone, Lower Saxony, and Hesse to the German People's party in southwestern Germany and the Free Democratic party in Bavaria, North Rhine-Westphalia, Bremen, and Hamburg. By 1948, the various state organizations in the western zones coalesced into a unified Free Democratic party (FDP). Unlike both the Social Democrats and the Christian Democrats, the FDP was led by several party notables rather than a single dominant figure. The party's undiluted economic liberalism and cultural secularism appealed predominantly to businessmen, independent professionals, and intellectuals. Thus, FDP electoral support was concentrated in areas of traditional liberal support, namely, southwestern Germany and cities.

Despite their common affirmation of constitutional government, social pluralism, and individual civil liberties, West Germany's three major parties thus espoused conflicting ideological priorities. Following the CDU's shift toward more conservative economic principles, SPD leaders began to defame Adenauer and other leading Christian Democrats as capitalist "reactionaries." Consequently, the two larger parties emerged as outspoken rivals within the Economic Council and the various state parliaments. This development was in part a natural consequence of the approximate electoral parity between the CDU/CSU and the SPD on a trizonal basis. In addition, Adenauer and Schumacher developed an intense personal antipathy toward each other based on differences in their individual temperaments, political styles, attitudes toward the occupation powers, and above all their belief that only their own political party was qualified to lead postwar Germany.

Following elections by the various state parliaments to the Parliamentary Council in August 1948, party disputes were enlarged to encompass prospective institutional arrangements and the distribution of power under the proposed constitution for a West German state. For complex ideological and political reasons (including their historical distrust of earlier Prussian dominance in national German politics), most Christian Democrats favored a decentralized form of federalism that would accord maximum legislative and financial powers to the individual states. The Social Democrats, in contrast, endorsed a strong national government and weaker state prerogatives. A potential impasse between these opposing positions was ultimately averted because of the mediating role performed by the Free Democrats and other smaller parties, Adenauer's negotiating skills as council president, and occasional intervention by watchful Allied officials.[5] The result was an eventual CDU/CSU-SPD-FDP agreement on a federal system characterized by a strong lower house and federal chancellor and the direct representation of state interests through an appointive upper house.

Following the ratification of the Basic Law in May 1949, the various parties launched a national campaign for elections to the first Bundestag in August by intensifying their debate on basic economic choices confronting the fledgling Federal Republic. Were economic planning and nationalization the best means to achieve economic recovery and alleviate Germany's physical destruction, housing shortage, and refugee problem—as the Social Democrats advocated? Or would the Christian Democratic and Free Democratic prescriptions for more limited forms of government intervention in the economy suffice to encourage economic growth and full employment? In either case, what was the Federal Republic's optimal strategy for seeking the restoration of German sovereignty and reunification with both the Saar and the Soviet zone? Schumacher repeatedly voiced maximum demands of the Allies in behalf of these external objectives, whereas Adenauer clearly indicated his preference for less dramatic private consultations with the occupation officials in defense of German national interests.

The Christian Democrats won 31 percent of the national vote in the August election, compared to 29 percent for the Social Democrats and nearly 12 percent for the Free Democrats. Trailing distantly were the Communists with nearly 6 percent, the German party (DP) and the Bavarian party with 4 percent apiece, and various smaller splinter groups. When the Bundestag convened in early September, Adenauer was narrowly elected to serve as federal chancellor in a CDU/CSU-FDP-DP coalition government. Members of the Bundestag met with an equal number of deputies from the state parliaments during their first week in session to elect Theodor Heuss, a prominent member of the FDP, the first president of the Federal Republic. Concurrently, the Länder governments appointed 42 deputies—plus 4 nonvoting delegates from West Berlin—to the upper house, or Bundesrat. Thus, by mid-September, the principal offices of the Federal Republic were occupied, and the new West German government assumed its awesome policy obligations as successor to the German Reich.

Economic and Social Recovery

With the formation of its first government, the Federal Republic embarked on a formative phase of policy innovation and regime consolidation that lasted from 1949 until Adenauer's retirement in 1963. During this period, the Christian Democrats achieved unprecedented policy and electoral successes in their pursuit of multiple programs of postwar recovery. The result was not only the institutionalization of a stable political order but also Germany's transition from a historically isolated and bellicose nation to a cosmopolitan and respected member of the Western community.

Domestically, the Adenauer government concentrated its preliminary efforts on means to encourage economic growth and social integration in accordance with libertarian maxims of free competition and association. Both objectives entailed an expansion of the legal competence and material resources of the new West German government. This required in turn extensive collaboration with the occupation powers and other West European nations. Accordingly, in one of his first foreign policy statements, Chancellor Adenauer declared in October 1949 that the Federal Republic wished to participate in regional efforts to promote economic reconstruction by joining the Organization for European Economic Cooperation (OEEC). The Western Allies responded to Adenauer's initiative a month later by agreeing to West German membership in both OEEC and the International Authority of the Ruhr when they concluded the first Allied-West German treaty agreement in the form of the "Petersberg Protocol."[6] In the same document, the United States, Britain, and France relaxed restrictions on West German shipbuilding, reduced the number of plants scheduled for dismantling, and halted dismantling in West Berlin altogether. In December the United States transferred authority to disperse Marshall Aid funds in West Germany from Allied occupation officials to the Federal Republic.

West German officials utilized the gradual relaxation of Allied economic controls and the parallel receipt of $4.4 billion in Marshall Aid and other forms of external assistance to encourage private industrial expansion. Consistent with the minimum interventionist principles of the CDU's concept of a "social market economy," Economics Minister Ludwig Erhard and his administrative staff pursued a cautious fiscal and monetary policy designed to engender increased confidence in the new West German mark (DM) and to promote the expansion of foreign trade. The results were initially mixed. On the one hand, the currency reform of 1948 and Allied investments contributed to a visible economic revival. Industrial production reached 100 percent of the 1936 level by the end of 1949, and industrial employment rose by 16 percent. On the other hand, the government's relative economic passivity helped sustain a stubbornly high unemployment level of more than 1.5 million workers through 1952. Many of the unemployed persons were political refugees and expellees from the East, whose numbers swelled to nearly 9.4 million by the beginning of 1951.

The outbreak of the Korean war in June 1950 provided an unanticipated stimulus to West Germany's incipient economic recovery. Demilitarization and the decline in industrial production during the occupation interlude meant that Germany possessed a greater industrial reserve capacity than most advanced capitalist nations. Moreover, the federal government's economic policies had in fact produced a stable currency and favorable balance of trade. Thus, the Federal Republic was in an unusually strong position to respond to the "spurt in foreign demand" that ensued in the wake of the Korean conflict.[7] Within a year, German exports nearly doubled, and the production index rose 39 points. The combined value of West German goods and services—which at 98.1 billion marks in 1950 approximated the gross national product of the entire German Reich in 1938—jumped to 120 billion marks in 1951, and continued to grow at an average annual rate of 18.3 billion marks through the remainder of the decade.

The Federal Republic's rapid economic recovery generated the material resources that both private industry and government officials needed to resolve the country's most vexing social problems: persisting unemployment, the integration of refugees, and indequate housing. With the expansion of West German industrial production and a simultaneous growth in public and private services, the number of unemployed workers steadily declined from 11 percent in 1950 to less than 1 percent a decade later. In absolute numbers, more than 1.5 million workers who had been unable to find a job in 1950 were employed by 1960.

Refugees and expellees were among those who benefited most from West Germany's economic growth. Their integration into West German society was the product of a combination of market forces and government activism. An example of the former was the establishment of new optical and textile industries in traditionally agrarian Bavaria; in the latter case, the various Länder had enacted a law as early as February 1947 calling for positive steps to integrate "the expellees into the indigenous German population with equal rights and obligations."[8] After the promulgation of the Basic Law, the federal government quickly enacted a national resettlement program to facilitate the voluntary relocation of some 300,000 displaced persons from the agricultural districts to industrial centers. A subsequent "Equalization of Burdens Law," which was endorsed by the Bundestag in August 1952, imposed a special levy on fixed property and capital to help finance the integration of refugees. By the end of 1957, these measures enabled national and state authorities to relocate more than 890,000 displaced persons and to contribute more than 5 billion marks toward their housing.[9]

Increased national wealth and government revenues enabled private investors and public officials to undertake the physical restoration of the war-shattered country. Between 1949 and 1951, more than 326,000 new housing units were completed; thereafter, the annual completion rate increased from 139,200 in 1950 to 217,800 in 1963. Concurrently, local, state, and national authorities undertook the reconstruction of West Germany's cities and transportation facilities. By the early 1960s wartime rubble and other scars of physical destruction had virtually disappeared from the major urban centers, many of which acquired broad new thoroughfares, green belts, and subway systems as noticeable improvements over prewar living conditions. The national railway system (the Bundesbahn) successively expanded its service during the formative 1950s, with the number of passengers and volume of freight transported by rail rising each year through 1957. Both subsequently declined in step with the expansion of the country's elaborate network of well-engineered expressways (the Autobahn) and an exponential growth in the ownership of private automobiles. Between 1946 and 1955, the number of cars increased from nearly a million to 1.8 million; by 1960 the number reached 4.5 million. A steady growth in the omnipotent presence of trucks on the densely traveled autobahns provided visible testimony to West Germany's phenomenal economic recovery and continuing growth.

Cooperation with the West and the Restoration of Sovereignty

Parallel with his coalition government's efforts to achieve economic and social recovery, Chancellor Adenauer utilized his considerable prestige and bargaining skills to promote two closely related foreign policy objectives: enhanced security and the restoration of West German sovereignty. In contrast to the emphasis of the opposition SPD on the primacy of all-German unity, Adenauer was quite willing to accept the division of Germany to achieve both of these goals. His choice was in part a product of his background as a Rhineland Catholic, which led him to profess a profound distrust of Germany "east of the Elbe." In addition, Adenauer's values as an erstwhile constitutional democrat reinforced his strong anticommunism and emotional identity with the West.

Equally important, Adenauer was a professed political realist. More than most West Germans, who naively perceived the socialist policies of land reform and nationalization in the DDR as merely provisional, Adenauer entertained no pretensions about maximum long-term Soviet and SED ambitions. On the contrary, he accepted at face value Communist assertions that the "socialist achievements" in the DDR were permanent, and therefore sought to draw as firm a line as possible between the two parts of Germany to prevent their "export" to the Federal Republic. This did not mean that Adenauer forswore the eventual attainment of German reunification. On the contrary, he and his fellow Christian Democrats staunchly proclaimed the "indivisible unity" of all Germans and their party's determination to achieve reunification under conditions of constitutional democracy and freedom of choice concerning Germany's foreign policy alignment. But until such conditions were attainable, Adenauer was unwilling to postpone the pursuit of West German security and political recovery.

In eschewing the utopian vision of a unified and demilitarized Germany, which some members of the SPD opposition thought could be achieved through four-power negotiations, Adenauer's views coincided closely with those of the Western powers (especially the United States). As a result, Western leaders viewed the German chancellor with considerable respect and proved receptive to his efforts to expand the scope of West German independence. The Petersberg protocol of November 1949 was but the first step in the gradual extension of the legal status of the Federal Republic within the international political community. Others followed in 1950 when the Bonn government joined the Council of Europe, the World Health Organization, the International Labor Organization, and the United Nations Economic and Social Council. In 1951 West Germany also became a member of the General Agreement on Tariffs and Trade, the World Bank, and the International Monetary Fund.

The only major discordant element in Allied-German relations remained the ambivalent status of the Saar. Following the region's detachment from the western zones in 1947, France had negotiated a unilateral agreement with the Saar government in March 1950 that provided for a 50-year lease of the Saar coal mines to France. In January 1952 the French government further underscored the international autonomy of the Saar by elevating its former high commissioner there to the rank of ambassador. Chancellor Adenauer strongly protested both moves, challenging the legality of French control of mines in the territory and asserting that "the Federal Government considers itself empowered and obligated to preserve German rights in their entirety."

Efforts to resolve the Saar controversy coincided with the escalation of the cold war to yield a combined economic and military solution to Adenauer's quests for West German sovereignty and increased national security. Responding to American pressure to settle the Saar issue on terms acceptable to both sides, French Foreign Minister Robert Schuman proposed in March 1950 that the two countries invite other interested European states to join them in combining their coal, iron, and steel resources in a common pool. Adenauer enthusiastically accepted, and in June representatives of the Federal Republic, France, Italy, and the Benelux countries convened in Paris to begin negotiations. The upshot was an innovative international agreement, signed by the six states in April 1951, to establish the European Coal and Steel Community (ECSC). Unlike the United Nations and the multitude of European economic and political organizations that had been established during the early postwar period, the ECSC treaty provided for the creation of a supranational rather than an intergovernmental organization. That is, the member states agreed to merge their coal and steel industries in a single market that would be governed by a Council of Ministers and a High Authority with independent executive authority. Once implemented, the ECSC would eliminate national controls over coal and steel production and would thus all but eliminate the possibility that any of the signatory powers could unilaterally launch a war.

The ECSC treaty was ratified by the six parliaments by June 1952 and went into effect in July. Its positive economic and political effects immediately facilitated reconciliation between the Federal Republic and its West European neighbors. The Europeanization of coal and steel production led, first, to the abolition of the now-redundant International Authority of the Ruhr; second, the move eliminated the need for France to maintain a separate government in the Saar. Accordingly, after a majority of the Saar's population rejected independence in a referendum held in October 1955, France and West Germany signed a treaty providing for the incorporation of the Saar into the Federal Republic. On 1 January 1957 the Saar thus rejoined Germany as the tenth official Land.[10] In addition, the success of the ECSC in stimulating coal and steel production among its member states prompted the same six governments to negotiate an even more ambitious treaty in 1957 to create a European Economic Community (the Common Market) encompassing all industrial goods, agricultural products, and services. The EEC treaty was implemented in 1958.

In step with West European efforts to integrate their national economies, American and European leaders embarked on a comprehensive program of collective security that ultimately transformed West Germany's legal status as an international actor. Escalating cold-war tensions prompted unilateral steps on each side that the other viewed as detrimental to its own security interests. In the East, Soviet occupation officials had sanctioned the creation of an armed German Border Police as early as November 1946 and a Garrisoned People's Police in July 1948—both as alleged means to defend socialist achievements against perceived domestic and external threats. Worried about the broader implications of these steps toward incipient remilitarization in East Germany, Chancellor Adenauer demanded adequate protection for the Federal Republic from the Western powers. Both he and SPD Chairman Schumacher declared during the summer of 1950 that they would sanction a West German contribution to Europe's defense—but only, in Adenauer's words, on the basis of "complete equality between Germany and the other European nations. Equal duties (presuppose) equal rights."[11]

American political and military advisers concurred on both the need for additional men and arms to buttress the defense capabilities of the North Atlantic Treaty Organization (NATO) and Adenauer's conditions for West German participation in the common defense effort. At a meeting in September 1950 in New York, the three Western foreign ministers agreed that the Federal Republic could form mobile police units along its border with the DDR. The United States, Britain, and France simultaneously relaxed some of the restrictions of the Occupation Statute and declared that they would treat any Soviet attack on West Germany or Berlin as "an attack on themselves."

The tripartite pronouncements of September 1950 initiated a strenuous diplomatic effort to establish a European army in which the various national military forces would be integrated under a supranational command. Delegates from the six ECSC states met in Paris in February 1951 to draw up a treaty for a contemplated European Defense Community (EDC), and continued negotiations until May 1952. In the interim the Western Allies issued a number of decrees extending still further the economic and political powers of the Federal Republic. On 27 May 1952, France, West Germany, Italy, and the Benelux countries formally signed the EDC treaty. In conjunction with the parallel ratification of the ECSC agreement, the six-power accord to establish a European army seemed to herald the dawn of a new era of European cooperation.

Unexpectedly, the French parliament dispelled such idealism when a majority of deputies voted an indefinite postponement of the EDC treaty in August 1954. Faced suddenly with the demise of an international legal basis for West German rearmament, British and American officials hastily fashioned an alternative arrangement in October whereby West Germany would join NATO directly as a member of the newly created West European Union. Simultaneously, the Western Allies removed nearly all remaining legal constraints on West German sovereignty, reserving for themselves only the defense of West Berlin and the right to intervene in internal German affairs in case of serious international or domestic disorder.[12]

Known as the Paris Agreements, both accords were ratified by the various legislatures of the countries concerned and formally enacted on 5 May 1955. Thus, nearly 10 years to the day following the capitulation of the Third Reich, the Federal Republic assumed historic Germany's place as an independent state in the international community. Unlike previous German regimes, however, it did so as an economic, military, and political partner of the West.

The Allied-German decisions on rearmament and membership in NATO were not without their political price. Throughout the protracted negotiations on West Germany's role in the Western defense effort, the Soviet Union had sought to curtail German rearmament by reopening the prospect of German reunification. Beginning with a Soviet declaration in December 1950 that Moscow wished to discuss all aspects of the German question, Russian and East German officials repeatedly offered to negotiate with the West to create "a unified, democratic, peace-loving Germany." [13] Accordingly, representatives of the four powers gathered in Paris in March 1951 to discuss an appropriate agenda. After 73 futile sessions, the conference came to an inconclusive end, with both sides as far apart on fundamental political and economic principles concerning postwar Germany as they had been at the Moscow foreign ministers meeting in 1947. The Soviet Union submitted a final proposal in May 1952 calling on the Western Allies to begin talks on a German peace treaty, free all-German elections, and German reunfication; the United States, Britain, and France rejected the note as a propaganda gesture designed to delay signing of the Contractural Agreements in Paris. In the face of Western intransigence, the Soviets and their East German clients therefore abandoned further efforts to impede the military integration of the Federal Republic within NATO or to disguise the DDR's own rearmament and membership in the Warsaw Pact. The division of Germany was henceforth irrevocable.

Consolidation and Legitimation

West Germany's rapid economic growth, its recovery of both legal sovereignty and the Saar, and its acceptance as an equal partner within the European Coal and Steel Community and the North Atlantic Treaty Organization rebounded to the partisan electoral advantage of the Christian Democrats and decisively affected the institutional consolidation of the Bonn Republic. Between 1949 and 1957, the CDU/CSU advanced in three national elections from 31 percent of the popular vote to an absolute majority of 50.2. Chancellor Adenauer's

TABLE 2.1

POPULAR PERCEPTIONS OF "GREAT GERMANS," 1950-56

(IN PERCENTAGES)

Responses based on question: *"Which German has done the most for Germany?"*

Leading Germans	1950	1952	1953	1955	1956
Bismarck	35	36	32	30	31
Hitler	10	9	9	6	7
Various kaisers, kings	14	14	10	11	8
Adenauer	—	3	9	17	24

SOURCES: Adapted from Elisabeth Noelle and Erich Peter Neumann, *Jahrbuch der öffentlichen Meinung, 1947-55* (Allensbach: Verlag für Demoskopie, 1956), 132; ibid., *1957,* 141.

personal popularity grew in tandem with his party's increase in electoral support. Whereas only 3 percent of a West German sample numbered the CDU leader among history's "great Germans" in 1952, by February 1956 the percentage had grown to 24. Simultaneously, positive public attitudes toward various kaisers and toward Hitler decreased in frequency, indicating growing popular support for the Federal Republic itself (see table 2.1).

Public behavior as well as attitudinal changes during the first decade and a half of the existence of the Federal Republic revealed the extent of Germany's most profound political revolution in modern times. Whereas the percentage of voters who had supported antisystem parties during the Weimar period increased steadily from nearly 12 percent in December 1924 to more than half in July 1932, the number of their counterparts in postwar Germany dramatically declined from 1949 onward. As indicated in table 2.2, the percentage of popular support for extremist and splinter parties fell from 27.9 percent in the first Bundestag election to less than 1.0 percent by the beginning of the 1970s. Concurrently, the three major parties increased their total support from 72 percent in 1949 to 99 percent during the 1970s. Political, social, and legal reasons for the demise of particular splinter parties—as well as the temporary resurgence of a rightist movement in the mid-1960s and the appearance of the Greens in the early 1980s—are explored in following chapters. But as a general behavioral tendency among West German voters, the decline in mass support for splinter movements constitutes a crucial index of the Federal Republic's progressive legitimation in the eyes of the electorate.

The underlying cause for the regime's early consolidation can be sought, first, in the government's domestic and foreign policy successes of 1949-57. A rising standard of living, the integration of the refugee population, and the Federal Republic's new status as an independent and respected member of the

TABLE 2.2

ELECTORAL SUPPORT FOR EXTREMIST AND SPLINTER PARTIES,
1920-33 AND 1949-87[a]

Elections	Percentage of Support
Reichstag	
June 1920	20.0
May 1924	19.2
December 1924	11.9
May 1928	13.2
September 1930	31.4
July 1932	51.6
November 1932	50.0
Bundestag	
1949	27.9
1953	16.5
1957	10.3
1961	5.6
1965	3.6
1969	5.4
1972	.9
1976	.9
1980	1.9
1983	6.2
1987	9.6

a. Percentage of second ballots cast in national elections to the Reichstag and the Bundestag, respectively.

Atlantic Community generated a perceptible increase in popular support for the postwar regime. According to a national opinion survey conducted in October 1951, only 2 percent of the population considered the postwar era to be Germany's best historical epoch. The percentage rose to 42 by 1959 and increased to 62 in 1963.[14]

A second factor encouraging system legitimation was leadership behavior. With several noteworthy exceptions, spokesmen for West Germany's three major parties embodied effective models of personal restraint, responsibility, and tolerance in their day-to-day political behavior. To be sure, Chancellor Adenauer frequently engaged in highly acrimonious parliamentary debates with Schumacher and other opposition spokemen over unemployment policies, rearmament, and other controversial issues. Moreover, Adenauer's popularity among his partisan supporters was more than matched by intense dislike for his leadership style and many of his policy choices among members of the SPD and the smaller parties. But the fact that Adenauer and most of his ideological opponents handled their disputes according to parliamentary rules and democratic norms established what has remained a binding precedent of elite consensus affirming the legitimacy of open competition and pragmatic compromise among diverse policy alternatives. As Robert Dahl has cogently noted, such an achievement is rare in a world characterized more by violent confrontation among political groups than "legal, orderly, peaceful modes of political opposition."[15]

Leadership respect for the Bundestag as a working democratic institution encouraged in turn increased popular support for the postwar political order. The percentage of adult Germans who were seriously interested in the Basic Law increased from 21 in 1949 to 30 by May 1955, while those who expressed a generally favorable attitude toward the Bundestag rose from 21 percent in January 1950 to 29 percent in June 1956. Fully 71 percent of the adult population asserted in June 1958 that West Germany "needed a parliament," compared to only 10 percent who said they would be willing to dispense with the lower house.[16]

Behavioral and attitudinal trends in West Germany after 1949 indicated nothing less—to use Sidney Verba's apt description—than "the remaking of a political culture."[17] Thanks to the complex interaction between political re-education during the occupation, the economic and policy successes of the 1950s, Adenauer's integrative role as the first postwar chancellor, and elite consensus on fundamental democratic norms, an overwhelming majority of West Germans came to affirm the pluralist socioeconomic order and democratic institutions of the Federal Republic. They became, in short, constitutional democrats out of conviction rather than convenience—in contrast to the shallow libertarian attachment of many of the Weimar era's *Vernunftrepublikaner*.

Admittedly, West Germany's leaders and voters have retained many attributes from their nation's autocratic past. Among them are a strong sense of self-righteousness, frequently officious behavior on the part of public officials, and an exaggerated preoccupation with legalism in political discourse and action. But none of these traditional qualities negates the larger achievement of fundamental political transformation since the end of World War II. Under Adenauer's tutelage, the Federal Republic achieved, in short, a working synthesis between two of the essential conditions of successful modernity: the attainment of recognized political authority and citizen participation on the basis of legal equality. The restoration of national unity eluded postwar Germany's first federal chancellor, but the internal consolidation of the Federal Republic yielded a more integrated society than any of its predecessor regimes. On this foundation, the Federal Republic entered the post-Adenauer era of recurrent international and domestic crises as a relative bastion of political stability.

Notes

1. Office of the U.S. High Commissioner for Germany, "Occupation Statute," *Report on Germany, 1st Quarterly* (21 September–31 December 1949): 56-57.

2. Elisabeth Noelle and Erich Peter Neumann, *Jahrbuch der öffentlichen Meinung 1947-1955* (Allensbach: Verlag für Demoskopie, 1956), 315.

3. Lewis Edinger provides a probing assessment of Schumacher's personality and leadership style in *Kurt Schumacher: A Study in Personality and Political Behavior* (Stanford: Stanford University Press, 1965).

4. For a good discussion of Adenauer's role during the formative years of Christian Democratic organization, see Arnold J. Heidenheimer, *Adenauer and the CDU: The Rise of the Leader and the Integration of the Party* (The Hague: Martinus Nijhoff, 1960).

5. Peter H. Merkl, *The Origin of the West German Republic* (New York: Oxford University Press, 1963).

6. Office of the U.S. High Commissioner for Germany, "Petersberg Protocol," *Report on Germany*, 69-71.

7. Henry C. Wallich, *Mainsprings of the German Revival* (New Haven: Yale University Press, 1955), 86.

8. Joseph Schectman, *Postwar Population Transfers in Europe 1945-1955* (Philadelphia: University of Pennsylvania Press, 1962), 302.

9. Ibid., 314.

10. As noted in the preceding chapter, 12 states were originally constituted in the western zones. The detachment of the Saar and the merger of Württemberg-Baden, south Baden, and Württemberg-Hohenzollern into the single state of Baden-Württemberg reduced the number of Länder to 9. The Saar's return increased the number to the present total of 10.

11. Konrad Adenauer, *Memoirs 1945-53* (Chicago: Regnery, 1966), 270.

12. The latter restriction was rescinded in 1968 when the West German parliament endorsed a series of constitutional amendments that accorded the federal government the authority to deal with a state of national emergency.

13. Office of the U.S. High Commissioner for Germany, *Report on Germany*, 21 September 1949-31 July 1952, 274.

14. Noelle and Neumann, *Jahrbuch der öffentlichen Meinung 1958-64* (Allensbach: Verlag für Demoskopie, 1965), 230.

15. Robert A. Dahl, ed., *Political Oppositions in Western Democracies* (New Haven: Yale University Press, 1966), xi.

16. Opinion data from Noelle and Neumann, *Jahrbuch der öffentlichen Meinung 1947-1955,* 162; and idem, *Jahrbuch der öffentlichen Meinung 1957* (Allensbach: Verlag für Demoskopie, 1958), 165, 177, and 261.

17. Sidney Verba, "The Remaking of Political Culture" in *Political Culture and Political Development,* ed. Lucian W. Pye and Sidney Verba (Princeton: Princeton University Press, 1965).

3. The Constitutional-Institutional Framework: Policy-Making Actors, Structures, and the Judicial System

West Germany's constitutional-legal order is an outgrowth of both German history and postwar reform. Earlier experiments with federalism between 1871 and 1933 decisively influenced the decision by delegates to the Parliamentary Council to establish a modified federal structure for the western zones in 1949. Conscious of fundamental historical flaws, such as dominance by a single state (Prussia) during the Imperial era and the concentration of emergency powers in the hands of the Reich president under the Weimar constitution, they took painstaking care to define a new constitutional order that would inhibit the centralization and potential abuse of political power. Similarly, they learned from the tragic disregard of human rights by the National Socialists to inscribe a basic catalogue of civil liberties in the Basic Law that may not be deleted through constitutional amendment. Following the American precedent, the founding fathers of 1949 also established an independent Federal Constitutional Court with powers of judicial review.

The result of institutional and legal innovation in postwar West Germany is a constitutional order that diffuses political authority vertically among national, state, and local levels of government as well as horizontally among executive, legislative, and judicial actors. In accordance with twentieth-century democratic concepts of activist government, this multitiered set of institutional arrangements called the German "state" serves more than to enforce domestic order and ensure external security—or even, in Marxist terminology, to "reproduce" the existing socioeconomic order. Instead, national and state statutes, administrative decrees, and court decisions also promote continuing processes of system change in accordance with competing ideological claims advanced by political parties, organized interests, and citizen action groups. Clearly evident in the form and substance of policy outcomes are corporatist decision-making arrangements that distinguish the Federal Republic from the Anglo-American democracies with their more fragmented decisional systems.

The Debate on Principles

In various guises, the structure of West German federalism proved the overriding issue during deliberations of the Parliamentary Council in 1948-49. As Peter Merkl recounts in his assessment of the council's sessions, deputies debated at length such fundamental principles as the nature of federal-state relations, the prospective political role of the upper house of parliament (the Bundesrat), and the federal government's financial powers.[1] Partisan differences were readily apparent between the Social Democrats, who favored a centralized political system with relatively limited Land autonomy; the northern Christian Democrats and the Free Democrats, who endorsed a decentralized federal system; and most CSU delegates, who strenuously defended the primacy of states' rights. "Centralizers" sought the creation of a strong national executive, extensive federal financial authority, and a subordinate legislative role on the part of the upper house. "Federalists" and states' rights advocates, in contrast, generally sought to impose discernible limits on national authority and the powers of the Bundesrat.[2]

The eventual outcome was a political compromise engineered in large measure by Konrad Adenauer in his capacity as council president. Ever mindful of external Allied interest in an agreement that would be acceptable to most West Germans, Adenauer astutely bargained with factions within the CDU/CSU and with members of the SPD, the FDP, and the smaller parties to achieve a synthesis among the different constitutional perspectives. The result was the creation of a constitutional order that combines centralized executive and legislative powers with decentralized state authority affecting public administration, education, culture, and most law-enforcement measures.

National, State, and Local Jurisdiction: The Legal Basis of Germany's "Cooperative Federalism"

Constitutional incentives for cooperative relations between the national government (the *Bund,* or Federation) and its constituent parts (the 10 Länder that legally constitute the Federal Republic) are contained in the formal distribution of government power and the financial provisions of the Basic Law. In the first instance, the constitution reserves certain matters of overriding policy significance to the national government but otherwise accords the states a positive role in the political process through provisions for concurrent and reserved jurisidiction. An additional constitutional provision encouraging a system of "cooperative federalism" is the requirement that the states rather than specialized federal agencies administer most national policy.[3] In the second instance, the Basic Law stipulates that state revenues "from income taxes, corporation taxes, and turnover taxes," which together comprise by far the largest category of government income, "shall accrue jointly to the Federation and the Länder" to the extent that a percentage of such revenue is not allocated directly to city and county government bodies for local use.[4] This provision accords the states considerable financial resources for investment in various public services, which they provide under their constitutional rights of concurrent and reserved jurisdiction.

Exclusive national jurisdiction, in which the Länder may legislate "only if, and to the extent that, a federal law explicitly so authorizes them," extends to the following policy areas:

- [ ] foreign affairs and national defense
- [ ] German citizenship
- [ ] passports, immigration, emigration, extradiction
- [ ] currency and monetary policy
- [ ] federal railroads and air transport
- [ ] mail and telecommunication
- [ ] industrial property rights and copyrights
- [ ] cooperation between the national government and the Länder in matters of criminal police, the "protection of the free democratic basic order," protection against actions on West German soil that might "endanger the foreign interests of the Federal Republic of Germany," and the establishment of a Federal Criminal Police Office.[5]

Even more extensive is the scope of concurrent jurisdiction in which both the federal government and the various states may enact laws and issue binding administrative decrees. These include

- [ ] civil law, criminal law, courts, the legal profession
- [ ] registration of births, deaths, marriages
- [ ] laws relating to association, assembly, residence, weapons
- [ ] refugee and expellee matters
- [ ] public welfare
- [ ] war damage and reparations, including benefits to war-disabled persons
- [ ] laws relating to economic matters, including mining, industry, and banking
- [ ] labor laws
- [ ] production and utilization of nuclear enery for peaceful purposes
- [ ] regulation of educational and training grants and the promotion of scientific research
- [ ] expropriation, socialization of land, resources, and means of production

☐ prevention of the misuse of economic power
☐ road traffic and highways
☐ various health-related measures[6]

In addition, under terms of a constitutional amendment adopted in 1969, the national and state governments share legal responsibilities for the "expansion and construction of institutions (and the) improvement of regional economic structures."[7] A simultaneous constitutional amendment also provided that the "Federation and the Länder may . . . cooperate in educational planning and in the promotion of institutions and projects of scientific research of supraregional importance."[8] Both amendments, as noted below, have encouraged the centralization and coordination of economic and social policy making under federal government aegis.

The constitutional principle determining whether the federal government or the Länder act in matters of concurrent legislation is essentially one of practicality. Article 72 of the Basic Law stipulates that the federal government shall legislate in matters of concurrent jurisdiction under the following conditions: (1) if legislation by a particular Land cannot effectively deal with an issue; (2) if "the regulation of a matter by a Land law might prejudice the interests of other Länder or of the people as a whole"; or (3) if "the maintenance of legal or economic unity, especially the maintenance of uniformity of living conditions beyond the territory of any one Land, necessitates such regulation."

The individual states exercise jurisdiction in policy areas that are not explicitly enumerated in the preceding catalogue of exclusive or concurrent legislation. These include public education, ranging from preschool facilities to universities;[9] local police protection; television and radio; as well as museums, theaters, libraries, and other cultural facilities. In practice, the states delegate responsibility for the implementation of purely local services — including public utilities, hospital care, and road construction — to West Germany's 10,718 city and county government units.[10] Constitutionally, the latter are guaranteed "the right to regulate on their own responsibility all the affairs of the local community within the limits set by law."[11] In most local communes, the style of local politics is reminiscent of traditional "parish-pump policies" dominated by local organized interests and influential "notables."[12]

The Structure of Parliament

West Germany's status as a federal political system is institutionalized in the bicameral structure of the national parliament. Made up of the Bundestag (lower house) and the Bundesrat (upper house), the German legislature embodies dual principles of representation. The 496 voting members of the Bundestag are directly elected for four-year terms on the basis of universal suffrage and modified proportional representation (as explained in chapter 3), while the 41 voting members who make up the Bundesrat are appointed by the governments of the various Länder. West Berlin, which legally remains under the occupation of the three Western Allies, is represented by 22 nonvoting members in the Bundestag and four nonvoting members in the Bundesrat.[13]

In terms of its representative base, the parliamentary system of the Federal Republic thus stands in marked contrast to unitary systems with bicameral legislatures such as Britain and France in which the lower house is constitutionally superior to a largely honorific upper house. The West German system most closely approximates Canadian federalism, one feature of which is an appointed Senate, and American federalism prior to the adoption of the Seventeenth Amendment in 1913 providing for the direct election of U.S. senators.

The Bundestag

Consistent with well-established traditions of parliamentary government throughout Western Europe and elsewhere, the Bundestag serves as the representative foundation for the formation of the national government. As such, it is unquestionably the more important of the two legislative bodies in the Federal Republic. Following each national election, or in the event of the voluntary resignation of an incumbent federal chancellor, members of the Bundestag convene to elect, by majority vote, a new chancellor.[14] In addition, they may force the resignation of a federal chancellor through a "constructive vote of no-confidence" if they simultaneously elect—again by absolute majority—his successor.[15]

Once a federal chancellor assumes office, he and his Cabinet colleagues become politically accountable for their actions (and their omissions) to the Bundestag. The Bundestag may demand the presence of any member of the federal government and exercises a variety of parliamentary control functions over executive and administrative activities. These include the right to pose "interpellations" about government policy (i.e., formal party queries) as well as questions raised by individual deputies during a weekly Question Hour; the authority to convene special committees of investigation; and the right to designate a military ombudsman, known as the *Wehrbeauftragter,* who has independent power to investigate alleged abuses within the West German armed forces.[16]

Internally, the Bundestag consists of a series of leadership groups and standing committees. The chief executive officer is an elected Bundestag president, who functions as the equivalent of speaker of the house and traditionally represents the largest political faction. He or she is assisted by four elected vice presidents, who jointly make up the executive committee *(Gremium)* of the lower house. The Bundestag president and vice presidents confer regularly with members of a Council of Elders *(Ältestenrat)*, which consists of 23 deputies representing the various parties in approximate proportion to their parliamentary strength, to coordinate general legislative activity and plan the day-to-day parliamentary agenda.

The parties themselves are organized in parliamentary factions *(Fraktionen)* that correspond to the American and British legislative caucus. Each is led by a chairman, whose dual task is to help forge party policy and factional unity on pending legislative matters. In addition, each factional chairman represents his party during floor debates and in consultation with parliamentary officers about such matters as the daily agenda. Members of the parliamentary factions are assigned to various party working groups *(Arbeitskreisen)*, each of which corresponds to important areas of national legislation. Among them are working groups on foreign and defense policy, German-German relations, economic policy, social policy, and legal affairs. The CDU/CSU maintains 18 working groups, the SPD has 8 groups, the FDP 5, and the Greens 8. These internal committees play a crucial role in determining the fate of prospective legislation, as their members are characteristically experts in their policy fields and can therefore strongly influence the formation of party policy before particular bills are formally debated in parliament. While the Bundestag is in session, the various party factions generally meet on at least a weekly basis to consider reports from their working groups, review their legislative strategy, and debate policy or internal questions of general interest.

The bulk of legislative deliberation, as is true of other representative democracies, occurs within the Bundestag's elaborate committee structure. During the eleventh legislative period (1987-90), for example, the Bundestag established 21 standing committees, most of them corresponding to the jurisdiction of Cabinet-level federal ministries (see below). Among the most important are committees on foreign policy; internal affairs; finance; laws; budgetary matters; economics; agriculture and forestry; labor and social order; defense; and youth, family, women, and health. Committee members are appointed on a proportional basis by the president of the Bundestag in consultation with the various party factions. The number of members has ranged from a low of 13 on a largely technical committee to certify election results to a high of 37 on the prestigious foreign affairs and budgetary committees.

THE BUNDESRAT

As the institutional representative of the 10 West German Länder plus West Berlin, the Bundesrat provides an important channel of regional influence on national policy formation. The upper house does not serve as a basis for government formation, nor is it empowered to perform day-to-day control functions comparable to those of the Bundestag. Nonetheless, the Bundesrat provides significant "correctives" to the legislative process; moreover, because of partisan alignments among its members, it can complicate the task of national policy formation enormously.

The various states are represented in the Bundesrat according to their population. The smaller states are allocated three seats apiece, while states with populations of at least 4 million are entitled to four deputies. Those with 5 million or more inhabitants designate five representatives. Thus, Bremen, Hamburg, and the Saar each have three deputies; Hesse, Rhineland-Pfalz, and Schleswig-Holstein have four; and Baden-Württemberg, Bavaria, Lower Saxony, and North Rhine-Westphalia each have five. As noted, West Berlin designates four nonvoting delegates. Unlike voting procedures in the Bundestag, members of the Bundesrat do not cast individual votes. Instead, they vote as a three-, four-, or five-person bloc on instructions from their state governments in Munich, Düsseldorf, and other state capitals.

In their role as national parliamentarians, Bundesrat deputies are constitutionally empowered to act on behalf of the Länder "in the legislation and administration of the Federation."[17] In practice, this means that all government bills must be submitted first to the Bundesrat for its opinion. Similarly, the Bundesrat has the constitutional prerogative to review all legislation passed by the Bundestag. In addition, members of the Bundesrat may initiate legislation on their own volition. As indicated in the description of the legislative process below, these provisions accord the Bundesrat multiple possibilities of legislative delay, the right of a suspensive veto, and, in certain cases, even the power of absolute veto over proposed legislation.

Structurally, the Bundesrat is organized along similar lines as the lower house. Its chief executive officers include an elected president and three vice presidents. The former office routinely rotates on an annual basis among the ministers-president of the various Länder. Bundesrat committees duplicate those of the Bundestag.

The direct participation of Länder representatives in legislative decisions enhances the potential significance of regional variations in party strength. As long as the parliamentary majority in the Bundestag corresponds approximately to the composition of the governments in most of the state parliaments and hence to the majority in the Bundesrat, the two houses of parliament will perform their legislative functions with minimum friction. But if one majority prevails in the lower house and another in the Bundesrat—by virtue of different electoral outcomes on the national and state levels—the result can be a parliamentary stalemate between opposing factions.[18] As I discuss in the next chapter, the latter situation characterized relations between the Bundestag and the Bundesrat from the late 1970s through the early 1980s.

The Dual Executive

Political leadership in the Federal Republic is vested in a dual executive whose roles, like the Basic Law itself, reflect the lessons that West Germans have drawn from their political history. Consistent with the precedents of the Weimar Republic and to a lesser extent the Imperial system, executive power is concentrated in the hands of the federal chancellor, who serves as head of government. Unlike his Imperial and Weimar predecessors, the federal chancellor enjoys considerable security of tenure once he is elected to office. Historical memories similarly shape the constitutional status of the other chief executive officer, the federal president. In a deliberate attempt to avoid a repetition of political rule by presidential decree, which characterized both the beginning and the end of the Weimar Republic, the framers of the Basic Law carefully circumscribed presidential powers in the Federal Republic. As a result, the president functions primarily as a symbolic and sometimes moral spokesman for the nation rather than as an active participant in the political process.

THE FEDERAL CHANCELLOR

The central leadership role accorded the federal chancellor is based legally on the constitutional maxim that the chancellor "shall determine, and be responsible for, the general policy guidelines" (Article 65). In practice, the chancellor's authority is considerably strengthened by a number of extralegal factors. Among them are his status as a prominent leader (if not the chairman) of the governing party, the strength of his parliamentary support, his visibility in the public media, and the prestige that accrues from periodic meetings with foreign statesmen. In addition, a chancellor's authority may expand or contract in accordance with less tangible elements of personal leadership style and policy effectiveness.

One of the major constitutional innovations in postwar Germany is the elaborate set of provisions, described in the preceding section on the Bundestag, that govern the election and potential dismissal of the federal chancellor. Designed to diminish the prospect of rapid executive turnover, which has characterized unstable parliamentary systems throughout twentieth-century Europe, the election procedures encourage extraordinary executive stability. As noted, the federal chancellor must, as a rule, be elected by an absolute majority. Moreover, a chancellor can be dismissed from office only if the Bundestag "(elects) a successor with the majority of its members" (Article 67). The only admissible exception to the majority principle is outlined in Article 63 of the Basic Law. In the remote event that a majority of the Bundestag is unable to agree on a chancellor, the federal president may, at his personal discretion, either (1) appoint the person receiving the largest number of votes within seven days of the election or (2) dissolve parliament and order a new national election. In the four decades since the Federal Republic was founded, none of the latter contingencies has ever materialized. All federal chancellors have been elected by an absolute majority, and only one was dismissed under provisions outlined in Article 67 for a constructive vote of no-confidence, namely, Helmut Schmidt in 1982 (as I discuss in chapter 5).

Once a federal chancellor has been elected by a parliamentary majority and duly appointed by the federal president, his first task is to recommend candidates for the president to appoint as members of the federal government. Ministerial assignments are typically the object of intense consultations both within the chancellor's own party and between it and his coalition partner(s). Cabinet seats are generally apportioned according to the parliamentary strength and policy priorities of the parties that make up the coalition. The most prestigious assignments are the vice-chancellorship and the ministers of foreign affairs, economics, finance, justice, defense, and the interior. The other Cabinet posts include agriculture and forestry; labor and social order; youth, family, women, and health; environmental affairs, protection of nature, and safety of nuclear reactors; traffic; mail and telecommunication; land use, construction, and city planning; inter-German relations; research and technology; education and science; and economic cooperation.

The policy role of the federal chancellor assumes diverse forms. As chief executive officer, he chairs regular meetings of the Cabinet to discuss evolving policy guidelines and resolve potential disputes among different ministers. In addition, the chancellor acts as the principal government spokesman during important plenary sessions of the Bundestag. The federal chancellor delivers an annual keynote address on the state of the nation, presents and defends the annual budget, and speaks to particular foreign and domestic issues as they arise. Assisting the federal chancellor in day-to-day policy formation and evaluation is a staff of lawyers, economists, political scientists, and other experts who serve in the Federal Chancery, a large modern building adjacent to the parliamentary complex.

The federal chancellor also performs important leadership tasks as chairman (or at least as a highly prominent member) of his party. He consults regularly about government and party policy with party stalwarts in the parliamentary caucus and Länder organizations, and campaigns actively in behalf of his party during national and many state elections. In recent years, chancellors and chancellor candidates have also assumed an increased interest in recurrent efforts to elaborate or revise their parties' programs.

THE FEDERAL PRESIDENT

The federal president is elected for a five-year term by a special electoral college known as the Federal Assembly *(Bundesversammlung),* which is composed of all the members of the Bundestag and an equal number of delegates chosen by the various Land parliaments. He may be reelected once. Because the public is not involved in the election of the federal president, the office lacks the prestige associated with the American Presidency and in mixed presidential-parliamentary systems such as France and Finland. This was also the intent of the framers of the Basic Law, who deliberately diluted the powers of the German head of state in order to strengthen those of the federal chancellor and members of his Cabinet.

The most important legal responsibilities of the federal president are to nominate a chancellor candidate following each election to the Bundestag; appoint the chancellor if he receives the requisite majority vote; appoint and dismiss members of the federal Cabinet upon the recommendation of the federal chancellor; and, under carefully prescribed conditions, order new national elections. The Basic Law foresees two such contingencies: (1) If, as noted, an absolute majority of the Bundestag is unable to agree on the election of a federal chancellor, the president may choose either to appoint the plurality candidate or dissolve the lower house and call a new election; or, (2) if a majority of the Bundestag rejects a motion of the federal chancellor for a vote of confidence. In the latter event, the chancellor may petition the federal president to dissolve the Bundestag. If the president concurs, a new election must be held within 21 days.

Other presidential powers include the formal authority to appoint and dismiss federal judges, civil servants, and military officers (albeit only on the recommendation of the chancellor and the Cabinet); the right of pardon for civil and criminal offenses; and the ceremonial right to represent West Germany within the international community. In the latter capacity, the president "shall conclude treaties with foreign states . . . (and) shall accredit and receive envoys" (Article 59). In practice, of course, actual decisions concerning the conduct of West German foreign policy are made at the Cabinet level.

Once elected, a federal president is expected to remain in office for the duration of his five-year term. For personal and/or political reasons, however, an incumbent may decide to resign early or not seek a second term. The president may be impeached by a two-thirds majority of either the Bundestag or the Bundesrat in case he "willfully violates" the Basic Law or federal statutes (Article 61).

Thus far, six men have served as federal president: Theodor Heuss, a prominent Liberal and a founding member of the FDP, from 1949 to 1959; Heinrich Lübke, a Christian Democrat and former minister of agriculture, from 1959 until 1969; Gustav Heinemann, a Social Democrat, from 1969 until 1974; Walter Scheel, a member of the FDP, from 1974 until 1979; Karl Carstens, a Christian Democrat, from 1979 to 1984; and Richard von Weizsäcker, also a Christian Democrat, who was elected in 1984.

The Legislative Process

The dual executive, the Bundestag, and the Bundesrat interact to determine West German national legislation and legal decrees. The federal government and parliament share legal responsibility for policy deliberation and enactment, although for constitutional and political reasons the federal chancellor and his ministerial colleagues perform the leading role in initiating the majority of federal decisions.

Formally, as indicated in figure 3.1, bills may be introduced by either the federal government, the Bundesrat, or the Bundestag.[19] Government bills must be submitted first to the Bundesrat, which is entitled to state its position on them within six weeks. Conversely, bills initiated by the Bundesrat must be re-

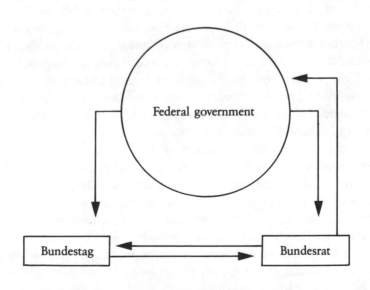

FIGURE 3.1
THE LEGISLATIVE PROCESS

ferred directly to the federal government. The latter is required to submit such proposals—along with its own views on their relative merits—to the Bundestag within three months.

Legislation initiated within the Bundestag itself, along with bills submitted by the federal government and the Bundesrat, are reviewed by members of the Council of Elders and then submitted to the lower house for a preliminary vote. If a bill passes the first reading, it is referred to the appropriate parliamentary committee for detailed deliberation and potential modification. If a committee majority endorses the bill, it is resubmitted to the Bundestag for a second and third (final) reading. Proposed measures thus endorsed by the Bundestag must then be sent without delay to the Bundesrat. If the upper house similarly approves a measure, the legislative process is completed, and the bill is referred to the federal government for the final steps in its formal enactment. If, however, the Bundesrat rejects a bill, the upper house, the federal government, or the Bundesrat may demand that a joint consultative committee —made up of members from both chambers—be appointed to reconsider the measure. If such a committee proposes any changes in a bill, it must be sent back to the Bundestag for renewed deliberation and endorsement by a majority vote.

In the overwhelming number of cases, the two houses concur on pending legislation. As shown in table 3.1 on page 60, the total number of bills ratified by the Bundestag and the Bundesrat has ranged from a high of 516 passed during the seventh parliamentary period (1972-76) to a low of 139 during the ninth session (1980-83). From the late 1950s through 1972, fewer than 50 joint consultative committees were convened to resolve policy differences between the Bundestag and the Bundesrat during each parliamentary session. Thereafter, the number jumped to 104 in 1972-76 but declined to only 6 in 1983-87. When the two chambers are unable to resolve their differences through the mediation of a consultative committee, the Bundesrat has recourse to two kinds of veto: (1) a suspensive veto, applicable in matters of ordinary legislation, which can delay a bill but can eventually be overriden by a corresponding majority in the lower house; or (2) an absolute veto, which may be exercised with respect to constitutional amendments and any laws affecting changes in the boundaries of the various Länder.

Once parliament endorses a measure, the bill goes to the federal government for signature by the minister in charge of that particular policy area. From there, a measure is sent to the federal president for his countersignature. A bill becomes law upon its publication in the Federal Registry of Laws. As noted, virtually all domestic legislation is delegated to the various states—rather than federal administrative agencies—for policy implementation.

TABLE 3.1
LEGISLATIVE ACTIVITY, 1957-87

Type of Activity	Legislative Periods							
	1957-1961	1961-1965	1965-1969	1969-1972	1972-1976	1976-1980	1980-1983	1983-1987
Bills initiated by								
Federal government	394	368	415	351	461	322	155	280
Bundestag	207	245	225	171	136	111	58	183
Bundesrat	5	8	14	24	73	52	38	59
TOTAL	606	621	654	546	670	485	251	522
Origins of ratified bills								
Federal government	348	326	372	259	427	288	104	273
Bundestag	74	97	80	58	62	39	16	42
Bundesrat	2	3	9	13	17	15	8	32
Joint	—	—	—	5	10	12	11	9
TOTAL	424	426	461	335	516	354	139	320
Consultative committees convened by								
Federal government	3	3	4	2	7	7	3	—
Bundestag	—	2	1	—	1	1	—	—
Bundesrat	46	34	34	31	96	69	17	6
TOTAL	49	39	39	33	104	77	20	6

SOURCE: *Statistisches Jahrbuch für die Bundesrepublik Deutschland 1988,* 91.

Executive Preeminence Versus Parliamentary Control

Throughout the legislative process, the federal government clearly dominates as West Germany's central policy actor. Cabinet members initiated an average of 61 percent of all legislation between 1949 and 1985, compared to an average of 34 percent submitted by Bundestag deputies and only 5 percent by members of the Bundesrat. The government's share of bills actually passed by parliament is even higher: an average of 78 percent of all bills ratified between 1949 and 1985. (Percentages are calculated from the absolute numbers presented in table 3.1.)

Underscoring the pivotal policy role of the federal government is a simultaneous increase in the number of legal ordinances *(Rechtsverordnungen)* issued by the chancellor's office and other ministries. Such decrees have the force of law and require only the consent of the Bundesrat before they become effective (Article 80). Typically, they take the form of executive elaborations of general statutes previously endorsed by parliament. From the late 1960s onward, the number of legal ordinances increased from 1343 during the sixth legislative session (1969-72) to 1726 during the seventh (1972-76), declining thereafter to 1229 during the tenth (1983-87). The majority of ordinances were in the areas of financial policy, traffic regulations, agriculture, and economics.

Executive preeminence in West Germany is hardly surprising, given the constitutional prerogatives of the federal chancellor and his considerable political resources as leader of the parliamentary majority. As in other stable parliamentary regimes such as Sweden and Norway, the chancellor can usually rely on the loyalty of the deputies within his own faction and those of his coalition partner(s) to mobilize majority support for the government's legislative program. Moreover, executive preeminence in the Federal Republic corresponds to similar patterns in other modern democracies. Comparable to postwar tendencies in the United States, Britain, France, and the Scandinavian countries, the West German executive has accumulated increased power as a consequence of diverse international and domestic developments. Among them are the growing complexity of legislation, recurrent foreign policy and economic crises, and a steady expansion of the economic and social roles of government—all of which have encouraged the centralization of executive power as a universal phenomenon.

At the same time, legal and political constraints within parliament mitigate against executive omnipotence. For one thing, members of the Bundestag have taken seriously their constitutional rights to exercise parliamentary controls over executive behavior. Both government and opposition factions utilize party interpellations and the Question Hour extensively as a means to extract information from Cabinet officers and to instigate periodic debates concerning foreign and domestic policies. The frequency of full-scale interpellations *(Grosse Anfragen)* has fluctuated from a high of 175 during the tenth legislative period (1983-87) to a low of 23 during the seventh (1972-76). The number of so-called lesser interpellations *(Kleine Anfragen)* and especially questions posed by individual members of parliament, meanwhile, dramatically increased through 1983 (see table 3.2). While the government, regardless of its composition, is predictably reluctant to yield to opposition demands that it change its policy course, interpellations and the weekly Question Hour provide a constant avenue of legislative pressure on executive officers. As a consequence, individual ministers have been occasionally forced to admit publicly that they erred in their judgment and to undertake minor policy correctives. In one dramatic instance, discussed in the next chapter, Bundestag deputies successfully utilized the question procedure as an indirect means to force the resignation of a prominent Cabinet official.

61

TABLE 3.2
PARLIAMENTARY CONTROL FUNCTIONS, 1957-87

Type of Activity	1957-1961	1961-1965	1965-1969	1969-1972	1972-1976	1976-1980	1980-1983	1983-1987
Interpellations	49	34	45	31	23	47	32	175
Lesser interpellations	410	3 08	487	569	483	434	297	1 006
Oral questions	1,536	4,786	10,733	11,073	18,497	23,467	14,384	22,864

SOURCE: *Statistisches Jahrbuch 1988*, 91.

In addition to legal channels of parliamentary control, various political factors constitute potentially significant constraints on executive discretion. One is the relative distribution of government and opposition strength in the two houses of parliament. A Cabinet that commands only a bare majority in the Bundestag is obviously in a weaker position to enact its program than one that rests on a more comfortable margin. Similarly, a government that lacks a majority in the Bundesrat is vulnerable to opposition efforts to delay or modify legislative decisions. Equally significant, the necessity to form coalition governments restricts the scope of discretionary executive action. Because both the CDU/CSU and the SPD have been dependent on other parties for their tenure in office, neither party has been wholly successful in dominating the national policy agenda to the same degree as majority single-party governments in, for example, Canada or the United Kingdom.

In addition, West Germany's federal structure itself constitutes a principal constraint on executive autonomy. Even during periods of a concurrent majority in support of the government coalition in both the Bundestag and the Bundesrat, the fact that the parliamentary opposition will inevitably command a majority in at least some of the Länder assemblies means that political power is always distributed among a variety of policy actors.

Public Administration

An important corollary of West German federalism is that policy implementation—similar to decision processes themselves—is institutionally fragmented. Historical tendencies toward administrative-bureaucratic centralization, which began with the founding of the Imperial Reich in 1871 and reached their terrifying apex under Adolf Hitler, were abruptly reversed in 1945 when Allied officials implemented their sweeping program of political and economic decentralization. Facilitating Allied efforts to dismantle the unitary administrative apparatus of the Third Reich (and simultaneously encouraging a "dereification" of the state in eyes of public officials and citizens) was their decision early in the occupation to dissolve Prussia and establish a number of smaller successor Länder (including North Rhine-Westphalia and Lower Saxony) in its place.

The result of Allied-sponsored reforms is the emergence of what Guy Peters has described as "(p)robably the most extreme version of . . . administrative devolution and administrative federalism" within the Western democratic community.[20] By this, Peters means that most legislation, executive decrees, and court decisions are enforced by Länder bureaucrats rather than by federal officials. The exceptions are foreign policy and national defense, as well as the administration of most of West Germany's railroads, the telephone system, and the post office. Other policy decisions—ranging from economic management to those affecting agriculture and the provision of social services—are delegated to the states for implementation. Empirically documenting this division of labor is the fact that in 1986 only 11 percent of all public officials worked for the Federation compared to 55 percent employed by the Länder and 34 percent by local county and city governments.[21]

An important consequence of "administrative federalism" is that policy implementation may vary somewhat from Land to Land. As Peters observes:

> Although the federal ministers must assure that the programs of their ministry are administered properly and uniformly throughout the country, in practice they have few means of enforcing such uniformity. The system allows for considerable autonomy in the *Länder* with respect not only to the organization of their own civil service systems, but also to the manner of executing public policies. The logic behind such a system—from the administrative rather than political point of view— is that different local conditions may require marginally different solutions. Further, different local historical factors and differences in the religious composition of the *Länder* may require variations in the internal procedures of administration.[22]

In practice, variations in policy implementation are not as great as they might seem, with the exception of policy areas in which the Länder exercise considerable decision-making autonomy in their own right, such as education and culture. One reason is the striking degree of conformity among senior civil servants—whether employed by the Federation or the states—with respect to social class and educational background. According to a national survey conducted in the mid-1950s, all West German public officials were recruited from the middle and upper social classes (compared to 63 percent in the United States and 77 percent in the United Kingdom). Moreover, fully 77 percent of West German civil servants had completed a college education (compared to 57 percent in the United States and 52 percent in the United Kingdom), with 69 percent of them having studied law. The comparable percentage in the United States was 52 percent and virtually zero in Britain.[23]

Policy Coordination

The day-to-day tension between leadership priorities and countervailing political constraints thus makes necessity out of constitutional virtue, with the formal division of power inherent in West Germany's "cooperative federalism" requiring continuous efforts to adjust conflicting national, regional, party, and group claims through the policy-making process. As I explain more fully in the assessment of government-opposition relations and macroeconomic management in chapters to come, the response by national decision makers to institutional complexity has been to establish a variety of decisional linkages designed to maximize policy coherence and effectiveness. The most sweeping arrangement, which signaled the emergence of a West German variant of democratic corporatism designed to cope with the domestic consequences of successive international economic crises from the mid-1960s onward, involved regular policy consultations attended by leading government, banking, industrial, and labor officials.

Efforts by policy actors to coordinate and rationalize the policy-making process have been accompanied by individual and group initiatives to challenge conformist political and legal tendencies. Therein lies the significance of the Federal Republic's elaborate judicial system as an important constitutional factor alongside political-administrative federalism, the decision-making role of the two houses of parliament, and the dual executive.

Civil Liberties and the Judicial System

Underlying the normative objectives in the Basic Law that define the executive and parliamentary prerogatives described above is an extensive catalogue of individual civil liberties and provisions governing the nation's courts. Common to both is the declared intent by the founding fathers of 1949 to secure "rule by law" as a means to prevent the personal abuse of power which characterized previous German regimes.

Fully 18 articles of the Basic Law prescribe a range of classical liberal and more modern individual and/or group rights. These include familiar guarantees of human dignity, liberty, legal equality, religious freedom, freedom of expression, freedom of assembly, freedom of association, the freedom to own property, the privacy of mail and telecommunications, the inviolability of the home against unreasonable searches, and the right of petition (Articles 1-9, 13, and 17). In addition, the Basic Law sanctions the legal rights of families, mothers, and illegitimate children (Article 6); affirms the right of all Germans "to choose (freely) their trade, occupation, or profession, their place of work and their place of training" (Article 12); accords conscientious objectors the right of performing an alternative public service to military conscription (Article 12a); prohibits the extradiction of German citizens to foreign countries (Article 13); and accords "persons persecuted on political grounds . . . the right of asylum" (Article 16).

An additional basic right—in this case one accorded the state rather than individuals—is that of economic socialization. Article 15 asserts: "Land, natural resources and means of production may for the purpose of socialization be transferred to public ownership or other forms of publicly controlled economy by a law which shall provide for the nature and extent of compensation." Finally, in marked contrast to the American constitutional tradition but similar to the practice of other West European countries, the Basic Law affirms religious instruction as an integral part of the "ordinary curriculum in state and municipal schools" (Article 7). Exceptions are allowed in secular schools and for parents or guardians who do not wish their children to receive religious training.

Assigned the formal task of enforcing and interpreting these and other constitutional provisions is a multitiered network of state and federal courts. A local court *(Amtsgericht)* serves as the first instance for minor civil disputes and criminal offenses. More important offenses, along with appeals from the local courts, are tried in state courts *(Landgerichte),* which are presided over by a single judge, or state civil or criminal "chambers" *(Zivil-* or *Strafkammern),* which are more complex structures made up of several judges. The highest court of review on the state level is the Provincial Court *(Oberlandesgericht).* Serving as the final instance for appeals involving ordinary civil and criminal matters is the Federal Court of Justice *(Bundesgerichtshof),* which is located in Stuttgart. In addition, specialized state and federal courts exist to settle disputes involving labor regulations, administrative decrees, and social questions. Judges on all levels are appointed for life by the relevant Cabinet minister, who is assisted by a committee of experts made up of the "competent Land Ministers and an equal number of members elected by the Bundestag" (Article 95).

The number of local and state courts, by type, is shown in table 3.3 on page 66. Presiding over them in 1987 were some 17,000 judges—2880 of them women (the overwhelming majority employed on the Land level).[24] In 1984, local and state courts passed first judgment in 1.9 million civil cases and heard nearly 174,000 appeals, while criminal courts tried 1.5 million cases and nearly 64,000 appeals. That same year, the Federal Court of Justice reached a verdict in 4260 civil disputes and 3800 criminal cases.[25]

Politically, the most important legal structure in West Germany is the Federal Constitutional Court *(Bundesverfassungsgericht),* situated in Karlsruhe in Baden-Württemberg. The Court is composed of two senates, each consisting

TABLE 3.3

TYPES AND NUMBER OF LOCAL AND STATE COURTS, 1988

State	Local Courts	State Courts	Local Civil Chambers	Local Criminal Chambers	State Civil Chambers	State Criminal Chambers
Schleswig-Holstein	30	4	49	33	27	4
Hamburg	6	1	52	43	15	5
Lower Saxony	79	11	137	135	44	9
Bremen	3	1	18	23	8	3
North Rhine-Westphalia	130	19	328	250	104	12
Hesse	58	9	120	104	32	8
Rhineland-Pfalz	47	8	73	59	22	4
Baden-Württemberg	108	17	158	218	39	8
Bavaria	72	21	197	203	67	13
Saar	11	1	20	13	9	2
Berlin	7	1	62	44	24	5
TOTAL	551	93	1214	1125	391	73

SOURCE: *Statistisches Jahrbuch 1988*, 330.

of eight judges. All of them are elected for 12-year terms, half by the Bundestag and half by the Bundesrat. They are formally appointed to office by the federal president. The Federal Constitutional Court is empowered to pass definitive judgment on the following issues (Article 93):

1. The constitutionality of federal and state laws
2. Disputes "concerning the extent of the rights and duties of a highest federal organ or of other parties concerned who have been vested with rights of their own by [the] Basic Law or by rules of procedure of the highest federal organ"
3. Legal disputes between the federal government and the states, as well as conflicts between the states
4. "Complaints of unconstitutionality" submitted by individuals, local governments, or associations of local government
5. The constitutionality of political parties

The Federal Constitutional Court frequently has been called on to exercise its sweeping jurisdiction. At the petition of the federal government, the court has twice outlawed political parties as unconstitutional, as noted in the next chapter. More recently, conservative political spokesmen have turned to the Court to challenge the constitutionality of controversial national legislation — including a state treaty between West and East Germany, which the CSU questioned in 1974, and the 1976 bill on codetermination, which various employer groups sought to annul through judicial channels in 1977. In both of the latter instances, the Constitutional Court ruled in favor of the federal government.

In aggregate terms, the caseload confronting the Federal Constitutional Court has progressively increased in recent decades. The number of cases, most of which generally involve "complaints of unconstitutionality" rather than judicial review, rose from 2300 in 1971 to 5493 in 1983, declining thereafter to 3124 in 1986.[26]

The increased frequency of legal disputes concerning the constitutional rights of individuals and groups is significant. For one thing, it indicates a growing inclination on the part of West Germans — similar to Americans — to look to the courts for the resolution of civil disputes rather than to the national and state legislatures. For another, the increased tendency toward litigation involving basic rights reveals growing public awareness of a persisting contradiction in West German society between constitutional ideals of human dignity, liberty, and equality, on the one hand, and the realities of socioeconomic inequalities and government efforts to curtail political dissent, on the other. Both trends point toward continued change in the constitutional-legal framework of the Federal Republic in the years ahead.

Notes

1. Peter H. Merkl, *The Origin of the West German Republic* (New York: Oxford University Press), 55-89.

2. Ibid.

3. Important exceptions are the ministries of foreign affairs and defense, both of which function as purely national administrative institutions.

4. Article 106 of the Basic Law. The principal constitutional source for this chapter is *Grundgesetz mit Grundvertrag. Menschenrechtskonvention, Bundeswahlgesetz, Bundesverfassungsgerichtsgesetz, Parteigesetz und Gesetz über den Petitionsausschuss.* Text edition with an introduction by Güer Düng, 19th ed. (Munich: Deutscher Taschenbuch Verlag, 1977). An English translation of the Basic Law can be found in Albert P. Blaustein, *Constitutions of the Countries of the World* (Dobbs Ferry, N.Y.: Oceana, 1974). Further citations in this chapter are to specific articles in the Basic Law.

5. Articles 71 and 73.

6. Article 74.

7. Article 91a.

8. Article 91b.

9. As noted, the various Länder and the federal government may negotiate agreements concerning educational planning and the promotion of scientific research.

10. For purposes of local government and administration, West Germany is divided into 8506 local communities *(Gemeinden)* and 328 cities and counties.

11. Article 28.

12. Kurt Sontheimer, *The Government and Politics of West Germany* (New York: Praeger, 1973), 159.

13. Although West Berlin deputies may not formally vote in either house, they participate fully in committee deliberations and cast advisory votes on the floor.

14. Article 63. If a majority of the members of the Bundestag are unable to agree on a candidate, the federal president has the discretionary authority either to appoint the plurality candidate as federal chancellor or to dissolve the lower house and call new elections.

15. Article 67.

16. The office of the *Wehrbeauftragter* was modeled after the Swedish office of the *justitieombudsman,* which was established in 1809 as a means to enforce bureaucratic accountability and legal impartiality. The West German effort to emulate the Swedish example, however, has proved less than a resounding success. Early CDU/CSU ambivalence toward the office and the second incumbent's criticism of the Bundeswehr as a "state within the state" have seriously undermined the institution's effectiveness. See H.P. Secher, "Controlling the New German Military Elite: The Political Role of the Parliamentary Defense Commissioner in the Federal Republic," *Proceedings of the American Philosophical Society* 109 (April 1965): 81.

17. Article 50.

18. For studies of regional elections and their consequences for national politics, see Lowell W. Culver, "Land Elections in West Germany," *Western Political Quarterly* 19 (June 1966): 304-36; and Linda L. Dolive, *Electoral Politics at the Local Level in the German Federal Republic* (Gainesville: University of Florida Press, 1976).

19. In the latter instance, at least 26 deputies must co-sponsor a proposed bill for

68

it to be officially considered.

20. B. Guy Peters, *The Politics of Bureaucracy* (New York: Longman, 1978), 111. Peters contrasts the West German administrative system with the "prefectoral system" in France, a less extreme version of devolution in the United Kingdom, and the American pattern of "deconcentration of administration" (111-12).

21. Statistisches Bundesamt, *Statistisches Jahrbuch 1988*, 440-41.

22. Peters, *Politics of Bureaucracy*, 111-12.

23. Ibid., 93-98.

24. *Statistisches Jahrbuch 1988*, 331-33.

25. *Statistisches Jahrbuch 1986*, 329-31.

26. Ibid., 335.

4. The Social Fabric of West German Politics: Organized Interest Groups and Political Parties

The emergence of corporatist policy-making arrangements in post-Adenauer West Germany, which is discussed primarily in the context of economic management in chapter 6, is closely related to the prior transformation of the country's interlocking systems of organized interest groups and political parties. Both systems are the product of history as well as postwar economic, social, and political change. All of the Federal Republic's major interest groups and political parties claim ideological and membership links with the past. At the same time, leadership choices and the effects of regime consolidation and legitimation during the formative 1950s and 1960s have profoundly affected their contemporary structural characteristics and their socioeconomic and political functions. The result is a process of what Gerhard Lehmbruch describes as organizational "concentration" affecting both interest groups and the political parties.[1]

Postwar structural concentration distinguishes West Germany from most other industrial democracies. Whereas the present-day interest-group and multiparty systems of the United Kingdom and Sweden closely resemble those that emerged in each of the countries by the early 1920s, the Federal Republic has experienced a clear break in historical continuity. In place of the three national trade union movements that existed during the Imperial and Weimar periods, a single trade union confederation now serves as the umbrella organization representing the majority of West Germany's industrial workers. Similarly, the multitude of ideological and regional parties whose very existence contributed to the instability of the Weimar Republic has given way to the electoral dominance of the Christian Democrats, the Social Democrats, and the Free Democrats.

The tendency toward structural simplification in the Federal Republic is by no means irreversible, as witnessed by the rise and fall of diverse splinter parties — including most recently the success of the Greens in the parliamentary elections of 1983 and 1987 — and factional conflicts within each of the three major parties. Taken together, structural concentration and recurrent fragmentation thus constitute contradictory themes of the "German model" in practice.

Socioeconomic, Cultural, and Demographic Differentiation

Comparable to similar organizations in other advanced democracies, organized interest groups and political parties in the Federal Republic are rooted in diverse occupational, class, and social strata. Germany's nineteenth-century transition from an agrarian to an industrial society has yielded a highly differentiated labor force in the Federal Republic. During the postwar decades, West Germany's population increased from 46.2 million in 1946 to a peak of 61.8 million in 1975, declining thereafter to just over 61 million by 1985. Nearly half of all citizens are gainfully employed (1984), 40 percent of them in manufacturing and construction, over a third in public and private services, and just under a fifth in transportation and commerce. Augmenting the native labor force of 26.4 million Germans are 2.4 million foreign workers, primarily Turks, Greeks, Italians, and Yugoslavs. Most of the latter *Gastarbeiter* (guest workers) are employed in lower-paid jobs in industry, construction, and services.

Since the early 1930s, as indicated in table 4.1, the distribution of West Germany's work force by occupation has undergone substantial change. Comparable to general European and North American trends during the same period, the number of persons employed in agriculture and other primary occupations has declined steadily, while those engaged in industry continued to grow

TABLE 4.1

DISTRIBUTION OF THE GERMAN LABOR FORCE, 1933-86
(IN ROUNDED PERCENTAGES)

Year	Agriculture, Forestry, Fishing	Manufacturing, Construction	Transportation, Commerce, Services
1933	29	40	31
1939	25	41	34
1950	22	45	33
1960	13	48	38
1970	9	49	43
1986	5	41	54

SOURCES: Statistisches Bundesamt, *Bevölkerung und Wirtschaft 1872-1972*, 142; World Bank, *World Development Report 1982* (Washington, D.C.: World Bank, 1982), 147; and *Statistisches Jahrbuch 1988*, 98.

at a relatively steady pace through the 1960s. West Germany's incipient move toward postindustrialization began in the 1970s when the number of industrial workers leveled off while the percentage of salaried employees increased by nearly a third. The latter group of workers—consisting of government officials, educators, professionals, and specialists in the field of research and development —will predictably increase in numbers through the remainder of the century.

Occupational differences are closely linked with three other socioeconomic variables: (1) levels of income, (2) the division of labor between men and women, and (3) education. According to government statistics, nearly a third of households can be classified as "working class" on the basis of net monthly incomes in 1986 of 1800 marks or less (approximately $1000). The largest social category, comprising 45 percent of households, are middle-class wage earners with net monthly incomes between 1800 and 4000 marks ($1000 to $2222). Upper-class households earning 4000 marks or more a month ($2222 and up) comprise 12 percent of the population. Among the latter are independent farmers, highly paid government officials *(Beamte)*, professionals, and self-employed businessmen.

Associated with differences in both occupation and levels of income are differences in male and female employment. First, fewer women than men work outside the home. In 1986, females made up only 40 percent of the labor force. Second, men and women typically perform different kinds of jobs, with males outnumbering females by ratios of two and more to one in manufacturing, construction, transportation, communication, and government administration. Similar to patterns in other advanced societies, more women than men are employed in traditionally low-income professions, such as home management, services, commerce, and agriculture.

A key determinant of both occupation and income in West Germany is formal education. Although virtually all Germans are literate, only a distinct minority of them have achieved specialized academic training beyond the compulsory minimum level of eight to nine years of elementary education. In 1980, for example, 66.5 percent of West Germans had advanced no further than elementary school, while 29.5 percent had received some sort of intermediate or professional training, and 4.3 percent had studied on the university level.[2] Differences in occupation, income, and education among West German employees and their families mutually reinforce one another to yield discernible class differences among the large middle and working classes and a smaller, less visible upper class—as measured by place and type of residence, car ownership, leisure activities, and even dialect.

Other important categories of socioeconomic differentiation among West Germans include religion, place of residence, and age.

RELIGION

Since the Reformation, religious differences have played a key role in defining social and cultural cleavages in German society. Religion assumed an important form politically with the creation of the Center party as a response by the nation's Catholics to the political dominance of largely Protestant Prussia. Throughout the Imperial and Weimar eras, the Center party functioned as the principal instrument for mobilizing Catholic voters and representing their socioeconomic interests within the legislative and executive branches of government. During the postwar period, in contrast, organized religion has declined in relative significance as a source of cultural and regional identity among adult Germans, due in combination to the separation of heavily Protestant East Germany from the rest of the nation, the influx of East European refugees, and the continuing secularization of West German society. Nonetheless, religious identity continues to influence political loyalties and electoral behavior, particularly among Catholics and women voters. Evangelical Protestants remain the largest religious group in postwar Germany, although their relative number has fallen marginally since 1950 as the number of dissenting Protestants and Catholics has grown (table 4.2).

TABLE 4.2

RELIGIOUS AFFILIATION, 1950-80 (IN ROUNDED PERCENTAGES)

Denomination	1950	1961	1970	1980
Protestant	52	52	49	46
Catholic	44	44	45	44
Other Christian	—	1	2	3
Jewish	—	—	.1	.1
No affiliation, other	4	4	4	8

SOURCES: *Statistisches Jahrbuch 1985,* 64; and David B. Barrett, ed., *World Christian Encyclopedia* (New York: Oxford University Press, 1982), 314.

PLACE OF RESIDENCE

Postwar population growth and economic development have yielded continuing urbanization and internal migration among the various Länder. In the first instance, the number of Germans living in urban areas with a population of 20,000 and more has grown from 20 million in 1950 to over 36 million in 1985. Some 43 percent of West Germans live in cities with populations exceeding 50,000. Three cities claim more than a million inhabitants: West Berlin, Hamburg, and Munich. Between half a million and a million citizens live in eight other major metropolitan centers: Cologne, Frankfurt, Düsseldorf, Dortmund, Essen, Bremen, Hanover, and Nürnberg.

Within the Federal Republic as a whole, the population is unevenly distributed among the Länder as a result of their different size and the regional dispersion of industry and services. The largest and most populous state is North Rhine-Westphalia, with 27 percent of the population. Following in descending order are Bavaria, Baden-Württemberg, Lower Saxony, Hesse, and—at a distance—the remaining states (see table 4.3). In recent years, industrialization and the expansion of the service sector have encouraged population growth in more than half of the Länder and a corresponding decline in the others. Between 1970 and 1980, the population increased between 6 and 9 percent in Schleswig-Holstein, Lower Saxony, Hesse, Baden-Württemberg, and Bavaria. Smaller advances of about 3 percent were recorded in North Rhine-Westphalia and Rhineland-Pfalz. Länder and city-states losing population during the same period were Hamburg, Bremen, the Saar, and West Berlin.

TABLE 4.3
POPULATION BY LÄNDER, 1987
(IN MILLIONS)

Schleswig-Holstein	2,612
Hamburg	1,567
Lower Saxony	7,189
Bremen	654
North Rhine-Westphalia	16,672
Hesse	5,552
Rhineland-Pfalz	3,606
Baden-Württemberg	9,350
Bavaria	11,043
Saar	1,041
West Berlin	1,884

SOURCE: *Statistisches Jahrbuch 1988*, 52.

AGE

Generational differences are also a significant element in the social fabric of contemporary West German politics. Historical memories of World War I, the economic chaos and political instability of the interwar period, and the traumas of National Socialism and World War II engender attitudes of skepticism and political caution among many older citizens. For most younger Germans, in contrast, postwar affluence and relative political stability are accepted ways of life, thus encouraging their acceptance of what Ronald Inglehart has described as "post-materialist" social and economic values emphasizing quality of life issues rather than material growth per se.[3]

Other economic, social, and political experiences will become formative for future generations, just as the general population itself will undergo continuing demographic change. Statisticians project that because of a falling birthrate, the West German population will decline from its present level of 61 million persons to between 59 and 60 million by 1990. As in other advanced nations, this trend will have two opposed social consequences, both of which will necessitate important policy adjustments in the years ahead: a decline in the number of young people and an increase in the number of elderly citizens. According to official calculations, the percentage of West Germans under 15 years of age will fall to 15 by 2000 (compared to 23 percent in the early 1970s), while the percentage of persons sixty-five years of age and older will grow from 14 (1972) to 18.[4]

Interest-Group Membership and Organization

Among the factors of socioeconomic differentiation, *occupation* is of primary significance in determining the organization and membership of West Germany's interest-group system. Income, education, religion, place of residence, and age, in contrast, are more important in accounting for political identities and electoral behavior.

The largest and most powerful associations represent employers and organized labor. Employers are organized in two national organizations: the Federal Association of German Employers *(Bundesvereinigung der Deutschen Arbeitgeberverbände,* or the BDA), which is responsible for questions concerning labor relations, and the Federation of German Industry *(Bundesverband der Deutschen Industrie,* or the BDI), which addresses itself primarily to economic policy. Speaking in behalf of organized workers with respect to both sets of issues is the German Confederation of Trade Unions *(Deutscher Gewerkschaftsbund,* or the DGB).

Both the BDA and the BDI claim direct institutional ties with equivalent pre-Nazi organizations. Employers are represented in each group on the basis of firms rather than individually. The Association of Employers consists of 46 national associations representing 384 local units and is organized in 6 economic sections, each corresponding to major productive categories such as manufacturing, construction, banking and insurance, and agriculture. The BDI is similarly organized on the dual basis of a federal structure and basic economic activities.

In contrast, the DGB is institutionally a postwar phenomenon. Its founding leaders—most of whom had been active in the socialist, Catholic, and liberal trade union organizations that spanned the Imperial and Weimar eras—resolved early during the occupation interlude to overcome the historical legacy of denominational and ideological rivalry and organization fragmentation. Thus they established the DGB in 1949 as a unitary federation representing the major national industrial unions, with membership on its governing board shared proportionately by Protestants (who are in the majority) and Catholics.

Today, the DGB encompasses 17 national unions that claimed in 1987 a combined membership of 7.8 million workers. Approximately 31 percent of West German employees belong to a union—compared to 80 percent in Sweden, 40 percent in Britain, and 23 percent in the United States.[5] The individual unions vary considerably in size. The largest is the Metal Workers' Union *(IG Metall)* with 2.6 million members, while the smallest is the Agricultural and Forestry Union with 42,000 members. Industrial workers make up the largest contingent of DGB members with 68 percent of the total. Salaried employees constitute 22 percent and government officials the remaining 10 percent.

The BDA, the BDI, and the DGB are "peak associations" exercising relatively little direct authority over their constituent units. That is, the organizations serve as national spokesmen for management and labor interests, with each seeking to maximize its members' political influence through research and publication activities, lobbying efforts vis-à-vis government officials, publicity campaigns, and, on occasion, legal action. Unlike comparable national organizations throughout much of the postwar period in Sweden, the DGB and the BDA do not negotiate national wage agreements. Instead, this responsibility is vested in the hands of regional or local trade unions and employer associations. The result is a pattern of more prolonged (and sometimes more acrimonious) wage negotiations than those characteristic of the "Swedish model" of advanced industrial society.

Other significant organized interest groups include the German Association of Farmers *(Deutscher Bauernverband),* with approximately 700,000 members; the Association of Public Officials *(Deutscher Beamtenbund),* with approximately 786,000 individual members; the German Union of Salaried Employees *(Deutsche Angestelltengewerkschaft),* with over 494,000; and the Federation of Free Professions *(Bundesverband der freien Berufe),* which consists of 67 national associations representing lawyers, doctors, dentists, engineers, and architects. Comparable to the larger employer and union federations, each of these associations seeks to bargain with public and private officials in behalf of their members to achieve maximum wages and favorable decisions concerning policy formation and implementation.

On the local level, an intricate network of industrial and commercial chambers *(Kammern),* composed solely of employers, performs important vocational training and certification tasks on behalf of the federal and state governments.

The local chambers are represented nationally by the German Industrial and Commercial Association (*Deutscher Industrie- und Handelstag,* or DIHT). Parallel local and national chambers represent craftsmen and farmers.

GROUP GOALS AND BEHAVIOR

With the emergence of the DGB as a unitary organization representing the majority of West Germany's organized industrial workers, the interest-group system has come to function as a principal factor in postwar economic and political stability. Officially, the DGB is committed to an ideological vision of economic democracy, which the Federation defines to mean social control of economic power through "the codetermination of organized workers . . . in all economic, social, and personnel decisions . . ." and, inter alia, the nationalization of "key industries and other market- and economically-dominant enterprises. . . ."[6] Of these dual objectives, union officials have thus far taken only codetermination seriously.

Throughout the postwar period, DGB and union spokesmen have continually sought to extend the participatory rights of workers in management decisions. Their efforts led, first, to the reinstatement in 1946 of elected company councils *(Betriebsräte)* on the level of individual firms.[7] A year later, union spokesmen prompted occupation officials in the British zone to endorse an even more sweeping change in the form of parity codetermination*(Mitbestimmung)* between workers and employers in iron and coal industries. This innovation, which provided for the equal representation of labor and shareholders on company supervisory boards, institutionalized shared responsibility (and hence authority) for decisions affecting production, investments, and personnel policy in the firms in question.

The experiment in parity codetermination in the British zone of occupation was extended to all coal, iron, and steel industries in the Federal Republic through national legislation implemented in 1951. The following year, parliament authorized a more diluted form of codetermination for the remaining industrial firms whereby worker representatives were accorded a third of the seats of the companies' supervisory boards. Although the 1952 bill fell far short of union demands for full equality between labor and capital, union spokesmen viewed it as an important step toward the ultimate realization of that goal.[8]

DGB officials redoubled their efforts to extend rights of parity codetermination to all major industries after the Social Democrats displaced the Christian Democrats as the senior coalition party in 1969 (see chapter 5). Union pressure on members of the government and parliament led finally to the adoption of a new codetermination bill in 1976, which introduced near-parity representation on the part of worker representations on the boards of all larger noncoal, iron, and steel industries. Various firms and employer associations filed suit in July 1977 to challenge the constitutionality of the measure, but the Federal Constitutional Court upheld its legality in 1979. Because the 1976 bill nonetheless fails to provide for complete equality between workers and shareholders, union officials signaled their determination in 1983 to launch a national campaign to achieve more comprehensive forms of codetermination in the future.[9]

Partly in return for rights of codetermination, DGB and union leaders have tabled any serious discussion of nationalization in favor of cooperation with the BDA and its member associations on behalf of economic recovery and growth. Accordingly, they have concentrated much of their day-to-day energies on bargaining sessions with employers concerning higher wages, improved social benefits, and a shorter workweek. To help ensure continued economic growth and maximum employment, union officials have proved generally willing to moderate their wage demands and to collaborate with management and public officials on measures to encourage price stability and contain domestic inflationary pressures. The result, as I discuss more fully in chapter 6, is the emergence of corporatist policy-making linkages that have promoted both economic stability and sociopolitical integration.

The Mainstream Political Parties: Functions and Programs

Socioeconomic differentiation also shapes the structure and membership of the West German political party system. Unlike organized interest groups, parties openly compete with one another for electoral support in their quest for seats and political influence in representative assemblies. Accordingly, political parties in the Federal Republic, as in other advanced democracies, are highly complex organizations whose political functions transcend the representation of particular occupational interests. Foremost among their political tasks are leadership recruitment, the representation of group interests, the simplification of policy alternatives, and the exercise of government responsibility or legislative opposition.

Throughout the postwar period, the Christian Democrats, the Social Democrats, and the Free Democrats have maintained themselves as West Germany's three dominant political movements. As early as the first Bundestag election in 1949, the CDU/CSU, SPD, and FDP together amassed more than 70 percent of the national vote. In both the 1972 and 1976 elections, their combined popular support peaked at 99 percent. The joint strength of the CDU/CSU, SPD, and FDP has declined in elections during the 1980s, due primarily to an increase in support for the Greens, but still exceeds 90 percent.

Two opposed political tendencies account for the shift from Germany's historical pattern of unstable multipartism toward today's more simplified party system: (1) the fusion of conservative and Catholic groups within the CDU/CSU, and (2) the virtual disappearance of a radical socialist alternative to the SPD. The demise of both an extreme right and the Communist left has permitted the Christian Democrats and the SPD to expand their electoral base from 31 percent and 29.2 percent in the 1949 election to a postwar average of 45.1 and 35.3 percent, respectively. That this tendency toward bipolarity has not resulted in the emergence of a full-fledged two-party system is due, first, to the ability of the FDP to maintain an average electoral following of 9.1 percent during the postwar period, and, second, to the success of the Greens in gaining and then maintaining membership in parliament with 5.6 percent and 8.4 percent of the popular vote in the 1983 and 1987 elections, respectively (see table 4.4).

TABLE 4.4

NATIONAL ELECTIONS IN THE FEDERAL REPUBLIC, 1949-87

(PERCENTAGE OF VOTES CAST ON SECOND BALLOT)

Year	Partici- pation	KPD/ KDP	Greens	SPD	FDP	CDU/ CSU	NPD, Radical Right	Other
1949	78.5	5.7	—	29.2	11.9	31.0	1.8	20.3
1953	86.0	2.3	—	28.8	9.5	45.2	1.1	13.1
1957	87.8	—	—	31.8	7.7	50.2	1.0	10.3
1961	87.7	—	—	36.2	12.8	45.3	0.8	5.7
1965	86.8	—	—	39.3	9.5	47.6	2.0	3.6
1969	86.7	0.6	—	42.7	5.8	46.1	4.3	0.5
1972	91.2	0.3	—	45.8	8.4	44.9	0.6	0.1
1976	91.0	0.4	—	42.6	7.9	48.6	0.3	0.2
1980	88.6	0.2	1.5	42.9	10.6	44.5	0.2	0.1
1983	88.4		5.6	38.2	7.0	48.8		0.5
1987	83.1		8.4	37.0	9.1	44.3		1.4

With their near-monopoly of seats in the Bundestag and the Länder parliaments, mainstream parties have become the exclusive basis for the selection of national political leaders. Similarly, they serve as the principal channel for transmitting and aggregating different citizen and interest-group demands for policy decisions. By performing the triple tasks of leadership recruitment, interest aggregation, and policy formation, the CDU/CSU, SPD, and FDP thus play a crucial role in the day-to-day effectiveness and legitimation of the West German political system. At the same time, each of the mainstream parties upholds distinctive ideological principles that serve to attract different sets of core electoral supporters and interest groups. Their contrasting programs provide in turn the basis for different policy choices and recommendations as they perform their remaining functions of governance and opposition.

THE CHRISTIAN DEMOCRATS

West Germany's Christian Democrats are formally organized in two independent parties that have remained in more or less permanent alliance throughout the postwar period. The larger party is the Christian Democratic Union (CDU) with local and state organizations in all Länder except Bavaria. A separate party exists in the latter state in the form of the Christian Social Union (CSU). Both groups were founded in the early months of the occupation regime as supraconfessional organizations. Each professes a bourgeois political credo based on "Christian responsibility" and libertarian principles of "freedom and justice." By seeking to mobilize voters from diverse social strata, both parties thus established themselves as mass-based "people's parties" with a broader electoral appeal than that of the much more sectarian Center party of the Weimar era.

The CDU and the CSU can be classified as conservative in that both are strongly supportive of capitalism and German nationalism. Key concepts in the CDU's party program include the celebration of democracy as a dynamic process of political development that "guarantees the participation of (all) citizens," the affirmation of the party's early postwar formulation of social market economic principles, the endorsement of a strong middle class, support for piecemeal educational reforms that encourage upward social mobility while maintaining the principle of certified individual competence, and demands for effective government measures against "attacks against society and the state" and "the abuse of social and political power." In addition, the CDU affirms "strengthened rights of workers in the workplace," but, significantly, the party stops short of supporting DGB demands for full parity between labor and capital on company boards. Finally, the CDU advocates continued alliance with the United States and other Western nations, German reunification, negotiations between "the two parts of Germany" to ease living conditions in both states, and relations with the Soviet Union based on "the mutual recognition of elementary rights and security needs."[10]

Similarly, the CSU proclaims its ideological foundation in "Christian faith" and affirms basic values of private ownership, libertarian democracy, law and order, German national interests, and European unity. In even more explicit terms than the parent CDU, the CSU proclaims its conscious identity with a "living historical European tradition (of conservatism)." Thus, the CSU "endorses the eminent technical possibilities of our time for improving the living conditions of mankind. At the same time (the CSU) opposes all political utopianism and the total technocratization of life which disregards the individual and freedom."

Since their parallel founding during the summer of 1945, the CDU and the CSU have maintained their regional separation. The Christian Democratic Union is by far the larger party, claiming a national membership of more than 714,000 members compared to 182,000 who belong to the CSU. The fact that the CSU is restricted to Bavaria, while the CDU competes in the remaining West German Länder (plus West Berlin), also accounts for the persisting disparity in their percentage of the national vote in successive elections and the number of their seats in the Bundestag, as seen in table 4.5.

TABLE 4.5

RELATIVE STRENGTH OF THE CDU AND THE CSU:

POPULAR ELECTORAL SUPPORT AND NUMBER OF BUNDESTAG SEATS

National Election	Percentage of Popular Support		Seats in Bundestag	
	CDU	CSU	CDU	CSU
1949	25.2	5.8	115	24
1953	36.4	8.8	191	52
1957	39.7	10.5	215	55
1961	35.8	9.6	192	50
1965	38.0	9.6	196	49
1969	36.6	9.5	193	49
1972	35.2	9.7	177	48
1976	37.4	10.6	190	53
1980	33.8	10.2	174	52
1983	38.2	10.6	191	53
1987	34.5	9.8	174	49

Although the CDU and the CSU have always governed together during periods of Christian Democratic rule, they nonetheless display important differences in leadership, party structure, and policy priorities. The CDU remains a confederation of state parties whose internal cohesion declined following Adenauer's retirement as federal chancellor in 1963. Once described by many observers during Adenauer's tenure as chairman as little more than a "chancellor's party," the CDU has experienced a rapid turnover of leadership in recent decades. Adenauer was succeeded by his economics minister, Ludwig Erhard. Within three years, Erhard was replaced by Kurt-Georg Kiesinger, the former minister-president of Baden-Württemberg. Since the late 1960s, various CDU notables have served as chancellor candidates and party leader. The current federal chancellor, Helmut Kohl, was prime minister of Rhineland-Pfalz from 1969 until 1976, and became chairman of the CDU in 1973.

The CSU, in contrast, claims a more centralized structure dominated from the 1960s to the late 1980s by one of West Germany's most willful, charismatic, and controversial figures: the late Franz Josef Strauss, a former minister of defense and minister of finance. An outspoken anticommunist, Strauss transformed the CSU into a perceptibly more conservative party than the CDU. One consequence of his disenchantment with the more moderate stance of national Christian Democratic leaders was Strauss's dramatic announcement in November 1976 that the CSU would sever its traditional parliamentary alliance with the CDU. The move was widely interpreted by the media and members of the other parties as a first step toward establishing the CSU as a national conservative party that would compete to the right of the parent CDU. In the face of the CDU's threat to retaliate by extending its own organization into Bavaria, Strauss relented and agreed to reestablish the joint CDU/CSU faction in the Bundestag, but only on the condition that the CSU could publicly disagree with the CDU on particular policy issues.[11]

With their accord of December 1976, the CDU and the CSU thus restored the outward political unity of the Christian Democratic movement. The prospect of another rupture within the alliance diminished when the CDU/CSU jointly nominated Strauss as their chancellor candidate in the 1980 Bundestag election. The parties once again joined ranks to support Kohl's election as federal chancellor in October 1982 and his subsequent bids for reelection in 1983 and 1987.

The Social Democrats

After its initial postwar advocacy of selective nationalization and economic planning failed to generate a parliamentary majority during the formative years of the Federal Republic, Germany's Social Democratic party (SPD) followed the lead of the CDU/CSU in establishing a new identity for itself as a "catchall" party with broad electoral appeal. The major milestone in this transformation was the adoption of a new program at an extraordinary party congress held in November 1959 in the Bonn suburb of Bad Godesberg. With the adoption of the Bad Godesberg program, the SPD explicitly affirmed traditional Judeo-Christian religious values, the legitimacy of the established capitalist economic system, European integration, and cooperation with the Western alliance. As a result, the SPD largely abandoned its ideological heritage as a doctrinaire class-based party. The SPD became, in short, more of a people's party in the image of the CDU/CSU. It still attracts most of its electoral support from among industrial workers, but the adoption of a more flexible program enabled party leaders to extend Social Democratic support to include middle-class voters as well.

The Bad Godesberg program is notable for its lack of traditional socialist rhetoric. Rather than emphasize historical stages of socioeconomic development or even the prospect of social "equality" comparable to demands advocated by Scandinavian Social Democrats, the SPD affirms "freedom, justice, and solidarity" as the "fundamental values of socialism." Its basic demands for a "humane society" include world peace, international solidarity between rich nations and poor ones, equal access to education, a full cultural life, and the enhancement of individual "social consciousness" through citizenship training "in the broadest sense." The only explicitly socialist demand in the party's catalogue of basic objectives is its call for a "new economic and social order" in which the "collective interest" would prevail "over special interests." The program reads further: "Democracy, social security, and freedom are endangered in a society and economic system dominated by the drive for profit and power."[12]

Substantively, the Bad Godesberg program contains a lengthy affirmation of parliamentary democracy, support for West German defense efforts within NATO, and an endorsement of a comprehensive system of social security benefits available to all citizens. In addition, the program endorses the trade union movement as an important element of democracy and advocates the extension of worker codetermination "throughout the entire economy." The party's educational objectives are distinctively libertarian in tone: "Education should give all persons the opportunity to develop their talents and skills in an unhindered fashion. (Its purpose should be) to strengthen (the individual's) resistance to conformist tendencies of our time. Knowledge of traditional cultural values as well as the formative social forces of the present are (necessary) principles of independent thought and free judgment." As concrete goals of educational reform, the SPD advocates an extension of the compulsory minimum number of years in school from 9 to 10, unhindered access to higher levels of education for "everyone who is qualified," and new opportunities for employed persons to pursue a university degree.[13]

The ideological objectives of the Social Democrats are distinguished from those of the Christian Democrats primarily with respect to the party's emphasis on long-term collective measures to achieve greater public control over the economic system. Criticizing the "concentration of economic power" in the hands of large privately owned firms and business interest groups, the Social Democrats urge measures to strengthen middle-size and small business firms; competition by various unspecified "public undertakings"; more extensive publicity about company policies as a means to mobilize public opinion against the potential abuse of private economic power; state-sponsored investment controls; and, even more vaguely, eventual "public ownership" as a "legitimate form of public control."[14]

The simultaneous shift toward a more libertarian profile and the advent of a new generation of party leaders in the late 1950s enabled the SPD to attract the support of an increasing number of salaried employees, women, and other traditional bourgeois voters. Under the chairmanship of Willy Brandt, the resolute mayor of West Berlin from 1957 to 1966, the SPD's share of the popular vote rose from 31.8 percent in 1957 to 36.2 percent in 1961. Its popular support continued to climb until it reached an all-time high of 45.8 percent in 1972. Thereafter, SPD strength leveled off at 42+ percent in the 1976 and 1980 elections before plummeting, for reasons to be explored in chapter 5, to less than 40 percent in the 1983 and 1987 elections. Through the 1970s the party's membership gradually expanded, approaching with 970,000 members in 1973 the historical zenith of 1 million party members registered in all of Germany in 1931. By 1987, party membership had declined marginally to 913,000.

In step with the SPD's electoral and political successes from the 1960s through the early 1980s, however, the Social Democratic movement became increasingly beset by internal conflicts. The party's apparent abandonment of traditional socialist values was adamantly criticized by younger activists in various auxiliary youth and student groups. The refusal of leaders of the Socialist German Youth Association (SDS) to accept the Bad Godesberg program caused the SPD to disavow the SDS and establish a new Social Democratic Association of University Students (SHB) in 1960. Later, younger ideological purists formed the Working Group of Young Socialists—known colloquially as the "Jusos"—within the parent party. From the early 1960s, the Jusos' self-proclaimed task has been to mobilize party and mass opinion on behalf of socialist transformation. With the adoption of 56 "theses concerning political economy and strategy" in 1971, the Jusos characterized postwar West Germany as a "mature capitalist" society beset by a "fundamental contradiction between social production and private acquisition" and ruled by a minority of wealthy industrialists. To achieve "an end to the power of capitalists to control the means of production," the Jusos demand an extension of direct worker influence over company decisions and the implementation of "democratic economic planning" through investment controls and the "nationalization of key industries as well as banks and credit institutions."[15]

Ideological agitation by the Jusos helped prompt the party's endorsement of a new set of programmatic principles in November 1975 that were designed to augment and clarify the SPD's concept of long-term system change. Known as an "economic and political orientation framework for the years 1975-85," the latest SPD statement reaffirms both the basic libertarian values of the Bad Godesberg program and the need to "subordinate economic power to democratic control." To achieve the latter objective, the party currently advocates the extension of worker codetermination and the implementation of state investment controls.[16]

THE FREE DEMOCRATS

Of all the mainstream parties in West Germany, the Free Democratic party (FDP) remains by far the smallest. Its share of the popular vote has fluctuated between a low of 5.8 percent in 1969 and a high of 12.8 percent in 1961, with national FDP membership (which numbered 65,000 in 1987) remaining a third of the CSU's membership. Like both the CDU/CSU and the SPD, the FDP is beset by recurrent internal ideological cleavages.

German liberalism reemerged during the initial months of the occupation as a highly diversified political force. Between 1945 and 1947, the movement was reconstituted on a Länder basis, with the name of the party varying from state to state, as previously recounted. The decentralized structure of German liberalism reflected in large measure the historic division between national liberals, who retained an ideological stronghold in North Rhine-Westphalia and Lower Saxony, and more progressive constitutional democrats, who dominated in Baden-Württemberg, Bremen, and Hamburg. These competing traditions were united in a loose alliance in December 1948 when the Liberals formed the Free Democratic party as a trizonal federation.

During the subsequent years of regime consolidation, the FDP identified itself primarily as a moderate bourgeois party espousing "personal freedom, individual responsibility, and respect for the rights of others." As heirs to the libertarian ideals of the American and French revolutions, the Free Democrats declared their opposition to Communism, early Social Democratic demands for economic planning, parochial schools, and all "collectivist tendencies" within society (including the growth of government bureaucracy). The Liberals' major programmatic contribution to postwar reconstruction was their emphasis on free-market economic principles, which the Christian Democrats borrowed in 1947 to justify their own social market economic doctrines. In addition, FDP leaders stressed a nationalistic foreign policy stance that distinguished the party marginally from the CDU/CSU. At the same time, the Liberals coupled their support for German unification with an endorsement of close cooperation between the Federal Republic and the Western powers.

From 1949 to 1957 and again between 1961 and 1966, the FDP played an important policy-making role as junior partner in a series of CDU/CSU-dominated national Cabinets. Early postwar leaders occupied important Cabinet positions under Chancellors Adenauer and Erhard, and the FDP's first chairman, Theodor Heuss, served two terms as federal president from 1949 to 1959. Due principally to their political success as one of West Germany's governing parties, the Free Democrats were able in 1957 to narrow the ideological cleavage between national liberals and constitutional democrats with the adoption of their first comprehensive program at a party congress in West Berlin. The Berlin program reiterated Liberal support for individual liberties and a free-market economy, and defined the party's parliamentary role as that of a "third force" between the CDU/CSU and the SPD. In practice, this meant that party leaders would utilize their centrist position in the Bundestag as a parliamentary lever to influence policy choices of the two larger parties. On several important occasions, they proved instrumental in affecting the course of national politics. Their pressure tactics backfired in 1966, however, when the FDP withdrew from the government in a dispute over taxation policy only to witness the formation of a Grand Coalition between the Christian Democrats and the Social Democrats (see chapter 5).

Forced unexpectedly into parliamentary opposition at a time of profound political unrest in West Germany and other industrial democracies, the Free Democrats entered a period of ideological transformation. Party spokesmen abandoned the FDP's earlier emphasis on militant anticommunism and the primacy of German reunification and embraced, with the adoption of a new action program in 1967, a positive program combining domestic reform and détente with Eastern Europe. Specifically, the Free Democrats advocated greater democratization at home—for example, through increased student representation in decision-making bodies at Germany's universities—and direct negotiations between the Federal Republic and the DDR concerning "all questions of mutual interest." Accompanying the party's reorientation as a progressive liberal movement was the election of Walter Scheel, who represented the constitutional democratic wing of the party, as the new FDP chairman in September 1967. The change in party leadership presaged a shift in its coalition strategy. In 1969 most FDP Bundestag deputies voted with the SPD to elect West Germany's first Social Democratic president, Gustav Heinemann, and then joined the SPD in a national coalition government following elections in September.

The Free Democrats codified their new ideological image as a social liberal movement when they adopted the "Freiburger theses" in 1979. In this document the FDP defined the next task of German liberalism as the attainment of a more democratic, open society. Specific proposals include the "democratization of society" through the extension of participatory rights by citizens "in the productive process," the "reform of capitalism" through government efforts to encourage more decentralized ownership of property, tax reforms to facilitate greater individual savings, and improved environmental protection. As a concrete means to promote "social democratization" and the "humanization of the world of labor," the FDP reaffirmed Germany's postwar experiment with codetermination. Rather than endorse the DGB's demand for full parity representation between workers and shareholders to all industries, however, the Freiburger theses advocated a more complex formula whereby the seats allocated worker representatives on company boards would be divided between industrial and salaried employees.[17]

During the late 1970s and early 1980s, the FDP experienced abrupt fluctuations in electoral support. For a combination of policy and political reasons to be discussed in chapter 5, the Free Democrats suffered devastating defeats in a succession of state elections. In an effort to recoup some of their losses, they renounced their national coalition with the SPD and joined the CDU/CSU in forming a new government in October 1982. The FDP's "betrayal," as it was promptly characterized by irate Social Democrats, nearly cost the party its parliamentary representation in 1983 when party strength fell from 10.6 percent to 6.9 and the number of FDP deputies in the Bundestag declined from 53 to 34. Subsequently, however, the Free Democrats posted gains in both national and state elections to reaffirm their status as West Germany's pivotal middle force.

The Greens

From 1961 until 1983, West Germany's three mainstream political parties wholly dominated the Bundestag. Their monopoly was broken when the antiestablishment Greens *(die Grünen)* mobilized 5.6 percent of the popular vote in the March 1983 election to win 27 Bundestag mandates, only 7 fewer than the FDP. Whether the Greens can maintain themselves as a permanent fourth party on the national scene will depend on their success or failure in affecting policy outcomes concerning controversial security and environmental issues through the remainder of the decade and in the 1990s.

The Greens are not a conventional political party. Indeed, party officials formally describe the movement as an "antiparty party." By this, they mean that the Greens articulate socioeconomic interests that they allege are not represented adequately in the mainstream parties. "(A)n antiparty party, a party of a new type," is essential, one of the movement's leaders has written, "to speak for those who are weak, the elderly, the handicapped, women, young people, the unemployed, and foreigners."[18] The Greens' principal objectives in behalf of such groups are (1) stringent conservation and pollution controls to protect the natural environment, and (2) opposition to the domestic use of nuclear energy as well as the deployment of nuclear weapons on West German soil.

Party spokesmen demand nothing less than a fundamental reconstitution of the Federal Republic's socioeconomic system on an "ecological basis." As the draft preamble to the Greens' national program of 1983 reads: "Proceeding from natural laws and especially the insight that limitless growth is not possible in a limited system, ecological politics means to understand ourselves and our environment as a part of nature. . . . In particular, ecological politics requires the renunciation of an economic system that exploits and destroys natural resources."[19] More concretely, the Greens demand "greater conservation of energy and raw materials," the "manufacture of durable and easily repaired consumer goods," the "reutilization of used products and waste materials," and the "renunciation of products and processes that destroy the ecological balance and endanger life and health."[20]

On an equally consequential note, the Greens declare that "cooperation with all people of the world is the highest principle of our foreign policy." To that end, the Greens advocate global disarmament, "controls to ensure the maintenance of human rights (especially those of minorities, women, and children)," and the immediate dissolution of military alliances—"especially NATO and the Warsaw Pact."[21] Specifically, the Greens oppose the "storage and production of atomic, chemical, and biological weapons throughout the world" and the production and installation of middle-range rockets within both the NATO and the Warsaw Pact regions. Looking to the future, the Greens advocate the creation of a nuclear-free zone in Central Europe, the withdrawal of "all foreign troops from foreign territory," and the eventual dissolution of the West German armed forces.[22]

The pro-ecology, pacifist stance of the Greens distinguishes them sharply from the mainstream parties. To cite the views of a distinguished West German journalist, their ideology constitutes a form of "parochial nationalism," one that is "Candide-like, inward-bound, almost escapist. Its message is not *Deutschland über alles,* but 'Leave us alone': if we could only get rid of the weapons, we will get rid of war; if we could only push back 'the superpowers,' we will live in peace and all-European harmony ever after."[23]

The Greens' ideological ambiguity reflects the movement's highly heterogenous structure. Rooted in the proliferation of citizen action groups established on the local level in the 1960s, the Greens began to coalesce as a recognized political force during the 1970s in the form of decentralized city and statewide organizations. Local and regional names varied widely, ranging from *die Alternativen* ("the Alternatives") in West Berlin to *die Bunten* (literally, "the Colorful") in Hamburg. While many local leaders and their supporters undertook direct actions against government efforts to expand West Germany's nuclear energy program, other adherents borrowed slogans (including "Swords into Plowshares") from an underground peace movement in East Germany to advocate nuclear disarmament. Out of these diverse strands was formed, not without considerable difficulty, a confederal political association in March 1979.

The Greens were subsequently established as a national political party the following January.

By the mid-1980s, the Greens succeeded in winning seats in eight West German Länder parliaments (Bremen, Baden-Württemberg, Bavaria, Hamburg, Hesse, North Rhine-Westphalia, Lower Saxony, and Rhineland-Pfalz) plus West Berlin. Simultaneously, more than 1000 Green candidates were elected to seats on local urban and county councils. The Greens established themselves as a national political force by scoring 5.6 percent of the vote in the 1983 Bundestag election, and subsequently increased their popular support to 8.3 percent in 1987. Their regional electoral successes enabled the Greens to displace the FDP as the third party in several state parliaments and even to govern temporarily in coalition with the SPD in Hesse (1986-87). At the same time, a bitter internal dispute between ideological purists who reject such coalitions and "realists" who favor them raises serious questions about the future viability of the movement.

Electoral Behavior

Electoral behavior in the Federal Republic is a function of three principal factors: (1) the ideological appeal of the various parties to partisan supporters among various socioeconomic groups; (2) constitutional-legal constraints imposed by the Basic Law and various parliamentary statutes; and (3) the parties' records of perceived policy success or failure in office. The first two of these factors are discussed in the remainder of this chapter; the third is the subject of chapters 6 and 7.

SOCIOECONOMIC GROUPS AND PARTY SUPPORT

As ideological associations seeking to maintain or change aspects of the existing sociopolitical system, each of the mainstream parties has established a distinct electoral identity. According to successive postwar surveys, both the CDU/CSU and the FDP appeal predominantly to more affluent members of the middle and upper classes, while the SPD recruits most of its support among industrial workers. In the January 1987 election to the Bundestag, for example, the Christian Democrats drew 60 percent of their voters—and the Free Democrats fully 83 percent—from among salaried employees, independent professionals, and landowners. The comparable percentage for the Social Democrats was only 47. Conversely, the SPD recruited 48 percent of its followers among skilled and unskilled workers compared to only 13 percent for the FDP and 36 percent for the CDU/CSU.[24]

Further evidence of the parties' appeal to different socioeconomic groups is provided by survey data on levels of income and education. Higher-income voters tend, on balance, to favor the FDP and the CDU/CSU, while a plurality of those with lower incomes endorse the SPD. In the 1983 election, for instance, 19 and 10 percent of persons with monthly incomes over 2500 marks supported the FDP and the CDU/CSU, respectively. At the opposite end of the income scale, 19 percent of those with incomes between 600 and 1000 marks a month endorsed the SPD, compared to 16 percent who favored the CDU/CSU and 14 who voted for the FDP.[25] Similarly, the Free Democrats and to a lesser extent the Christian Democrats drew most of their electoral support in 1987 from persons who had completed secondary school and/or pursued university studies (67 percent and 40 percent, respectively, compared to 32 percent for the Social Democrats). In contrast, the SPD attracted 68 percent of its electoral clientele among those with only elementary and vocational training compared to 60 percent for the CDU/CSU and 33 percent for the FDP.

In addition, religion and to a lesser extent place of residence and age influence partisan electoral choice. Throughout the postwar period, the Christian Democrats have generated most of their support among Catholics (56 percent in 1987), while both the SPD (with 56 percent) and the FDP (with 63 percent) attract a larger percentage of their followers among Protestants. Urban-rural contrasts, meanwhile, underscore the influence of occupation, income, and religion on party preference. In 1987, the Social Democrats mobilized by far their largest number of voters (41 percent) in industrial areas with populations of 100,000 or more. Similarly, the FDP drew most of its support (40 percent) in large metropolitan areas, where many professionals and other affluent citizens reside. In contrast, a significant plurality of 46 percent of voters residing in communities with fewer than 20,000 citizens—where organized religion continues to play a more important role in the day-to-day lives of citizens than in the larger, more secularized cities—favored the Christian Democrats.[26]

Finally, the mainstream parties attract marginally different levels of support among various age groups. In the 1987 election, the Christian Democrats attracted their largest share of support (51 percent) among persons fifty years of age or older and their smallest percentage (17) among voters between eighteen and twenty-nine. Both the SPD and the FDP also appealed primarily to older citizens but attracted more younger voters (21 and 24 percent, respectively) than was the case with the CDU/CSU.[27]

In summary, the CDU/CSU appeals predominantly to middle- and upper-class citizens, Catholics, and older voters. In comparison, the SPD has made significant inroads among members of the middle class and younger voters but remains a party representing primarily industrial workers, persons with lower incomes and less formal education, and Protestants. The FDP, meanwhile, attracts a comparably affluent and better-educated clientele than the Christian

Democrats and simultaneously mobilizes a larger percentage of salaried employees, younger voters, and Protestants.

These socioeconomic characteristics generally confirm the proclaimed ideological nature of each of the mainstream parties. As professed conservatives, Germany's Christian Democrats are skeptical of utopian proposals to change the established economic and social system; the Social Democrats are advocates of piecemeal economic and social reforms designed to enhance the security and prospects of upward social mobility on the part of industrial workers and lower-level salaried employees; and the Free Democrats represent highly diverse socioeconomic groups who oppose the concentration of both political and economic power.

As the maverick political movement of the 1980s, the Greens attract an overwhelming percentage of their support among younger Germans (63 percent of their support in January 1987 came from those under twenty-nine years of age). Their adherents are concentrated among salaried employees and skilled workers and in more densely populated urban areas.[28]

LEGAL CONSTRAINTS

Although ideology and socioeconomic factors are the most important determinants of partisan political choice in the Federal Republic, various legal constraints also help shape electoral behavior. Foremost among them are national and state laws governing the electoral process and a constitutional prohibition against antidemocratic parties.

Current legislation defining the national electoral system dates from 1956 when parliament endorsed a "permanent" electoral law that incorporated, with some modifications, electoral practices that had been in effect since 1949. The 1956 legislation provides for a dual system that combines the German tradition of proportional representation with the Anglo-American practice of plurality elections from single-member districts. Thus, in elections to the Bundestag, West Germans eighteen years and older cast two votes on a single ballot: the first is for the direct election of one representative from each of the country's 248 constituencies, while the second is for the election of an equal number of delegates drawn from so-called Land lists of candidates nominated by the various parties on the state level. The second ballot is the more important of the two, as the relative percentage of a party's popular support determines its total number of parliamentary seats. The d'Hondt electoral system is used to allocate seats among the various parties whereby the number of votes cast for each party is successively divided by 1, 2, 3, et cetera, to yield a quotient that is approproximately equal to its proportional share of the vote. The number of constituency seats won by each party on the first ballot is deducted from the total number of seats to which it is entitled on the basis of its performance on the second ballot; the remainder of the seats are then distributed among the party candidates in the order in which they are listed on the various Land lists.[29] If a party wins more seats in a given state than it would deserve on the basis of its proportional share of the vote, the number of seats in the Bundestag is increased accordingly. This occurred in the January 1987 election in the case of the CDU/CSU. As a result, the size of the Bundestag was increased by one mandate (to 497 voting members) during the 1987-90 legislative session.

A distinctive feature of the West German electoral law is the requirement that a party must win either at least 5 percent of the popular vote or three constituency seats by direct election in order to share in the proportional representation of seats. Failing either contingency, a party cannot gain entrance to the Bundestag and therefore any votes cast on its behalf are "lost." A similar 5 percent barrier exists for party representation on the state level as well.

The West German electoral law has several highly significant political consequences. Most important is the 5 percent clause. This feature has strongly encouraged the postwar tendency toward party concentration. Time after time, splinter parties have failed to mobilize the minimum number of voters and have thus disappeared from the political landscape. Among them have been a variety of regional, special-interest, and narrowly ideological groups ranging from the German party to the Refugee party, the German Communist party (West German successor to the former KPD), and the radical right National Democratic party (NPD).

In addition, the dual ballot system has encouraged tactical cooperation among various parties, with voters frequently dividing their constituency and Land votes between two parties in order to maximize the prospect that both will be elected to parliament. The Christian Democrats established an early precedent for interparty electoral collaboration when they abstained from nominating candidates of their own in two districts in North Rhine-Westphalia in 1953, thereby enabling CDU supporters in both districts to cast their constituency votes for Center party candidates. As a result, the Center party was able to maintain nominal representation in the Bundestag prior to its final absorption by the end of the decade into the CDU. More recently, both Social Democrats and Christian Democrats have divided their votes between their own party on the constituency ballot and the FDP on the Land list in an effort to ensure the latter's survival as a junior coalition partner in successive SPD and CDU/CSU-led Cabinets.

An additional legal constraint restricting political parties is the constitutional requirement that all parties must conform in their organization and policies to democratic principles. According to Article 21 of the Basic Law:

1. The political parties shall participate in the forming of the political will of the people. They may be freely established. Their internal organization must conform to democratic principles. They must publicly account for the sources of their funds.

2. Parties which, by reason of their aims or the behavior of their adherents, seek to impair or abolish the free democratic basic order or to endanger the existence of the Federal Republic of Germany shall be unconstitutional. The Federal Constitutional Court shall decide on the question of constitutionality.

Party Stability and Change

The postwar tendency toward simplification of the party system is a product of multiple political-legal and socioeconomic factors. Among them was the decision by Allied officials to license only a limited number of parties during the initial stage of the occupation. Thus, the Christian Democrats, the Social Democrats, and the Free Democrats established themselves as early as 1945-46 as effective governing parties on the local and state levels, well before more narrowly defined political movements were permitted to organize and compete for public support.

In addition, the constitutional prohibition against nondemocratic parties was instrumental in the demise of two splinter groups. Citing Article 21 of the Basic Law, the federal government filed a brief with the Federal Constitutional Court in November 1951 questioning the legality of the right-wing Socialist Reich party. Because the SRP advocated a unitary state and a mystical form of "folk socialism" strongly reminiscent of National Socialist ideology, the Court declared the party unconstitutional the following year. The West German KPD was similarly banned as unconstitutional in August 1956.

A more general legal factor encouraging party concentration is the 5 percent barrier for winning seats in the Bundestag. This threshold proved the ultimate nemesis for most of the minor parties reestablished or founded in the early postwar period, including the Center party and various regional groups.

More important than legal constraints affecting splinter parties for explaining the postwar simplification of the German party system are broader socioeconomic and political factors that have contributed to the consolidation and legitimation of the Bonn republic. These include West Germany's impressive record of economic reconstruction and growth and Chancellor Adenauer's formidable domestic and foreign policy successes during the 1950s and early 1960s. In addition, Germany's division and the establishment of the DDR as a separate regime have encouraged simplification of the West German party system. The forced pace of Communization in East Germany not only undermined the KPD's electoral appeal in the West; it also exerted a significant unifying effect within the Federal Republic. The very existence of the DDR, combined with recurrent Soviet and East German threats against the autonomy of West Berlin, have served to encourage the acceptance of the established sociopolitical order in the Federal Republic as a preferred alternative to the political system east of the Elbe River.

Political consolidation is, of course, by no means an irreversible process, as witnessed by the temporary surge of electoral support for the right-wing NPD during the latter half of the 1960s and the success of the Greens in the 1980s. Moreover, the mainstream parties themselves can conceivably undergo political decomposition. A short-lived precedent was the legislative split between the CDU and the CSU in 1976, discussed above. More recently, the electoral successes of the Greens helped deprive the Free Democrats of their seats in several state parliaments during the early 1980s and very nearly cost them their representation in the Bundestag in 1983-87. Within the SPD, successive defeats in the 1983 and 1987 national elections have prompted potentially divisive debates among party leaders concerning ideological priorities and coalition strategies for the future.

In the short run, the two-and-a-half party system that emerged in Germany by the early 1960s has given way to a more complex four-party system. The mainstream parties of the Christian Democrats, the Social Democrats, and the Free Democrats continue to dominate the national and state political agendas but have had to yield legislative space to the Greens in both the Bundestag and most of the state parliaments. Whether this transformation of the party system will persist depends on multiple political and economic factors. Among them are the substance of the chapters that follow: patterns of government-opposition relations and the adequacy of policy choice in response to complex domestic and foreign issues.

Notes

1. Gerhard Lehmbruch, *Parteienwettbewerb im Bundesstaat* (Cologne: Verlag W. Kohlhammer, 1976).

2. Forschungsgruppe Wahlen Mannheim, *Wahlstudie 1980* (Cologne: Zentralarchiv für empirische Sozialforschung der Universität zu Köln, 1981), 342-43.

3. Ronald Inglehart, *The Silent Revolution: Changing Values and Political Styles among Western Publics* (Princeton: Princeton University Press, 1977).

4. Statistisches Bundesamt, *Statistisches Jahrbuch 1986 für die Bundesrepublik Deutschland* (Stuttgart: W. Kohlhammer GmbH, 1986), 67.

5. Membership percentages are from 1975 and are derived from Keith Fitzgerald, "Economic, Social, and Political Indicators," in *Futures for the Welfare State*, ed. Norman Furniss (Bloomington: Indiana University Press, 1986), 434.

6. DGB-Bundesvorstand, *Grundsatzprogramm des Deutschen Gewerkschaftsbundes* (Frankfurt: Union-Druckerei, 1981), 10.

7. Works councils were initially established in Germany in 1920 to accord employees an indirect voice in management decisions. They were suppressed by the Nazis during the early 1930s. Following the capitulation of the Third Reich in 1945, industrial workers spontaneously reestablished the councils in numerous firms throughout the western zones.

8. Early descriptions of codetermination include Abraham Schuchman, *Codetermination: Labour's Middle Course in Germany* (Washington, D.C.: Public Affairs Press, 1965); and Gerard Braunthal, "Codetermination in West Germany," in *Cases in Comparative Politics,* 3d ed, ed. James Christoph (Boston: Little, Brown, 1976).

9. See chapter 6.

10. CDU-Bundesgeschäftsstelle, *Das Berliner Programm, mit Beschlüssen des Hamburger Parteitages 1973* (Bonn: CDU, 1973).

11. Zelime Amen Ward, "The Split and Reunification of the CDU/CSU" (paper presented at the annual meeting of the American Political Science Association, Washington, D.C., September 1977).

12. Bundesvorstand der S.P.D., *Das Grundsatzprogramm der Sozialdemokratischen Partei Deutschlands* (Bonn: SPD, 1959).

13. Ibid.

14. Ibid.

15. *Thesen zur Politischen Oekonomie und Strategie — ausserordentlichen Bundeskongress der Jungsozialisten in Hannover 11. bis 12. Dezember 1971* (Bonn: n.d.).

16. Bundesvorstand der S.P.D., *Oekonomisch-politischer Orientierungsrahmen für die Jahre 1975-1985* (Bonn, 1975). Many German skeptics view demands for more extensive state controls over the economy as mere "window dressing" designed to appease the party's left-wing supporters without constituting a serious mandate to proceed with radical reforms. For a critical assessment of the "orientation framework 85," see Wilhelm Hennis, *Organisierter Sozialismus. Zum "strategischen" Staats- und Politikverständnis der Sozialdemokratie* (Stuttgart: Ernst Klett Verlag, 1977).

17. Bundesvorstand der F.D.P., *Freiburger Thesen der F.D.P. zur Gesellschaftspolitik* (Bonn, n.d.).

18. Petra K. Kelly, *Um Hoffnung kämpfen. Gewaltfrei in eine grüne Zukunft* (Bornheim-Merten: Lamuv Verlag, 1983), 21.

19. Die Grünen, "Präambel (Entwurf)," *Das Bundesprogramm* (Munich: Verlag die Grünen, 1983), 4.

20. Ibid., 7.

21. Ibid., 18-19.

22. Ibid., 19.

23. Josef Joffe, "The Greening of Germany," *New Republic* 188 (14 February 1983): 20.

24. Forschungsgruppe Wahlen, *Politik in der Bundesrepublik Deutschland. Mannheimer Wahlstudie 1987. 2. Welle. Januar 1987* (Mannheim: Forschungsgruppe Wahlen, 1987), 314. For a comparative assessment of the social bases of electoral politics in West Germany, the United States, Britain, and France, see Russell J. Dalton, *Citizen Politics in Western Democracies* (Chatham, N.J.: Chatham House, 1988), 151-76.

25. Forschungsgruppe Wahlen, *Politik in der Bundesrepublik Deutschland. Februar 1983* (Mannheim: Forschungsgruppe Wahlen, 1983).

26. *Politik in der Bundesrepublik Deutschland. Mannheimer Wahlstudie 1987*, 316-17.

27. Ibid.

28. Ibid.

29. Proportional representation was introduced in Germany during the Weimar Republic, whereby a party could win a parliamentary seat with as few as 30,000 votes. Weimar's system of proportional representation and the low threshold for electoral representation have been commonly cited as partial causes for the extreme fragmentation and volatility of the Weimar party system. See Gerhard Loewenberg, "The Development of the German Party System," in *Germany at the Polls. The Bundestag Election of 1976,* ed. Karl H. Cerny (Washington, D.C.: American Enterprise Institute for Public Policy Research, 1978).

5. Government and Opposition: Coalitions, Issues, and Policy Choices

A succession of coalition governments has shaped the course of postwar West German politics. The Christian Democrats dominated national affairs during the initial phase of regime consolidation and legitimation, as recounted in chapter 2. Following an extended transition period that began with Adenauer's retirement as federal chancellor in 1963 and culminated in the formation of a Grand Coalition made up of the CDU/CSU and the SPD in 1966, the Social Democrats assumed political leadership in alliance with the Free Democrats in 1969. The SPD-FDP "social-liberal" coalition lasted until October 1982 when the Free Democrats withdrew their support in favor of a renewed alliance with the Christian Democrats. West German voters subsequently accorded the CDU/CSU-FDP coalition an executive mandate through at least the early 1990s in successive national elections in 1983 and 1987. Each of these alternating phases of Christian Democratic and Social Democratic governance has been characterized by distinctive policy priorities and achievements in the continuing evolution of West Germany's sociopolitical and economic systems.

The Adenauer Era, 1949-63

By the 1980s, nostalgia buffs had already begun to celebrate the 1950s as West Germany's "golden age." This formative decade encompassed most of the decisive economic and political events in postwar German political history, with the first and second Adenauer Cabinets (1949-53, 1953-57) engineering crucial policy decisions on the nature of the economic system and the Federal Republic's integration into the Atlantic Community. The country's impressive economic recovery after 1951 seemed to vindicate Christian Democratic domestic and foreign policy choices and substantially contributed to the political legitimation of the new German republic.

The Christian Democrats sustained their claim to executive leadership through an adroit coalition strategy. Because the CDU/CSU had achieved only a bare plurality of seats in the 1949 election, they invited the Free Democrats and the German party (DP) to join them in forming the first postwar government. The Christian Democrats increased their number of seats substantially in the second national election in 1953, but Chancellor Adenauer nonetheless broadened his coalition to include the Refugee party (GB/BHE) as a means to ensure a sufficient parliamentary majority to endorse the constitutional amendments required to implement West German rearmament. In the 1957 Bundestag election the Christian Democrats achieved an absolute majority and thus were able to dispense with the support of the Free Democrats (who had begun to raise embarrassing questions about Adenauer's advancing age and his capacity to continue serving as federal chancellor). Instead, the CDU/CSU relied on the minuscule and more easily manipulated German party as its only coalition partner.

Domestic and external factors converged to spell an end to the Adenauer era and eventually Christian Democratic rule altogether. Adenauer's age and autocratic style of leadership became increasingly distracting factors that the Social Democrats and later the Free Democrats exploited to their partisan electoral advantage. In every Land election held between 1958 and 1963, the SPD advanced in popular support, while the Christian Democrats lost votes in nearly half of them. CDU losses were particularly acute in the peripheral states of the Saar and West Berlin as well as in the pivotal industrial state of North Rhine-Westphalia.

Decisively influencing Adenauer's political demise was a dramatic move by the East German regime literally to cement Germany's postwar division by erecting a wall through the heart of Berlin on 13 August 1961. This step culminated a prolonged effort by SED and Soviet Union officials to stem a swelling tide of refugees from the DDR to West Germany, most of whom utilized the transportation facilities and open thoroughfares of the former capital city to escape the forced pace of communization in their part of Germany. When the Western powers thwarted Russian efforts between 1959 and 1961 to transform West Berlin into a "demilitarized free city," the Warsaw Pact nations endorsed an SED initiative to close the sector border between the two parts of the city.

Clearly taken aback by the East German action, Chancellor Adenauer failed to respond beyond merely endorsing ineffectual Western protests. By default the political spotlight thus fell on the lord mayor of West Berlin, Willy Brandt, a popular and articulate Social Democrat who had embarked on a stellar political career in the city after returning to occupied Germany in 1945 following 12 years of political exile in Norway and Sweden. As the chief executive officer in West Berlin, Brandt effectively diffused an angry mass protest march against the wall and succeeded in prompting a series of positive American responses to bolster the defense and morale of the beleagured city. Belatedly, Chancellor Adenauer flew to Berlin to demonstrate his solidarity with its citizens, but by then his prestige had suffered an irreparable loss in the eyes of the West German electorate. In the September 1961 election, CDU/CSU strength fell from its previous absolute majority to 45.2 percent, while the Social Democrats increased their support from 31.8 percent to 36.2 percent. Campaigning under the slogan "With the CDU/CSU but without Adenauer," the Free Democrats consolidated their status as West Germany's third force by increasing their share of the popular vote from 7.7 percent to 12.8 percent. No splinter party survived the contest.

Despite their pledge that they would not serve again under the aging CDU chairman, the Free Democrats reluctantly agreed to endorse Adenauer's bid for a fourth term as federal chancellor in exchange for renewed membership in the national Cabinet. The junior coalition party was able to impose a firm limit on his remaining time in office within a year, however, in the aftermath of West Germany's first serious domestic political crisis: the so-called *Spiegel* affair.

The crisis began on 10 October 1962 when *Der Spiegel,* the leading German weekly newsmagazine and a long-time critic of the Adenauer government, published a lengthy article alleging that recent NATO manuevers had revealed serious deficiencies in the preparedness of the German armed forces. The author of the piece was a regular *Spiegel* contributor named Conrad Ahlers. Claiming that the article betrayed state secrets, state secretaries in the ministries of justice and defense ordered local police units to raid the *Spiegel* offices in Hamburg and Bonn. The *Spiegel*'s editor and five assistants were arrested, and reams of editorial material were impounded by the police. Simultaneously, the Defense Ministry issued an order for the arrest of Ahlers, who was vacationing in Spain. The order was transmitted through the military attaché at the West German embassy in Madrid to Spanish authorities, who detained Ahlers and turned him over to embassy officials for deportation to the Federal Republic.

The rapid reprisals against *Spiegel* prompted a serious breach between the coalition partners. Furious that his subordinates had not informed him in advance of the scheduled raid, Minister of Justice Wolfgang Stammberger, a Free Democrat, threatened to resign. The principal target of both his own wrath and that of the opposition SPD was Defense Minister Franz Josef Strauss, who blithely disclaimed any personal involvement in preparations for the raid or the arrest of Ahlers. The SPD utilized the Question Hour in the Bundestag to instigate a full-scale Bundestag debate on the *Spiegel* controversy in early November. When Strauss finally conceded during a heated parliamentary exchange that his ministry had in fact arranged for the arrest of Ahlers, the Free

Democrats dramatically quit the Cabinet. Party Chairman Erich Mende declared that the FDP would rejoin the government only if Strauss were dismissed.

Since the FDP's action meant that the federal government no longer commanded a parliamentary majority, Adenauer was compelled to meet Mende's condition. He agreed to relieve Strauss of his duties as defense minister and informed the Free Democrats in early December that he would step down himself in 1963. The following week, the CDU/CSU and the FDP concluded negotiations on the formation of a new Cabinet that excluded both Strauss and the embittered former Justice Minister Stammberger.

From Erhard to the Grand Coalition

The resolution of the political crisis caused by the *Spiegel* affair marked the beginning of the end of the initial phase of CDU/CSU ascendancy in West German politics. Adenauer remained in office until his designated retirement date in October 1963, at which time he was succeeded by Ludwig Erhard, his former vice-chancellor and a principal architect of Germany's postwar economic recovery. Long championed by the free-enterprise-minded Free Democrats, Erhard nonetheless proved a disappointing choice to both coalition partners. Admittedly his reputation as an "electoral locomotive" enabled the CDU/CSU to reverse its previous electoral decline by advancing to 47.6 percent of the popular vote in the September 1965 election. But a lack of confidence in his leadership abilities among prominent Christian Democrats, an incipient crisis of West German foreign policy, and an unsettling groundswell of electoral support for the right-wing National Democratic party (NPD) combined to terminate Erhard's chancellorship within a scant three years.

Fatefully, Erhard assumed power at a time of convulsive political change throughout the industrialized world. He was in office barely a month when American President John F. Kennedy was assassinated. An indirect consequence was the onset of prolonged public dissent over basic political values and public policy choices in all advanced democracies. Within Western Europe, Erhard confronted multiple tensions rooted primarily in resurgent nationalism. French President Charles de Gaulle instigated a boycott of the Common Market's Council of Ministers in 1965 in an effort to block the implementation of majority decisions in the executive body, as prescribed by the Treaty of Rome of 1957. Simultaneously, de Gaulle declared his opposition to an American proposal to establish a Multilateral Nuclear Force (MLF) as a means to increase military integration within the Atlantic Alliance. To the east, SED officials launched another war of nerves over West Berlin in an effort to force the Western Allies and the Federal Republic to accept the DDR as an equal negotiating partner.

A personally affable man, Erhard's instinctive laissez-faire attitudes proved inadequate to the times. Rather than lead or even reassure an increasingly troubled nation, Erhard was content to delegate political authority to party chieftains. He proved relatively more active in foreign affairs in that he traveled extensively within the Atlantic Community. Yet even in attempting to reconcile diverse foreign policy demands on the Federal Republic, Erhard's style was more responsive than forceful. Thus he acted to reaffirm established tenets of West German relations with its allies rather than break new ground. In the interest of Franco-German reconciliation, his coalition government tacitly went along with de Gaulle's insistence on the unanimity principle in important Common Market decisions. On both the MLF issue and East-West relations, Erhard deferred to American leadership. Accordingly, he agreed in principle to some form of West German participation in the proposed multilateral force and stubbornly refused to enter into any sort of dialogue with the East German regime in the absence of a prior American-Soviet agreement on the German question.

Erhard's passivity invited the ill-concealed scorn of leading party cohorts. Both Adenauer and CSU Chairman Strauss openly expressed their dissatisfaction with Erhard's leadership style and policy priorities. Adenauer utilized his status as CDU chairman (which he retained until March 1966) to help formulate binding directives on government policy and publicly disagreed with his successor's European policy. In parallel fashion, Strauss acted to undermine public confidence in Erhard by covertly opposing his choice of Cabinet personnel after the 1965 parliamentary election. As a measure of Strauss's negative influence within the joint Christian Democratic faction, Erhard received only 272 votes out of a combined total of 294 Christian Democrats and Free Democrats when he was reconfirmed as federal chancellor—7 fewer than when he was elected for the first time in 1963.

A precipitous increase in NPD electoral strength, beginning with municipal elections in Bavaria in March 1965, prompted Erhard's fall. Although the radical right party mobilized only 2 percent of the popular vote on a statewide basis, NPD candidates scored notable successes in a number of cities. Tapping a growing mood of German nationalism, which was largely emulative of the Gaullist precedent, the NPD sustained its electoral momentum later that month when it received four seats in the Hamburg state election. The next test of the party's fortunes was set for November when NPD candidates were scheduled to compete with the mainstream parties for representation in the Hesse and Bavarian assemblies.

Faced with a gathering rightist revival, party elites seized on a government crisis in late 1966 to reconstitute executive leadership. The immediate impetus was a conflict between the coalition partners over taxation policy, with the

Christian Democrats favoring a tax increase to cover a projected deficit in the 1967 budget while the Free Democrats endorsed an alternative plan to reduce government expenditures. When a Cabinet majority decided in favor of the CDU/CSU plan, the Free Democrats resigned from the government. The two larger mainstream parties promptly exploited the Cabinet's minority status to force Erhard out of office. On 8 November the Social Democrats successfully moved a parliamentary resolution calling on the chancellor to submit to a vote of confidence in the Bundestag. Even though Erhard declared that he would not comply with the resolution, his position as federal chancellor had clearly become untenable. As a result, the CDU executive committee convened to nominate a successor. Out of a field of four candidates, Kurt Georg Kiesinger, who had served as minister-president of Baden-Württemberg since 1958, emerged as the victor.

Negotiations commenced in mid-November among the three parliamentary factions on the formation of a new government. After rejecting a proposed coalition with the Free Democrats on the grounds that the FDP and the SPD would together command only a six-seat majority in parliament, SPD Chairman and Berlin Mayor Willy Brandt then surprised most informed domestic and foreign observers by agreeing to a "partnership (with the CDU/CSU) for a limited time." Thus was born the Grand Coalition of the CDU/CSU-SPD. Erhard submitted his resignation on 30 November, and the next day an overwhelming majority of Bundestag deputies elected Kiesinger as his successor. Serving alongside him in the national unity Cabinet were Brandt as vice-chancellor and foreign minister; Gustav Heinemann, a founding member of the CDU but a convert in the early 1950s to the SPD, who was appointed minister of justice; Karl Schiller, a Social Democrat and a professor of economics, who was named head of the powerful Ministry of Economics; and the controversial Franz Josef Strauss, who received the coveted Ministry of Finance.

The formation of the Grand Coalition came too late to reverse the immediate electoral fortunes of the NPD. Rightist candidates captured 7.9 and 7.4 percent of the popular vote in the Hesse and Bavarian elections, respectively, in November. In 1966 the National Democrats expanded their regional strength to include seats in the parliaments of Rhineland-Pfalz, Schleswig-Holstein, Bremen, and Lower Saxony. Flushed with success, party activists began to gird themselves for the 1969 parliamentary election and the NPD's anticipated entrance into the Bundestag.

With time, however, the concentration of political forces under the joint leadership of Chancellor Kiesinger and Foreign Minister Brandt signaled a qualitative shift in national politics that contributed to the ultimate demise of the NPD. For one thing, the Grand Coalition constituted an unprecedented degree of elite unity on fundamental political principles. In contrast to the unwilling-ness of democratic leaders to join forces in rebuffing National Socialism dur-ing the early 1930s, the CDU/CSU-SPD alliance displayed a shared resolve to defend the established political system against its radical critics. For another, the new Cabinet included men of exceptional competence and moral stature. As events proved, pivotal members of the Cabinet—notably Brandt and Schiller—revealed extraordinary skill and imagination in dealing with complex foreign policy and economic issues, respectively. The result was the restoration of a badly needed sense of executive competence at a time of escalating political disorder at home and abroad.

THE LATE 1960S: ISSUES AND TRENDS

The Grand Coalition spanned a number of crucial events in postwar German political and economic development. Symbolically, one of its major achieve-ments was to legitimize the claim of the SPD to executive leadership. For the first time since the late 1920s, the Social Democrats exercised national authority, thereby proving to skeptical middle-class voters that they were a responsible government party. As a result, the SPD was able through the remainder of the decade and into the early 1980s to extend its electoral appeal among Catholics, salaried employees, and other voters who had traditionally endorsed the Chris-tian Democrats.

Politically, the Grand Coalition underscored anew the close linkage in West Germany between national and state politics. Its formation inspired similar CDU-SPD combinations in 1967 and 1968 in Lower Saxony and Baden-Württem-berg. In both instances, the Free Democrats lost their previous status as the CDU's junior coalition partner. Partially counterbalancing the concentration of national and regional power in the hands of the two larger parties, however, was the fall of a minority CDU Cabinet in early December 1966 in North Rhine-Westphalia and its replacement by a SPD-FDP coalition—an event that pointed beyond the Grand Coalition to yet another stage in the evolution of interparty relations.

Substantively, the Kiesinger-Brandt Cabinet initiated a number of impor-tant domestic and foreign policy changes. The most pressing issue concerned financial and economic matters. In his first policy statement, Chancellor Kie-singer declared that one of the Cabinet's principal priorities was to achieve a balanced budget—a feat that had eluded Erhard during his final weeks in office. Complicating this task was the Federal Republic's first economic slowdown. Foreign demand for German exports had begun to fall as early as 1965. By the end of the Grand Coalition's first year of office, the domestic effects of the international recession were clearly apparent. Between 1966 and 1967, the value of the gross domestic product fell 1.0 percent, prompting a jump in the rate of unemployment from 0.7 percent to a potentially ominous 2.1 percent.

The Cabinet responded to the incipient economic crisis by undertaking a significant departure from established social market economy policies. As early as 1964, Chancellor Erhard had endorsed a modest retreat from his own neoliberal economic principles when his short-lived administration established an independent Council of Economic Experts whose task was the preparation of a comprehensive annual report on West German economic performance.[1] In response to the recessionary trends of 1966-67, the Grand Coalition intensified the shift toward greater state intervention in economic activities by introducing a comprehensive Law for Promoting Stability and Growth in the Economy.[2] The bill, which was endorsed by the Bundestag in June 1967, defined four principal economic objectives: the maintenance of stable prices, full employment, external financial equilibrium, and adequate economic growth. To achieve these goals, the bill called on the federal government to formulate a five-year financial plan (to be revised annually) that "relates the projected development of federal revenues and expenditures . . . to the nation's economic and social priorities."[3] Accompanying the plan were long-range macroeconomic target projections encompassing each of the four principal economic objectives. In addition, the bill prescribed the introduction of an innovative system of "concerted action" *(Konzertierte Aktion),* which would involve voluntary consultations among representatives of the Ministry of Economic Affairs, the Council of Economic Experts, the Federal Bank, employer associations, and the German Federation of Trade Unions (DGB) on measures to maintain stable economic growth and prices.[4]

The implementation of the 1967 Law on Stability and Growth brought prompt results. Through a combined program of increased public expenditures and tax relief for private businessmen, the federal government facilitated recovery from the prevailing recession. In return, business and labor representatives pledged to exercise price and wage restraint at the newly instituted "concerted action" consultative sessions. An important result of these simultaneous actions by public and private leaders was a decline in the number of unemployed workers from 629,000 in the spring of 1967 to 341,000 by the end of October. Within a year the unemployment level fell to less than 1 percent as the national economy achieved an annual growth rate of 5 percent. Justly earning much of the credit for orchestrating the Federal Republic's rapid economic recovery was Economics Minister Karl Schiller, whose resolute advocacy of short-term anticyclical measures and longer-range budgetary planning was perfectly attuned to the prevailing functional requirements of West Germany's increasingly complex industrial-capitalist system.

Far more problematic was a parallel initiative by the Grand Coalition to resolve a long-standing parliamentary dispute over proposed constitutional amendments governing the potential exercise of national emergency powers. As previously recounted, the three Western Allies had reserved two residual rights from the occupation regime under terms of the Paris Agreements of May 1955: the defense of West Berlin and the authority to intervene in domestic affairs in the event of a serious threat to the established sociopolitical order. The United States, Britain, and France insisted on retaining the first of these obligations as long as Germany remained divided. In view of the effective consolidation and legitimation of the Federal Republic after 1949, however, the three Allies declared their willingness to transfer the second of their reserved powers to the West Germans. As early as 1958, the Adenauer Cabinet had submitted a set of proposed constitutional amendments to the Bundestag that would establish the legal basis for an emergency West German parliament. The proposal was rejected by a majority of deputies on three occasions during the next 8 years, largely because many Social Democrats and Free Democrats were reluctant to introduce emergency provisions into the Basic Law after the tragic abuse of Article 48 of the Weimar Constitution some 30 years previously.

The formation of the Grand Coalition promised an end to the parliamentary impasse. Together, the CDU/CSU and the SPD drafted a new version of emergency legislation, which they submitted to the Bundestag in June 1967. The joint proposal called for the creation of a 33-person "joint commission," two-thirds of whose members would be appointed by the Bundestag and one-third by the Bundesrat, that would assume legislative powers in the event of a national emergency. In addition, the proposed constitutional amendments would authorize the federal government to curtail individual civil liberties if international or domestic disorder seriously threatened domestic tranquility; employ the West German military to put down armed uprisings; and order military conscripts to fill vacancies in the border guards, civil defense units, and hospital staffs.

Over the joint opposition of the FDP, trade unions, and student protesters, the CDU/CSU-SPD majority in the Bundestag endorsed the emergency legislation by an overwhelming majority in late May 1968. Two weeks later, the Bundesrat unanimously affirmed the constitutional amendments as well.

Alongside its domestic economic intiatives and emergency legislation, the Grand Coalition also undertook the first halting steps toward a more active foreign policy. With respect to Western Europe, Chancellor Kiesinger declared in December 1966 that the Federal Republic would pursue "the consistent development of the European Economic Community (the Common Market) and its institutions. The Community of the Six should be open to all those European states who agree with its aims." In explicit criticism of de Gaulle's opposition to British membership in the Common Market, Kiesinger added: "We should in particular be gratified if Great Britain and other (European Free Trade Association) countries were to become members of the European Communities."[5] Simultaneously, Chancellor Kiesinger offered the prospect of improved relations with Eastern Europe. He reaffirmed an earlier invitation by the Erhard Cabinet to exchange declarations renouncing the use of force, and emphasized his government's special interest in seeking reconciliation with Poland and Czechoslovakia.

The principal architect of the Grand Coalition's greater flexibility in foreign policy was the new foreign minister, Willy Brandt. A political exile in Scandinavia during the years of Nazi dictatorship, Brandt had acquired a strong sense of both internationalism and political pragmatism through his close contacts with Norwegian and Swedish Social Democrats. Thus, in contrast to his Christian Democratic predecessors in the Foreign Ministry, Brandt assumed office intent on seeking a practical accommodation with the socialist regimes of Eastern Europe. His concrete objectives were by no means clear in late 1966; the full implementation of a comprehensive new *Ostpolitik* (eastern policy) would have to await his own chancellorship three years later. But even as the junior partner in a Christian Democratic-dominated Cabinet, Brandt moved to end West Germany's isolation from the Soviet bloc. His first step was to establish diplomatic relations with Romania in early 1967 — a revolutionary break with the Federal Republic's long-standing policy not to accord recognition to states that recognized the DDR. In August, Brandt's Foreign Ministry negotiated a trade pact with Czechoslovakia as a further step toward normalizing West Germany's relations with the Warsaw Pact nations.

The Extraparliamentary Opposition

The Grand Coalition's domestic and foreign policies yielded contradictory results. A majority of West Germans honored the Cabinet's solid economic achievements with a resounding vote of public confidence. But the government's political acts and omissions were accorded a highly critical reception, both at home and abroad.

Domestically, the coalition's efforts to achieve parliamentary ratification of the proposed emergency legislation provoked widespread opposition among students and trade union leaders, many of whom saw in the constitutional amendments a potentially dangerous concentration of executive power. Their apprehensions were heightened by the virtual disappearance of an effective parliamentary opposition with the formation of the Grand Coalition. To voice their mounting concern, critical students and workers began staging mass protest demonstrations during the summer and fall of 1967. The extraparliamentary protest movement culminated in a massive march on Bonn just prior to the amendments' passage in May 1968.

The rise of an extraparliamentary opposition coincided with the emergence of an international student protest movement directed—in West Germany as in other advanced democracies—against individual statesmen, specific policies, and even the established sociopolitical system. In the particular case of the Federal Republic, critical students first massed in West Berlin in June 1967 to protest a visit by the shah of Iran. Shortly thereafter, ad hoc coalitions of left socialists, radical liberals, and their sympathizers joined forces at most universities to agitate for sweeping policy and structural changes. Their demands ranged from the democratization of university administration to the introduction of democratic socialism and the abolition of an influential chain of conservative newspapers owned by a Hamburg publicist named Axel Springer. In pursuit of these objectives, the student dissidents frequently engaged in violent confrontations with local police forces and university personnel. The result was a rapid escalation of ideological conflict between "new left" and establishment political leaders that seemed to some observers to portend a return to the political instability of the Weimar Republic.

External Criticism

Simultaneous with the emergence of the extraparliamentary opposition movement in West Germany, the Grand Coalition confronted increased criticism to its policies abroad. Although Kiesinger had managed to restore a measure of de Gaulle's personal confidence in the leadership of the Federal Republic, his government provoked concern within the broader international community. A principal reason was its refusal to sign an American- and Soviet-backed nuclear nonproliferation treaty designed to prevent the spread of nuclear weapons. The accord, which had been negotiated over a three-month period in early 1968 by members of an international disarmament committee, was overwhelmingly endorsed by the United Nations General Assembly in June 1968. Its major provisions prohibited nuclear states from transferring nuclear weapons to "have-not" countries; prohibited "have-not" countries from manufacturing or buying nuclear weapons; assigned the responsibility for enforcing the pact to the International Atomic Energy Agency (IAEA) in Vienna; and assured nonnuclear states the right to benefit from the peaceful application of nuclear devices. West German leaders endorsed the intent of the treaty but hesitated to sign it because of their opposition to the supervisory role accorded the IAEA. Moreover, Chancellor Kiesinger and other prominent Christian Democrats believed that the treaty discriminated against "have-not" countries (such as the

Federal Republic) in that the "have" nations were not subject to inspection by the IAEA.

By refusing to sign the nonproliferation treaty, the federal government invited criticism in both West and East. Without West German endorsement of the accord, neither of the superpowers could be expected to ratify the treaty, thus opening the prospect of an ominous new stage in the international arms race. For this reason, critical observers in the Soviet Union, Scandinavia, and even some of the NATO countries interpreted the German omission as a veiled attempt by the Federal Republic to acquire nuclear arms of its own.

Equally seriously, the Soviet Union and most of its Warsaw Pact allies reacted with open hostility to Foreign Minister Brandt's efforts to extend West German diplomatic and trade links with Eastern Europe. Fearing that Bonn's initiatives would undermine ideological cohesion within the Soviet bloc, Russian leaders strove, with strong East German backing, to discredit the political credibility of the Federal Republic. Soviet officials repeatedly condemned the National Democratic movement, hinting darkly that the USSR retained the legal right under the Charter of the United Nations to intervene in domestic West German affairs to suppress the "revival of fascism." Within their direct sphere of influence, the Soviets convened a meeting of East European Communist party officials in April 1967 to call for the convocation of a European-wide security conference and West German recognition of both postwar political boundaries and the legal invalidity "from the beginning" of the 1938 Munich accord that had transferred sovereignty over the Sudetenland in Czechoslovakia to the Third Reich.

A move toward political liberation in Czechoslovakia under the leadership of Alexander Dubcek, who became Communist party chairman and premier in 1968, greatly intensified Soviet and East German fears concerning West German foreign policy objectives in the region. Party chieftains in both countries charged the West Germans with encouraging the revival of a competitive party system in the Czech republic. To underscore their growing concern over the Federal Republic's alleged "revanchistic" aims in Eastern Europe, Soviet and SED officials began again to apply political pressure on West Berlin.

Mounting tension over the Federal Republic's eastern policies eased in August 1968 when Soviet and other Warsaw Pact troops invaded Czechoslovakia in a successful move to abort Dubcek's liberalization program. But even in the aftermath of this effort to shore up socialist solidarity by resort to force, Soviet and other East European leaders remained antagonistic toward the Grand Coalition's diplomatic initiatives. As minimum conditions for accepting the Federal Republic's overtures for improved East-West relations, they demanded West German endorsement of the nuclear nonproliferation treaty and recognition of existing boundaries (including the existence of the DDR as an independent state).

Thus, despite its recovery from the recession of 1966-67, the Federal Republic confronted a serious legitimation crisis by the end of the decade. External distrust of the Grand Coalition's foreign policy goals, combined with domestic attacks on established political institutions and policies, dramatically underscored the end of postwar political reconstruction in West Germany. After two decades of institution building and largely consensual national politics, the West Germans confronted the necessity to decide anew the course of national policy.

The SPD-FDP Coalition

The Bundestag election of September 1969 provided a tentative resolution of the Federal Republic's domestic and foreign policy impasse. Overshadowed by the prospect that the NPD might succeed in its bid to gain entrance to parliament, the campaign nonetheless crystallized emerging policy differences among the mainstream parties. The Christian Democrats contented themselves with celebrating the accomplishments of the Grand Coalition, particularly in the field of economic policy. In contrast, both the Free Democrats and the Social Democrats stressed the need for change in domestic and foreign policies. As noted in chapter 4, the FDP had embraced a more activist program in 1967 in which they espoused social democratization and direct negotiations with the DDR. With the election of a progressive southwestern liberal, Walter Scheel, as party chairman in January 1968, the FDP embarked on a new coalition strategy as well: one favoring alliance with the Social Democrats rather than with the more conservative CDU/CSU. Their shift in alliance strategy was confirmed in March 1969 when the Free Democrats joined the Social Democrats in the Federal Assembly to elect the SPD candidate, Gustav Heinemann, West Germany's third federal president. For its part, the SPD adopted an electoral program in April 1967 that endorsed the extension of codetermination in industry, the recognition of the DDR as an independent state "within the German nation," and the Federal Republic's signature to the controversial nuclear nonproliferation treaty.

Election results on 28 September dealt a crippling blow to NPD aspirations. Rightist candidates amassed only 4.3 percent of the popular vote, which was too little to enable the party to gain admission to the Bundestag. As a consequence, the National Democrats began to dissipate, with most of their leaders and followers abandoning hope of establishing themselves as a viable splinter movement to the right of the Christian Democrats.

Simultaneously, the election revealed a basic electoral realignment in favor of progressive system change. The Social Democrats advanced to 42.7 percent, while the Christian Democrats fell to 46.1 percent. Although the Free Democrats also declined in public support (they received 5.8 percent compared to 9.5 percent in 1965), the SPD and the FDP together commanded a 12-seat majority in the new parliament. Over the strenuous objections of the CDU/CSU, the SPD and the FDP thus agreed on the formation of a coalition ministry. On 21 October, Brandt was elected West Germany's fourth federal chancellor by a scant three-vote majority in the Bundestag.

The SPD-FDP Cabinet was a more streamlined government body than any of its predecessors. A significant symbolic change was the transformation of the former Ministry for All-German Affairs into the Ministry of Inter-German relations. This step signaled the new government's willingness to accept the East German republic as a separate state rather than merely a usurper regime with no claim to international legal recognition. Among the important members of the coalition government were the FDP Chairman, Walter Scheel, who became vice-chancellor and foreign minister; Karl Schiller, who retained his position as economics minister; Helmut Schmidt, the SPD floor leader, who became minister of defense; and Hans-Dietrich Genscher, a founding member of the FDP, who was named minister of the interior.

The formation of the SPD-FDP government initiated a discernible third stage in the political development of the Federal Republic. In contrast to all previous ministries, the Brandt Cabinet lacked a majority in the Bundesrat; moreover, it was beset by a gradual erosion of parliamentary support in the lower house. Nonetheless, Chancellor Brandt and Foreign Minister Scheel sustained their governing alliance into the mid-1970s to implement West Germany's most sweeping policy innovations since the republic's formative first decade.

Consistent with SPD and FDP campaign promises, Chancellor Brandt declared in his first policy statement that the federal government would seek improved relations with the Soviet bloc. He renewed West Germany's interest in negotiating renunciation-of-force agreements with the Soviet Union, Poland, and other East European countries. Significantly, he added that such agreements would "acknowledge the territorial integrity of the respective parties."[6] Toward the West, Chancellor Brandt reaffirmed the Federal Republic's allegiance to both NATO and the European integration movement. His major departure from the foreign policy stance of the Grand Coalition was his declared willingness to sign the nuclear nonproliferation treaty once his government received adequate clarifications from the superpowers concerning enforcement provisions.

The domestic portion of the new government's program constituted an ambitious catalogue of political, economic, and social reform measures. Among them were an extension of rights of codetermination and increased educational opportunities for middle- and working-class children.

FOREIGN AND DOMESTIC INNOVATION

The very scope of the SPD-FDP program inevitably invited widespread skepticism. Christian Democratic critics denounced Brandt's inventory of proposed and domestic changes as "insulting" and "vague." Of particular concern to opposition spokesmen was Brandt's declared willingness to accept East Germany as a separate state. Such a move, in former Chancellor Kiesinger's view, would encourage *de jure* recognition of the DDR by other countries, thereby unleashing, in his words, "a landslide that we have tried together to hold back for 20 years."[7]

At the opposite end of the ideological spectrum, suspicious East German officials were equally distrustful. Their initial response to Brandt's address was to dismiss it as nothing more than a repetition of previous West German policy and to insist, as on many occasions in the past, on full diplomatic recognition by the Federal Republic.

Despite the joint opposition of Christian Democrats at home and Marxist-Leninists in Eastern Europe, the SPD-FDP government proceeded to implement a new *Ostpolitik*. An essential step toward overcoming East German and residual Polish and Czech apprehensions was to achieve prior agreement on the relaxation of East-West tensions. To that end, Chancellor Brandt dispatched his close personal adviser on foreign policy matters, Egon Bahr, to Moscow in January 1970 to initiate a formal exchange of views on a renunciation-of-force agreement. By the end of May, both sides concurred on the general outlines of such an accord and formally initialed a treaty in August. The German-Soviet agreement called on both countries to "settle their disputes exclusively by peaceful means" and "to respect without restriction the territorial integrity of all States in Europe within their present frontiers."[8]

Chancellor Brandt and his foreign policy advisers were acutely aware that the accord with the Soviet Union formally sanctioned the postwar revision of boundaries in Central Europe and therefore, in effect, the division of Germany. To help defuse domestic opposition to official West German recognition of both these political realities, Federal Minister Scheel submitted a simultaneous "Letter on German Unity" to the Soviet Foreign Ministry in which he affirmed that the treaty "does not conflict with the political objectives of the Federal Republic to work for a state of peace in Europe in which the German nation will recover its unity in free self-determination."[9]

Parallel with the negotiations in Moscow, the federal government initiated talks in Warsaw on a similar renunciation of force. A treaty to that effect was signed in December 1970, calling on both West Germany and Poland to "settle all their disputes exclusively by peaceful means." Most important, the German-Polish treaty explicitly affirmed the Oder-Neisse boundary between East Germany and Poland. Both parties pledged to respect "the inviolability of their existing frontiers now and in the future and . . . each other's territorial integrity without restriction."[10]

The negotiation of the Soviet and Polish treaties unleashed a storm of protest in West Germany. Although a solid majority of citizens endorsed Brandt's and Scheel's efforts to promote détente, conservative critics in parliament raised serious objections to the accords themselves. CSU Chairman Strauss, CDU Floor Leader Rainer Barzel (who succeeded Kiesinger as party chairman in 1971), and others seized on the government's recognition of established frontiers in Central Europe as a "betrayal" of German national interests. In their view, the federal government had conceded too much to the Soviets and the Poles without extracting tangible political benefits in return.

In defense of its actions, the federal government was resolutely determined to obtain just such a concession from the Soviet Union in the form of a four-power agreement securing free access to West Berlin. Although West Germany could claim no legal jurisdiction over the former capital, Chancellor Brandt and Foreign Minister Scheel informed the Soviets that formal ratification of the Russian and Polish treaties by the Bundestag was contingent on the successful conclusion of quadripartite negotiations among the wartime Allies concerning the legal status of West Berlin. From 1948 onward, the Soviets, and later the East Germans, had repeatedly harassed Western traffic to and from Berlin in successive efforts to delay political events in the West and/or to underscore the DDR's sovereignty. But as a delayed consequence of the erection of the Berlin wall in 1961, which had contributed to the internal consolidation of the East German regime, and in response to an exchange of notes between the Western powers and the Soviet Union in 1969, the United States, the Soviet Union, Britain, and France began talks in March 1970 on means to "(improve) the situation with regard to Berlin and free access to the city."[11] Specifically, the Western powers sought an international agreement with the Soviet Union on guaranteed access for civilian traffic to and from West Berlin and improved communication and transportation links between the two parts of the city. In return, the Soviets sought an Allied agreement to curtail official West German functions in the western sectors of the divided capital.

The four ambassadors met repeatedly during 1970 and 1971. Several times the negotiations threatened to break down, but a West German declaration that the eastern treaties would not be approved without an accord on Berlin prompted the four powers to resume talks. Their efforts finally culminated in a comprehensive "Agreement on Berlin," which they signed in September 1971. Its principal features included Soviet acceptance of "unimpeded (civilian) access . . . between the Western Sectors of Berlin and the Federal Republic of Germany" and a Western declaration that "the ties between the Western Sectors of Berlin and the Federal Republic will be maintained and developed, taking into account that these Sectors continue not to be a constituent part of the Federal Republic of Germany and not to be governed by it."[12]

The achievements of the SPD-FDP government in implementing a new *Ostpolitik* were accompanied by equally historical initiatives in the West. With de Gaulle's peevish resignation from the French presidency in April 1969 after a majority of the French electorate had rejected his plan to reform the Senate of the Fifth Republic, a long-standing impasse over the proposed expansion of the Common Market was unexpectedly resolved. Since the early 1960s, Great Britain, Ireland, Denmark, and potentially Norway and Sweden had sought admission to the European Economic Community only to be stymied by de Gaulle's stubborn opposition. But once he relinquished executive power—to be succeeded by a more moderate Gaullist, Georges Pompidou—British prospects of joining the EEC were greatly improved.

Chancellor Brandt took advantage of de Gaulle's departure to urge both an intensification of the West European integration movement and the territorial expansion of the Common Market. The upshot, at a summit meeting of the heads of government of the six EEC countries in December 1969, was a unanimous reaffirmation of the Community's long-range objective to achieve political unity as well as a new agreement on enlarging the EEC. To this end, the six governments authorized the EEC's Commission to begin negotiations with the various applicant states. Talks ensued in early 1970 with Britain, Ireland, Denmark, Norway, and Sweden, and culminated in January in full membership treaties with all but the latter. Britain, Ireland, and Denmark ultimately ratified the agreements and formally joined the European Communities on 1 January 1973.

Domestic reforms assumed a lesser, though still important, priority in the SPD-FDP's attempt to rechart the direction of West German politics. In an effort to promote industrial democracy, the coalition partners intitiated interparty consultations in 1970 on means to implement the DGB's long-standing demand to extend rights of worker codetermination. On the educational front, the Social Democrats and the Liberals encouraged Land officials to introduce a new unitary school system, known as the *Gesamtschule,* as an experimental move to expand educational opportunities. To accommodate a burgeoning growth in West Germany's student population, the coalition partners also lent their legislative support to the establishment of a number of new universities.

On a more punitive note, Chancellor Brandt met with the ministers-president of the various Länder in January 1972 to confer about steps to curtail political extremism. The upshot was a federal-state agreement on guidelines restricting admission to the civil service. Although Article 12 of the Basic Law guarantees that all Germans have the right "freely to choose their trade, occupation or profession, their place of work and their place of training," the January 1972 edict excluded civil servant candidates who were members of an extremist political movement, e.g., either the NPD or the newly founded German Communist party (DKP). Specifically, the guidelines state that "if a candidate is a member of an organization that pursues goals inimical to the constitution, such membership justifies doubts whether he will defend the free democratic order at any time. As a rule, these doubts justify a rejection of his application for appointment."

Underlying the adoption of the new restrictions were ostensibly two motives: first, government reports that up to 2000 Communists "were already working as federal and state officials"; and, second, the SPD's resolve to demonstrate its political reliability at a time of resurgent ideological controversy. Whatever its genesis, the *Berufsverbot* (or "occupation ban," as it came to be known colloquially) signaled a further escalation of domestic conflict in the Federal Republic.

GOVERNMENT CRISIS

None of the domestic reform initiatives met with uncritical acclaim. Although the student protest movement declined in intensity once the social-liberal coalition assumed office, radicals retained a vocal presence in the administrative governance of such universities as Heidelberg, Hamburg, and the Free University in West Berlin. On the right, tradition-minded educators and Christian Democratic legislators criticized the government's educational reform efforts as inimical to quality education, especially the introduction of the *Gesamtschule*. Simultaneously, West Germany's recovery from the recession of 1966-67 prompted union efforts to achieve catch-up wage increases through a spate of wildcat strikes. Employers responded with lockouts at the affected firms. As a result, the postwar pattern of relative labor peace gave way, at least temporarily, to joint belligerence in the labor market.

Eclipsing both labor and lingering student unrest was sustained CDU/CSU criticism of *Ostpolitik*. Opposition resistance to the Soviet and Polish treaties unleashed a political crisis of profound importance. Even the fact that Chancellor Brandt was awarded the Nobel Peace Prize in December 1971 failed to deter Christian Democratic efforts to postpone the implementation of the eastern agreements. The new CDU chairman, Rainer Barzel, did not reject détente per se, but he, Strauss, and other Christian Democrats maintained that the treaties "were lacking in safeguards and that the Federal Republic had conceded far too much."[13]

The Christian Democrats were in a strategic position to impede ratification of the treaties because of the nearly equal division between government and opposition forces in the two houses of parliament. The CDU/CSU had commanded a single-vote majority in the Bundesrat even when the SPD-FDP coalition assumed office and gradually approached parity with the government parties in the lower house as well. The reason was that three Liberals and one Social Democrat deserted government ranks to join the CDU/CSU faction in opposing the treaties. Thus, the Cabinet's initial majority of 12 seats was reduced to a precarious 4-seat margin by the end of 1971. In April 1972 the government's majority disappeared altogether when two more members of the social-liberal coalition defected to the opposition camp.

In the light of the resulting parliamentary impasse, CDU/CSU leaders decided to force the government's resignation. CDU Chairman Barzel declared himself a candidate for the federal chancellorship, and his party colleagues moved a constructive vote of no-confidence against Brandt on 27 April. Employing Article 67 of the Basic Law for the first time in the history of the Federal Republic, Christian Democratic spokesmen fully expected a narrow victory and thus their return to executive power. On that assumption, Barzel, Strauss, and others vaguely promised that they would renegotiate the Soviet and Polish treaties on terms allegedly more favorable to the West Germans.

To the consternation of the CDU/CSU floor leaders, the no-confidence motion failed when two members of their faction abstained in the crucial vote on Barzel's election. Thus, by the slimmest of margins, the Brandt-Scheel government survived West Germany's most serious political crisis since the *Spiegel* controversy over a decade earlier.

FROM BRANDT TO SCHMIDT

Brandt's victory enabled the SPD-FDP coalition to proceed with legislative ratification of the treaties. Since the failure of the no-confidence motion clearly indicated that the Christian Democrats would be unable to block the treaties without resorting to obstructionist tactics in the Bundesrat, opposition leaders decided to instruct their parliamentary factions to abstain during the ratification procedure. Accordingly, the Bundestag endorsed the pivotal German-Soviet treaty on 17 May 1972 by a vote of 248 in favor, 10 opposed, and 238 abstentions. A similar majority voted in favor of the Polish treaty.

Despite their victory in the debate over the eastern treaties, the coalition partners confronted the certainty that they could no longer govern in the absence of a parliamentary majority. The only resolution to the continuing legislative deadlock, then, was to dissolve parliament and schedule new elections. Chancellor Brandt engineered this outcome with the tacit approval of the CDU/CSU when he called for a simple vote of confidence on 22 September. Predictably, the motion failed, thereby providing President Heinemann with a legal pretext to order a dissolution election on the basis of Article 68 of the Basic Law.

The electoral campaign of September-November 1972 proved the most animated in postwar German history. Foreign policy remained the dominant theme of government-opposition conflict. By early November the government had negotiated a comprehensive "Germany treaty" *(Deutschlandvertrag)* with the SED regime whereby both countries agreed to "settle their disputes exclusively by peaceful means," acknowledged the "inviolability now and in the future of (their common border)," and explicitly recognized the independent territorial jurisdiction and autonomy of each German state.[14] Although the Western powers praised the Germany treaty as a positive extension of the Berlin Agreement, the CDU/CSU declared that it reserved the right to renegotiate it after the election. Strauss and to a lesser extent Barzel attacked the treaty on the grounds that it indeed recognized the "independence" of the two German states, whereas Chancellor Brandt retorted that this provision by no means meant that the two Germanies were "foreign countries to one another."

Alongside the continued debate on the Federal Republic's *Ostpolitik,* various domestic issues galvanized the 1972 campaign. One was the escalation of an international terrorist campaign against the established political and economic order that was instigated by a small group of urban guerrillas known as the Red Army Faction. Inspired to undertake direct political action by the example of the student protest movement of the 1960s, the new breed of dissidents adopted a distinctively more radical profile. In contrast to their more idealistic student forebears, the urban terrorists openly proclaimed themselves revolutionary Marxists and cultivated close ideological links with counterpart movements in Italy, France, and the Middle East. In pursuit of their declared objective to overthrow Western capitalism, the terrorists adopted increasingly violent hit-and-run tactics. West German authorities captured several founding members of the Red Army Faction in 1972, but the persistence of terrorist activities prompted CDU/CSU spokesmen to raise serious questions about the adequacy of existing legal codes, surveillance techniques, and security measures as instruments for containing the terrorist campaign.[15] Indeed, many Christian Democrats openly charged the governing coalition with being "soft on terrorism."

West Germany's economic performance proved a third campaign issue. After having achieved widespread public acclaim for his efforts to lead the nation out of its economic doldrums of 1966-67, Economics Minister Schiller surprised government and opposition officials alike by stepping down as minister of economics because of a Cabinet dispute over monetary policy. His subsequent resignation from the SPD and his attacks on the economic policies of his successor, Helmut Schmidt, provided an unexpected boost to the CDU/CSU. Opposition leaders pointed to the recent spate of wildcat strikes and the prevailing inflation rate of 6 percent as evidence of the government's alleged economic mismanagement, asserting throughout the campaign that they could manage the economy more effectively themselves.

Apart from the intensity of partisan differences over foreign and economic policy, the 1972 campaign proved distinctive because of the proliferation of ad hoc "citizen lobbies" *(Bürgerinitiativen)* on the grass-roots level of politics. Such groups, composed primarily of younger middle-class professionals, had begun to emerge by the beginning of the decade as a result of mass affluence and increased citizen awareness of multiple unfulfilled social needs. Among them were a shortage of places in public kindergartens, inadequate attention by government officials to the special problems of foreign workers and other "marginal groups" (including handicapped persons), and insensitivity on the part of both political and administrative officials to pressing local issues such as environmental protection.[16]

Election results on 19 November confirmed the realignment of 1969 and thereby vindicated both the *Ostpolitik* and domestic policies of the social-liberal coalition. The Social Democrats advanced to 45.9 percent of the popular vote, while the Free Democrats increased their share to 8.4 percent. The CDU/CSU fell to 44.8 percent, for a loss of 15 seats. The outcome accorded Brandt a comfortable 269-233 parliamentary majority when he was reelected federal chancellor in mid-December.

The resolution of the 1972 government crisis enabled the social-liberal coalition to complete the implementation of its eastern policies. The two Germanies signed the *Deutschlandvertrag* on 21 December, and the federal government submitted both the treaty and a bill authorizing West Germany's application for membership in the United Nations to parliament for its approval. A majority of the Bundestag endorsed both items the following May. During 1973 the Federal Republic subsequently established diplomatic relations with Hungary, Bulgaria, and Czechoslovakia and exchanged "plenipotentiaries" (as opposed to ambassadors) with the DDR. In addition, the federal government negotiated a renunciation-of-force agreement with Czechoslovakia that declared the Munich accord of 1938 "invalid" in accordance with earlier Warsaw Pact demands.

The ratification of the eastern treaties yielded several unanticipated domestic political results. One was Barzel's resignation as CDU chairman in May

1973. The reason was his defeat on an intraparty motion to endorse West German membership in the United Nations. Barzel had agreed with his party colleagues in voting against the Germany treaty, but he argued strongly in favor of the government's bill to authorize the Federal Republic to join the UN. CSU Chairman Strauss and other conservative party spokesmen opposed his argument on the grounds that West German membership in the world organization would mean membership by the DDR as well. When a narrow majority of the Christian Democrats endorsed Strauss's position, Barzel resigned. Helmut Kohl, a moderate who had served as minister-president of Rhineland-Pfalz since 1969, was elected his successor.

A second consequence of the successful conclusion of the eastern offensive was Chancellor Brandt's gradual disenchantment with the demands of executive leadership. Once he had accomplished his principal foreign policy goals, his zest for the day-to-day political struggle that is incumbent on all modern party leaders began to wane. Brandt's growing fatigue with executive office coincided with the beginning of a new international economic crisis in 1973-74 that fueled domestic inflationary pressures and caused another surge in unemployment (see chapter 6). West Germany's growing economic difficulties prompted in turn a decline in Social Democratic electoral fortunes in state elections from 1974 onward. As a result, the Social Democrats decided to refrain from nominating a candidate of their own to succeed Gustav Heinemann when he announced that he would not seek a second term as federal president. Instead, SPD leaders declared they would support the Liberal candidate, Walter Scheel (the incumbent foreign minister).

Increasingly beset by these discouraging economic and political trends, Brandt stunned his countrymen by announcing his resignation as federal chancellor on 6 May 1974. The immediate reason for his decision was the arrest two weeks earlier of one of his close personal aides, Günter Guillaume, on charges of espionage on behalf of the DDR. Conceding that he had been remiss in granting Guillaume access to confidential party and foreign policy documents, Brandt stepped down as an act of political contrition. He did, however, retain his position as chairman of the SPD. Brandt's departure initiated a wholesale change in West German leadership. The SPD's executive committee promptly nominated Finance Minister Helmut Schmidt as his successor. A day before the Bundestag formally elected Schmidt the country's fifth postwar chancellor, the Federal Assembly convened to select Walter Scheel the new federal president. Succeeding Scheel as foreign minister was Hans-Dietrich Genscher, a long-time member of the FDP and minister of the interior in the social-liberal coalition. Thus, in a manner unprecedented in German political history, the Federal Republic simultaneously obtained a new head of government, head of state, and foreign minister.

THE SCHMIDT-GENSCHER GOVERNMENT

Chancellor Schmidt's rise to power capped an inordinately successful political career. Following his election to the Bundestag in 1953, Schmidt became interior minister of his native city of Hamburg in 1961 and SPD floor leader in 1967. He was elected vice-chairman of the party in 1968 and served under Brandt as minister of defense and later minister of economics and finance. In each of these positions, Schmidt demonstrated a talent for assertive leadership based on pragmatic policy considerations.

These qualities characterized the performance of the new federal government. In his inaugural policy address, Chancellor Schmidt announced that his Cabinet would concentrate its energies on restoring domestic economic stability. He spelled out the details later in the year with the promulgation of a comprehensive program designed to stimulate renewed economic growth. Among its principal features were increased public expenditures on highway construction and coal production, government subsidies to private firms, a modest reduction in individual tax rates, and an increase in government support to families with children.

Parallel with its efforts to encourage economic expansion, the Schmidt-Genscher Cabinet completed parliamentary negotiations on the long-standing issue of extended rights of codetermination. Responding to DGB pressure to achieve equal representation between workers and shareholders on the boards of all large industrial firms, the government submitted a bill in December 1975 that approached full parity. The measure provided for ostensible equality between labor and capital in that it empowered workers and shareholders each to elect one-half of the members of the supervisory boards of joint stock companies employing 2000 or more workers. The bill fell short of mandating full parity between capital and labor, however, in that it stipulated that each board must elect its chairman by a two-thirds vote. Since this meant that the chairman could not be chosen in opposition to the shareholders, the bill in effect ensured the continued dominance of private ownership in the West German productive process.

Despite DGB reservations about the latter feature of the government's proposal, the Bundestag endorsed the measure in March 1976. The bill was implemented in July with the proviso that any affected party would have a year's time to challenge its legal status through the court system. The DGB greeted the legislation as "an expansion of the rights and influence of workers and their unions,"[17] but vowed to continue efforts by organized labor to achieve full parity in the future.

In foreign policy matters, Chancellor Schmidt embarked on a less ambitious agenda than his predecessor. His primary task was twofold: to seek restored confidence within the Atlantic alliance, and to promote economic benefits promised by the new *Ostpolitik*. In pursuit of these objectives, Schmidt conferred with high-ranking American officials, initiated an agreement with Moscow on behalf of expanded economic cooperation between West Germany and Russia, and concluded a treaty with Poland whereby the federal government would provide an immediate payment of $500 million and a long-term loan of $400 million to the Polish government in exchange for the right of some 125,000 Poles of German extraction to emigrate to the West.

The electorate honored the domestic and foreign policy initiatives of the social-liberal coalition in the Bundestag elections of 1976 and 1980. Similar to the electoral contest of 1972, both campaigns were fought on personal as well as ideological grounds. Schmidt and Foreign Minister Genscher defended the Cabinet's achievements against joint attacks by CDU Chairman Kohl and CSU leader Strauss, who served as the Christian Democratic chancellor candidate in the two campaigns, respectively. Schmidt's demonstrated executive competence tipped the electoral balance narrowly in favor of the governing coalition in both instances. The two parties lost support in 1976 relative to 1972, but with a combined total of 50.6 percent of the vote they managed to retain a narrow parliamentary majority. Four years later, they mobilized 53.5 percent compared to 44.5 percent for the Christian Democrats—with Strauss's candidacy playing a significant role in the latter's defeat. Following each contest, Schmidt was easily reelected federal chancellor.

THE DECLINE OF THE SOCIAL-LIBERAL COALITION

Despite its electoral victories, the Schmidt-Genscher government confronted multiple policy challenges that ultimately spelled an end to the social-liberal alliance. One was the continuation of the terrorist campaign. German terrorists launched an increasingly violent series of attacks against prominent government officials in November 1974 when members of the Red Army Faction murdered the president of the West Berlin Supreme Court. They intensified their efforts to discredit established authority in 1977 when urban guerrillas killed the West German prosecutor-general and a prominent banker. In September 1977 terrorists kidnapped Hans Martin Schleyer, president of the German Employers' Association (BDA) and the German Federation of Industries (BDI). When their demand for the release of various leaders who had previously been sentenced to prison was refused, the terrorists retaliated by killing their captive.

The government's response to the terrorist campaign provoked criticism on both the right and the left. Conservative critics faulted Cabinet officials for their failure to halt the attacks. When the federal government responded with bills in 1974 and 1978 designed to facilitate the surveillance of suspected and imprisoned terrorists, various Social Democrats, trade unionists, and intellectuals attacked the measures as excessive and undemocratic.

An important indirect consequence of growing public apprehension about the terrorist issue was an electoral backlash directed above all at the Free Democrats (who controlled the federal ministry of interior responsible for maintaining domestic security). FDP candidates failed to win the necessary minimum of 5 percent of the popular vote in state elections in Lower Saxony and Hamburg in June 1978 and the party was thereby deprived of its previous representation in both state parliaments.

A simultaneous harbinger of increased sociopolitical conflict was a surprise initiative in June 1977 by 30 employer groups and 9 industrial firms to challenge the constitutionality of the Bundestag's codetermination bill of 1976 before the Federal Constitutional Court. Alleging that the extension of employee representatives on company boards undermined "the capacity of shareholders and companies to function effectively," the employers denounced the bill as an attempt to establish a new economic and labor system that was "incompatible with the basic constitutional principles and guidelines governing the legal order and nature of the economy and labor relations today."[18] The DGB chairman, Heinz Oskar Vetter, responded by declaring that he was outraged at this "blow" from the employers. In protest he demonstratively boycotted the scheduled July 1977 "concerted action" session in Bonn. The Federal Constitutional Court affirmed the constitutionality of the codetermination bill in 1979, but by then the DGB and its member unions were in no mood to revive the concerted action meetings, at least on a formal basis.[19]

Overshadowing public concern about both terrorist attacks and the conflict between organized capital and labor over codetermination was the state of the West German economy. The government's expansionary fiscal policies had helped stimulate a pattern of slow but steady growth from 1976 onward. Simultaneously, the country's annual inflation rate had fallen from a high of 7 percent in 1972 to 4 percent or less between 1975 and 1979. Stubbornly resisting government efforts to achieve full economic recovery, however, was the highest level of unemployment since the early 1950s. The number of persons out of work jumped from 2.6 percent in 1974 (when Schmidt assumed office) to 4.7 percent in 1975, and remained at over 4.0 percent through 1978—much to the consternation of organized labor. Economic conditions suddenly worsened in 1979 when the oil-exporting countries imposed a new round of price increases for petroleum products. The result, in West Germany as elsewhere in the industrialized world, was a renewed inflationary spiral accompanied by a short-term decline in economic expansion and a precipitous jump in unemployment.

Germany's economic slump deepened through the early 1980s, causing sharp policy disputes between the Social Democrats and the Free Democrats despite their electoral victory in 1980. Leaders of the SPD sought to restore economic growth and reduce unemployment through increased public borrowing and higher taxes, while FDP officials advocated reductions in taxes and public services in an effort to stimulate recovery through private initiative. The result of the policy impasse was a political crisis triggered by the Free Democrats' resignation from the Cabinet in September 1982 in favor of a renewed alliance with the Christian Democrats.

The Restoration of Christian Democratic Leadership

Directly contributing to the FDP's switch in coalition allegiances was a persisting pattern of electoral and political volatility. A decline in regional support for the social-liberal coalition in Bonn had induced FDP leaders in Lower Saxony and the Saar to form local coalitions with the CDU as early as 1974. The Free Democrats fell below the minimum requisite of 5 percent of the popular vote in Lower Saxony and Hamburg four years later but managed to retain their representation in the Hesse Landtag in a crucial state election in October 1978. Advancing at the expense of both the FDP and the SPD in most of the state elections throughout the 1970s were the Christian Democrats, who by the beginning of 1977 commanded an imposing 26-to-15-seat majority in the Bundesrat. One result of the CDU/CSU's growing regional strength was that the Christian Democrats were able to recapture the federal presidency from the Free Democrats in May 1979. When the Federal Assembly convened to select a successor to President Scheel, a majority of delegates chose Karl Carstens, a veteran member of the CDU from north Germany, over the joint opposition of the SPD and the FDP. Another Christian Democrat, Richard von Weizsäcker, was overwhelmingly elected federal president in 1984.

Significantly complicating the FDP's electoral prospects was the groundswell of public support for the Greens. Following an initial regional breakthrough in the 1979 election in Bremen, the Greens succeeded in winning seats in Berlin, Baden-Württemberg, Lower Saxony, and Hamburg by 1982 as well. In combination with parallel gains by the CDU in most of the regional contests during 1981 and the first half of 1982, FDP leaders became increasingly convinced that they needed to change their alliance strategy to ensure their party's survival. When opinion polls indicated that the CDU would win an absolute majority in the September 1982 election in Hesse, regional FDP leaders announced they would campaign with the CDU rather than renew their pact with the SPD. The stage was set for the dramatic turn of events that fall in Bonn.

Chancellor Schmidt sought to salvage the SPD's claim to executive leadership by seeking a vote of confidence as a prelude to a possible dissolution election. Schmidt's tactic failed when FDP Chairman Genscher and his colleagues resigned from the Cabinet on 17 September and joined with the CDU/CSU in calling for a "constructive vote of no-confidence" against Schmidt in favor of the Christian Democratic chairman, Helmut Kohl. The Social Democrats promptly assailed their former coalition partners and seized on the 26 September election in Hesse as an opportunity to mobilize public opinion against the "treason in Bonn." Their efforts proved successful in that the Hessen electorate acted to deny the CDU its anticipated majority and the FDP its previous representation in the Landtag altogether. Nationally, however, the new alignment between the CDU/CSU and the FDP prevailed in the crucial parliamentary vote on the chancellorship on 1 October. Despite the fact that 20 out of the 53 members of the FDP Bundestag faction were opposed to their party's abrupt switch from one coalition to another, Kohl was elected federal chancellor by a margin of 256 to 235. The new chancellor reappointed FDP chairman Genscher as foreign minister along with two other Free Democratic members of the former SPD-FDP coalition. Of the remaining 12 Cabinet members, 8 belonged to the CDU and 4 to the CSU.

Chancellor Kohl swiftly sought to legitimize the change of government by petitioning President Carstens to dissolve the Bundestag and call new elections. The president complied, and elections were scheduled for 6 March 1983. The resulting campaign offered the West German electorate a series of important political choices. The most fundamental one concerned the composition of the federal government. Opinion polls indicated an electoral plurality in favor of the Christian Democrats, but if a sufficient number of voters chose to "punish" the FDP for its role in instigating the downfall of the still highly popular former Chancellor Schmidt, as the Hessen electorate had done in September, the likely result would be an absolute CDU/CSU majority. Such an outcome would lead in turn to a significant increase in the influence of CSU Chairman Strauss and other conservatives on the formation of domestic and foreign policy. Alternatively, success by the Green movement in gaining entrance to the new Bundestag could conceivably result in the emergence of a minority (and therefore weak) SPD government that would be dependent on indirect (and hence unpredictable) Green support for remaining in office.

Policy issues and personalities dominated the electoral contest. Foremost among the former was West Germany's sluggish economic performance. Since the previous Bundestag election in 1980, the annual rate of economic growth had dropped from 1.8 percent to −1.2 percent by the end of 1982, while the number of unemployed workers jumped to more than 2 million (8.4 percent).

The accompanying loss of tax revenues and sharp increase in unemployment benefits had resulted in a growing budgetary deficit that forced both the SPD-FDP coalition and the new Kohl government to enact reductions in the provision of public services.[20] During the campaign, CDU/CSU and FDP officials vigorously defended budgetary initiatives by the Kohl ministry to cut social spending, while the Social Democrats attacked such measures on the grounds that they harmed lower-class economic strata. Looking to the future, the government parties promised more of the same restrictive policies. Spokesmen for the SPD, in contrast, emphasized (with the highly vocal support of the DGB) the need to institute a shorter work week and to extend economic democracy as necessary measures to reduce both long-term unemployment and the concentration of private economic power.

Even more controversial, especially in the view of outside observers, was an emotional campaign debate over the proposed stationing of 560 American Pershing II and Cruise missiles within Western Europe, beginning in late 1983. The debate had ensued after NATO leaders agreed in 1979 to install the missiles in response to the prior installation of 300 Soviet SS-20s in the Soviet Union. Only in the event that the Soviet Union agreed to dismantle its own missiles would the NATO decision not take effect. Chancellor Schmidt had endorsed the so-called dual track decision by the NATO alliance, but during the early 1980s West German pacifists began to voice serious reservations about accepting the American missiles on West German soil. The Greens in particular seized on the missile issue as part of their antinuclear, antiestablishment campaign. Their determination to oppose further nuclear armament guaranteed political conflict regardless of which party or coalition won the election.

In addition, individual personalities played a key role in the 1983 campaign. Unexpectedly, the SPD lost its chief electoral asset when Schmidt announced in late October 1982 that he would not compete for the chancellorship for reasons of health. He was succeeded by Hans-Jochen Vogel, a competent but uncharismatic former minister of regional planning and urban development and minister of justice in the Brandt and Schmidt Cabinets, respectively. Clearly eclipsing Vogel's unknown leadership qualities was Chancellor Kohl, who, as long-term chairman of the CDU/CSU parliamentary faction, former minister-president of Rhineland-Pfalz, and chancellor candidate in 1976, had established a reassuring public image for himself as a stolid middle-of-the-roader in the tradition of Adenauer and Erhard. Genscher, FDP chairman and foreign minister, complemented Kohl's strengths in that he, too, was a recognized national leader, although his official status was marginally undermined when only 56 percent of FDP delegates reelected him party chairman at a special party conference in early November 1982 (compared to more than 90 percent in 1980).

The election results on 6 March 1983 vindicated the coalition shift the previous fall. Together, the CDU/CSU and the FDP received 55.7 percent of the vote, with the Free Democrats' 6.9 percent guaranteeing them another legislative term while depriving the CDU/CSU of an absolute majority. The Social Democrats fell to 38.2 percent — their lowest share of the national vote since 1961 (36.2 percent) — while the Greens amassed 5.6 percent to gain entrance to the Bundestag as the first splinter party in more than two decades. Kohl was reelected federal chancellor on 29 March to confirm formally the Federal Republic's shift to renewed Christian Democratic dominance during its fourth and current phase of executive leadership.

Kohl and his coalition partners utilized their popular mandate to implement a national tilt in favor of more conservative foreign and domestic policy choices. The federal government affirmed the earlier NATO decision to deploy Pershing and Cruise missiles and in 1985 endorsed the Reagan administration's Strategic Defense Initiative ("Star Wars"), the latter in part to enable West German scientists and industry to share in the development of new space age technology. Economically, the CDU/CSU-FDP coalition pursued relatively restrictive fiscal and monetary policies designed to promote slow but steady domestic growth under conditions of low inflation. In the process, the federal government proved willing to accept a further increase in unemployment levels (which rose to 9.1 percent by the middle of the decade).

A dramatic economic and social crisis ensued in April 1986 when a nuclear explosion at Chernobyl in the Soviet Union released massive clouds of radioactive material that contaminated agricultural produce and dairy products throughout much of the Federal Republic (as well as other European countries). The Chernobyl disaster intensified opposition among the Greens and a growing number of Social Democrats to the domestic use of nuclear energy. In recognition of the increased importance of environmental issues, the federal government responded by establishing in June a new ministry of the environment, nature conservation, and reactor safety. Appointed as its first head was a popular CDU mayor of Frankfurt.

Economic performance, armaments, and environmental issues thus dominated Germany's political agenda through the mid-1980s. The Social Democrats sought to capitalize on public unrest in the wake of continuing high unemployment and Chernobyl to attack the CDU/CSU-FDP coalition in the months preceding the January 1987 Bundestag election. The SPD nominated Johannes Rau, a party centrist who has served as minister-president of North Rhine-Westphalia since 1978, as their chancellor candidate in hopes that he could succeed where Vogel had failed four years previously to dislodge Kohl. Throughout the campaign Rau steadfastly rejected the prospect that the SPD might form a governing coalition with the Greens if the two parties together were to win a legislative majority, although other prominent Social Democrats (including SPD Chairman Brandt) suggested that such an alliance might prove desirable. For their part, the Christian Democrats campaigned primarily on their record of economic stability and alliance loyalty, while the Free Democrats emphasized the need for bolder government action to stimulate higher levels of growth, e.g., in the form of tax cuts.

Election results on 25 January 1987 yielded a mixed message. The coalition partners jointly amassed 53.4 percent of the popular vote to obtain a renewed legislative mandate for another four years, while the Social Democrats dropped to their lowest level (with only 37.0 percent) since the early 1960s. The Greens continued their electoral advance by gaining 9.1 percent of the vote. Within the coalition, the distribution of popular support shifted marginally from the Christian Democrats, whose national strength declined from 48.8 percent in 1983 to 44.3 percent), to the Free Democrats, whose support rose from 7.0 percent to 9.1 percent. Thus, the election reaffirmed the FDP's status as West Germany's pivotal third party and simultaneously revealed increased public apprehension about Chancellor Kohl's personal qualities as executive leader.

In the aftermath of the election, the prospects of a future SPD-Green coalition seemed to recede. Brandt's resignation as Social Democratic chairman in March 1987 and the election of Vogel as his successor strengthened the status of party moderates, who are pointedly skeptical about a possible coalition with the Greens.

Despite his relatively weakened political status, Kohl acted decisively during his second full executive term to achieve several important policy outcomes. He endorsed the results of a U.S.-Soviet summit conference in December 1987 calling for the mutual reduction of intermediate-range missiles in Western and Eastern Europe and unilaterally agreed, over initial objections by members of the CSU, to the dismantling of 72 older Pershing 1A rockets under joint American-German command.[21] Early in 1988 Chancellor Kohl utilized West Germany's six-month status as institutional president of the European Community to press successfully for a breakthrough budgetary agreement on financing the EC's highly complex and expensive farm program. The budgetary agreement among the 12 members of the EEC paves the way toward implementing some 300 detailed legal provisions that will culminate in the creation of a comprehensive economic union within the EEC by 1992.[22]

Indicators of Policy Outcomes and System Change

The successive stages of Christian Democratic and Social Democratic executive leadership reveal a number of salient characteristics about the West German political process:

1. No party has consistently dominated the national policy agenda. To be sure, each of the two larger parties maintains discernible regional strongholds: the Christian Democrats in Baden-Württemberg, Bavaria, Rhineland-Pfalz, the Saar, and Schleswig-Holstein, and the Social Democrats in North Rhine-Westphalia, Hesse, Bremen, and Hamburg. But on the national level, only the Christian Democrats have ever won an absolute majority (1957), and even then they were required, for policy reasons, to form a coalition government. The most persistent junior coalition partner for both the Christian Democrats and the Social Democrats has been the FDP; only during the initial years of regime consolidation was Adenauer able to choose among other parties for coalition purposes (see table 5.1).

2. The ubiquity of national coalition governments has several important political consequences. One is that the coalition strategy of the FDP is decisive in determining the composition of the federal government. The FDP's prefer-

TABLE 5.1

NATIONAL COALITIONS AND FEDERAL CHANCELLORS, 1949-87

Party Leadership	Governing Coalition	Federal Chancellor
Christian Democratic		
1949-53	CDU/CSU-FDP-DP	Adenauer I
1953-57	CDU/CSU-FDP-DP-GB/BHE	Adenauer II
1957-61	CDU/CSU-DP	Adenauer III
1961-63	CDU/CSU-FDP	Adenauer IV
1963-65	CDU/CSU-FDP	Erhard I
1965-66	CDU/CSU-FDP	Erhard II
Transitional		
1966-69	CDU/CSU-SPD	Kiesinger
Social Democratic		
1969-72	SPD-FDP	Brandt I
1972-74	SPD-FDP	Brandt II
1974-76	SPD-FDP	Schmidt I
1976-80	SPD-FDP	Schmidt II
1980-82	SPD-FDP	Schmidt III
Christian Democratic		
1982-83	CDU/CSU-FDP	Kohl I
1983-87	CDU/CSU-FDP	Kohl II
1987-	CDU/CSU-FDP	Kohl III

ence for the Christian Democrats enabled Adenauer and Erhard to retain power through the mid-1960s. Thereafter, the Liberals' shift in coalition strategy made possible, first, the elections of Brandt and Schmidt, and in 1982-83 that of Chancellor Kohl. A second consequence of sustained coalition rule is that the Free Democrats are accorded a degree of political influence that is disproportionate to their share of the popular vote. At several critical junctures during alternating periods of CDU/CSU and SPD rule, the Free Democrats have utilized their pivotal legislative status to induce substantial changes in Cabinet personnel and/or policy formation.

3. As in all parliamentary democracies, executive stability in the Federal Republic is dependent on the strength and cohesiveness of the federal government's parliamentary majority. Among the 15 Cabinets that have held office from 1949 through the late 1980s, the most stable was the Grand Coalition, which rested on the joint support of 447 CDU/CSU and SPD deputies and was opposed by only 49 Free Democrats. During less exceptional periods of single-party leadership, the CDU/CSU has consistently enjoyed a more comfortable margin of legislative support than the SPD-FDP. During Adenauer's tenure, the Christian Democrats increased their numerical majority from 34 seats during the first legislative session (1949-53) to 185 during the second (1953-57). From the late 1950s through late 1966, CDU/CSU-led coalition governments commanded majorities ranging from 77 to 119 seats. In contrast, the five SPD-FDP Cabinets of 1969-82 rested on far narrower majorities that fluctuated between 12 seats in 1969-72 and 46 in 1972-76. The more precarious parliamentary status of the various social-liberal governments significantly complicated Brandt's and Schmidt's leadership tasks relative to the earlier and later periods of CDU/CSU ascendancy.

4. West German parliamentary democracy is, at the same time, distinctive by virtue of the constitutional structure of federalism. As explained in chapter 3, the 10 Länder that formally constitute the Federal Republic are accorded a direct role in federal legislation through their representation in the Bundesrat. Accordingly, regional elections yield political results that transcend the immediate boundaries of any particular state. Land elections not only affect the composition of the Bundesrat and hence the prospects of proposed federal legislation; they also serve as a leading indicator of incipient electoral realignments, comparable to midterm congressional elections in the United States and bye elections in the United Kingdom. Important examples include the resurgence of Christian Democratic strength during the mid-1970s and the simultaneous advent of the Green movement.

5. Exerting a key influence on the ebb and flow of mainstream electoral fortunes on both the regional and national levels is the personal prestige of

the federal chancellor and, in the case of the principal opposition party, the chancellor candidate. Adenauer's reputation as an effective and forceful leader contributed significantly to the early gains by the CDU/CSU during the initial phase of regime consolidation and legitimation. Later, Brandt's charisma and international recognition as a peacemaker facilitated the social-liberal coalition's victory in 1972. In similar fashion, Schmidt's popularity proved a decisive factor in the SPD-FDP's succcesses of 1976 and 1980, just as Chancellor Kohl's reassuring personal attributes contributed to the Christian Democratic advance in March 1983.

The alleged "chancellor bonus" of incumbency does not automatically rebound in favor of the governing party, as evidenced by the increase in NPD support during the 1960s as a partial response to the perceived weakness of Chancellor Erhard and the CDU's slippage in the January 1987 election. Instead, incumbency is an asset only when the chancellor is perceived by his party colleagues and the public at large as decisive, innovative, intelligent, and politically astute.[23] If a leader fails to display these qualities to a sufficient degree, critics within the ranks of his own party will inevitably voice demands for his ouster. Such was the fate of Chancellor Erhard in 1966.

6. Finally, as in other industrial democracies, political change in the Federal Republic assumed unanticipated directions from the mid-1960s onward in response to the emergence of new forms of ideological controversy. The student protest movement and the citizen lobbies contributed indirectly to the electoral victories of the social-liberal coalition from 1969 through 1980, just as the escalation of the terrorist campaign during the 1970s helped fuel a growing climate of political conservatism that presaged the later electoral realignment in favor of the CDU/CSU. Similarly, the emergence of the Greens as a fourth national political party during the 1980s helped initiate an extended public debate on fundamental principles of economic, social, and security policies that will inevitably continue into the 1990s.

Notes

1. For a more detailed description of Germany's transition "from neoliberalism to interventionism," see Allan G. Gruchy, *Comparative Economic Systems,* 2d ed. (Boston: Houghton Mifflin, 1977), 152-55.

2. *Gesetz zur Förderung des Wachstums und der Stabilität* (Bonn: 1967).

3. Ibid.

4. As is explored more fully in the next chapter, "concerted action" constituted West Germany's most highly institutionalized form of democratic corporatism.

5. Press and Information Office of the German Federal Government, "The New Government's Policy," *The Bulletin,* 20 December 1966.

6. Government declaration of 27 October 1969.

7. *New York Times,* 29 October 1969.

8. Press and Information Office of the Federal Republic, *The Treaty of August 12, 1974, between the Federal Republic of Germany and the Union of the Soviet Socialist Republics* (Bonn, 1970), 8.

9. Ibid., 10.

10. Press and Information Office of the Federal Republic, *The Treaty between the Federal Republic of Germany and the People's Republic of Poland* (Bonn, 1971), 8-9.

11. Honore M. Catudal, Jr., *The Diplomacy of the Quadripartite Agreement on Berlin* (Berlin: Berlin-Verlag, 1977), 65.

12. Ibid., 281.

13. Peter H. Merkl, *German Foreign Policies, East and West. On the Threshold of a New European Era* (Santa Barbara, Calif.: ABC-Clio Press, 1974), 166.

14. Press and Information Office of the Federal Republic, *Vertrag über die Grundlagen der Beziehungen zwischen der Bundesrepublik Deutschland und der Deutschen Demokratischen Republik* (Bonn, 1972).

15. Opposition demands for more stringent law-and-order measures were tragically reinforced on the eve of the dissolution election when eight Arab commandos killed two Israeli athletes and seized nine others as hostages during the Olympic games in Munich. The Arab guerrillas demanded the release of 200 ideological kinsmen in Israel but Israeli authorities refused to comply. As a result, the commandos sought to leave Germany with their hostages for Egypt. When West German police ambushed them at a military airport, all nine of the Israeli hostages and three of the Arabs were killed.

16. Quoted in Jutta Helm, "Citizen Lobbies in West Germany," in *Western European Party Systems,* ed. Peter H. Merkl (New York: Free Press, 1980), 582.

17. Quoted in Dieter Schuster, *Die deutsche Gewerkschaftsbewegung,* 5th ed. (Düsseldorf: Deutscher Gewerkschaftsbund, 1976), 108. For a complete text of the codetermination bill of 1976, see the Federal Minister of Labour and Social Affairs, *Codetermination in the Federal Republic of Germany* (Bonn, 1978).

18. The employers based their claims on Article 14 of the Basic Law, which declares that "property and the right of inheritance are guaranteed."

19. Informal equivalents were established, however, in the form of so-called Bungalow discussions at the chancellor's residence in Bonn. See chapter 6.

20. See chapter 7.

21. Policy differences persist between the federal government and its NATO allies, however, with respect to the modernization of remaining missiles and negotiation strategy vis-à-vis the Warsaw Pact. See "NATO Strives to Keep Germany in Fold on East-West Arms-Negotiations Stance," *Wall Street Journal,* 25 February 1988, 12.

22. For a comprehensive summary and assessment of the steps involved in the pending creation of an EEC-wide free market, see "They've Designed the Future and It Might Just Work," in *The Economist,* 13 February 1988, 45-49.

23. Elisabeth Noelle and Erich Peter Neumann, *Jahrbuch der öffentlichen Meinung 1965-1967* (Allensbach: Verlag für Demoskopie, 1967), 207.

6. Democratic Corporatism in Practice: Economic Management and Performance

Defined in the introduction to this volume as an institutionalized arrangement whereby government officials, business groups, and labor representatives jointly participate in making and implementing national policy decisions, democratic corporatism in West Germany has assumed diverse forms over time. That is, the scope and intensity of corporatist arrangements have expanded and later contracted in response to changing economic and political conditions. Moreover, the public debate over employment and industrial policies in the mid-1980s points toward the potential development of alternative modes of corporatist arrangements in the future.

Corporatist tendencies in the Federal Republic, while based on various historical antecedents, are primarily a product of multiple postwar structural and political changes described in preceding chapters. Among them are the reconstitution of autonomous organized interest groups during the occupation interlude (including the formation of a unified trade union movement in the form of the DGB) and the institutionalization of effective decision-making and administrative structures. Together, these factors constitute basic prerequisites for the advent of democratic corporatism in West Germany. Yet, as this chapter demonstrates, deliberate actions by key policy actors determined the form and consequences of corporatism in practice.

Growth and Affluence

For most of the postwar period, the Federal Republic has maintained a pattern of economic performance characterized by largely continuous growth and unprecedented prosperity. As indicated in table 6.1 on page 132, the country's average annual growth rate of 6.5 percent significantly exceeded that of both its European neighbors and the United States during the formative 1950s. The West German growth rate declined marginally to a still-respectable annual average of 4.4 percent during the 1960s and then fell to an annual average of 2.4 percent during the 1970s and 2.2 percent during the first half of the 1980s as

TABLE 6.1

AVERAGE ANNUAL GROWTH IN GROSS DOMESTIC PRODUCT
IN LEADING OECD COUNTRIES, 1950-86

Country	1950-60	1960-70	1970-80	1980-86
Canada		5.6	3.9	2.7
France	3.5	5.7	3.5	1.6
Germany	6.5	4.4	2.6	1.8
Japan		10.5	5.0	3.8
Sweden	2.6	4.4	1.7	1.7
United Kingdom	2.2	2.9	1.9	1.5
United States	1.6	4.3	3.0	2.2

SOURCES: OECD *Economic Surveys*; World Bank, *World Development Report 1982;* and OECD, *Economic Outlook,* June 1988.

a consequence of a rapid increase in the price of oil and a general international economic slump that began in 1979. During the same period, West Germany's per capita wealth increased dramatically—rising from $563 in 1951 to $1506 in 1960 and $14,611 in 1986—to exceed that of France and Britain (see table 6.2).

Accompanying growth and affluence in the Federal Republic has been one of the world's lowest inflation rates. Inflation averaged 3.2 percent a year during the 1960s, which was slightly below the average rate of 3.8 percent among the seven leading industrial democracies listed in table 6.3. The average annual rate rose to 5.9 percent in the 1970s but was significantly lower than the

TABLE 6.2

PER CAPITA GROSS DOMESTIC PRODUCT
IN LEADING OECD COUNTRIES, 1951-86
(IN DOLLARS)

Country	1951	1960	1970	1983	1986
Canada		1,910	3,883	12,310	14,174
France	840	1,519	2,790	10,500	13,077
Germany	563	1,506	3,106	11,430	14,611
Japan		531	1,912	10,120	16,109
Sweden	1,078	1,931	4,095	12,470	15,661
United Kingdom	794	1,494	2,188	9,200	9,651
United States	2,122	2,889	4,840	14,110	17,324

SOURCES: Compiled from International Monetary Fund, *International Financial Statistics;* OECD, *Main Economic Indicators: Historical Statistics, 1955-71* (Paris: OECD, 1973); OECD, *Main Economic Indicators: Historical Statistics, 1960-75* (Paris: OECD, 1976); World Bank, *World Development Report 1985,* 175; and OECD, *Economic Surveys, 1987/1988.*

TABLE 6.3

AVERAGE ANNUAL RATES OF INFLATION, 1960-86

Country	1960-70	1970-80	1981-86
Canada	3.1	9.3	6.9
France	4.1	9.2	8.5
Germany	3.2	5.1	3.2
Japan	4.8	7.5	2.4
Sweden	4.3	12.1	8.2
United Kingdom	4.1	14.4	6.6
United States	2.8	7.1	4.9

SOURCE: World Bank, *World Development Report 1982* and OECD, *Economic Outlook,* June 1988.

average rate of 9.2 percent for the seven industrial democracies as a group (see table 6.3). During the 1980s, Germany's inflation rate fell to its lowest level in two decades.

Two additional indicators of economic stability are low unemployment and labor peace. In the former instance, West Germany sustained an average annual unemployment level of less than 1.0 percent from 1969 through 1973. During the same period, unemployment averaged nearly 5.0 percent a year in the United States, 5.7 percent in Canada, and 3.0 percent in the United Kingdom. Only in 1974 did Germany's unemployment rate begin to climb, with important economic and political implications to be discussed below. The postwar pattern of long-term labor peace, meanwhile, remains largely intact. West Germany has by no means escaped labor conflict, but in comparison with most other advanced capitalist nations its frequency of industrial strikes and retaliatory lockouts has been low. From the early 1950s through the 1970s, West Germany experienced significantly fewer strikes than the United States, the United Kingdom, Canada, and France. Only the Scandinavian countries, Austria, the Netherlands, and Switzerland sustained comparable or better records of labor peace.

To a degree, these performance outcomes can be attributed to a variety of technological and economic factors. Among them are the modernization of Germany's factories in the wake of wartime destruction, the influx of $4.4 billion in Marshall Aid funds during the early postwar period, a consistent trade surplus from the early 1950s into the early 1980s, and the strength of the German mark in international currency transactions. The West German economy has benefited, too, from the influx of abundant cheap labor in the form of 13.7 million expellees and political refugees from the DDR and Eastern Europe during the 1940s and 1950s and, later, some 2.4 million foreign workers from southern Europe. Yet, ultimately, *political* acts have proven decisive in shaping the course of West German economic performance. Foremost among them have been decisions by public officials to endorse institutional reform and/or modify the scope and degree of government economic activism in response to the demonstrated need for systemic and policy innovation.

Organized Interest Groups and Policy Efficacy

Democratic corporatism, as opposed to "state" (or coercive) corporatism, presupposes voluntary compliance with authoritative policy decisions on the part of organized interest groups.[1] A key incentive for compliance lies in institutional and individual efficacy among group members with respect to economic and other policy decisions that affect their lives. This condition was met with respect to both organized labor and employer associations in the formative years of postwar political transformation.

As recounted in chapter 4, union activists succeeded in reestablishing works councils on the floorshop level as early as 1946 and achieving parity or nearparity representation of workers' interests on the supervisory boards of all larger industrial firms through legislation passed in 1951 and 1976. Although the DGB and its member unions are far from satisfied with these steps toward industrial democracy, West Germany's experiment in codetermination has nonetheless served to integrate the labor movement and its union representatives firmly into the established socioeconomic and political order. The result has been not only to increase worker loyalty to particular firms and thereby lessen potential sources of employee discontent but also to induce labor leaders to adopt a positive attitude toward cooperation with other policy actors in pursuit of common economic objectives.

The parallel reconstitution of regional and national associations modeled on pre-Nazi structures enabled employer representatives to establish counterpart organizations to the DGB and its member unions in the form of the National Association of German Employers (BDA), the National Federation of Industry (BDI), and the Diet of German Industry and Commerce (DIHT).[2] Given their anchorage in private ownership and their considerable financial support, the various employer groups exercise significant economic and political leverage vis-à-vis both organized labor and political authorities. Similar to union officials, employer representatives have proven willing to utilize their resources on behalf of cooperative strategies of economic reconstruction and growth. At the same time, they have resisted DGB initiatives and legislative measures that seem to restrict rights of private ownership, as indicated by the 1977 challenge by various firms and employer associations to the 1976 codetermination bill.

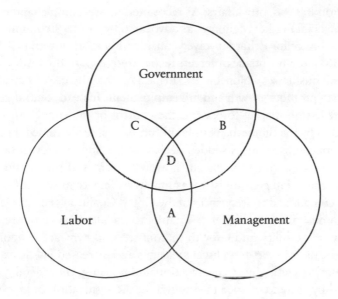

FIGURE 6.1

PATTERNS OF POLICY LINKAGES

NOTES: Area A = management-labor consultations and negotiations; area B = government-management consultations; area C = government-labor consultations; and area D = government-management-labor consultations.

Throughout the initial decade and a half of regime consolidation and post-war recovery (1949-66), policy linkages among government, employer, and labor actors were largely restricted to areas A, B, and C depicted in figure 6.1. That is, management and labor bargained directly in negotiating labor-market decisions affecting wages, hours, and other bread-and-butter issues (area A), just as central government officials (e.g., in the various federal ministries) conducted bilateral talks with employer groups and unions in the latter's attempts to influence the formation and implementation of economic, labor, social, and other policies through familiar institutional lobbying efforts (areas B and C). A move toward trilateral policy consultations (area D) occurred only with the formation of the Grand Coalition government.

The Rise and Fall of Concerted Action

Chancellor Kiesinger's election as head of a CDU/CSU-SPD coalition in December 1966 signaled the beginning of a policy shift toward greater government intervention in economic affairs. As recounted in preceding chapters, the concept of a "social market economy" as advocated by former Economics Minister and later Chancellor Erhard involved considerably more government economic activism than many outside observers recognized (e.g., in the form of tax benefits to small businesses). Nonetheless, Erhard resisted the use of Keynesian fiscal measures to promote growth and full employment. Instead, central government officials relied on market forces and the control of the supply of money and interest rates by the Bundesbank in Frankfurt to ensure continued, noninflationary economic expansion. A sudden decline in the annual growth rate, accompanied by a rise in unemployment, however, prompted the Grand Coalition to initiate more interventionist measures from late 1966 onward.

The content and consequences of the Grand Coalition's economic initiatives have been described in chapter 5. Thanks to its authority under terms of the 1967 Law on Stability and Growth to counteract downward economic cycles through the use of short-term fiscal measures and increased public expenditures on such projects as highway construction and housing, the federal government succeeded by the end of 1968 in stimulating the restoration of growth and reversing the trend toward greater unemployment. Simultaneously, Economics Minister Karl Schiller moved to institutionalize "concerted action" as a means to reduce domestic inflationary pressures through a coordinated program of wage and price stability.

Concerted action *(Konzertierte Aktion)* proved to be West Germany's most highly formalized experiment in democratic corporatism. Designed to facilitate the attainment of economic stability, concerted action brought together high-level government, employer, and labor officials to discuss macroeconomic trends and policy issues. Schiller convened six sessions of the concerted action partners in 1967 to discuss a wide range of topics including macroeconomic goals, structural policies, and income policies. Four sessions were held the following year to enable government and interest-group officials to review the annual economic report of the Council of Economic Experts, additional macroeconomic projections, social policies, and wage developments. Participants convened three times during the final year of the Grand Coalition in 1969 to continue their discussions of general economic goals and to assess factors of price stability and the pros and cons of a possible revaluation of the D-Mark.

Through 1968, concerted action helped facilitate the federal government's economic recovery program. In the first two years after the inception of concerted action, representatives of both organized labor and employer groups declared their willingness to act on the government's economic projection data to promote economic stabilization. Thus, union officials restricted the average rate of wage increases to 6.5 percent in 1967-68 in regional negotiations with employer associations. Wage restraint contributed in turn to the resumption of economic growth and an accompanying decline in the rate of unemployment by the end of 1968.

Beginning in 1969, however, concerted action sessions became increasingly acrimonious. One reason was political. As the various parties began to gird themselves for the September Bundestag election, Social Democratic and Christian Democratic leaders increasingly bickered over economic policy and the DGB's renewed initiative to extend rights of codetermination. When the Christian Democrats went into parliamentary opposition following the election, employer groups participating in concerted action proved less willing to exercise price restraint at the behest of the more prounion Social Democratic Cabinet leadership. Economic calculations proved a second factor weakening the effectiveness of concerted action. Angered that wage restraint had resulted in higher profits in a number of firms in the wake of economic recovery, rank-and-file workers and union officials staged a number of wildcat and official strikes in 1969 and 1970 to demand catch-up wage increases. The result was a jump in average annual wage increases to 12.6 percent in 1970 and 13.6 percent a year later. West Germany's annual rate of inflation increased in tandem to 5.3 percent in 1971 (compared to an average rate of 3.2 percent during the 1960s).

Despite new sources of political and economic tension between the principal labor market partners, Economics Minister Schiller continued to convene concerted action sessions at regular intervals through 1971. Repeatedly, the major agenda item proved to be trilateral discussions concerning appropriate means to promote stabilization under conditions of continued (albeit somewhat sluggish) economic growth. In January 1970 union representatives submitted for the first time their own economic projection data to supplement official projections prepared by the Federal Bank and the Ministry of Economics and Finance. At each of the three sessions in 1970 and the four meetings in 1972, concerted action participants exchanged views and declared their willingness, in principle, to support the federal government's efforts to achieve stable expansion through a combination of fiscal, monetary, and foreign economic measures.

Schiller's resignation from the Cabinet in 1972 marked the decline of concerted action as a formal instrument of democratic corporatism. Government officials continued to convene the sessions on an irregular basis through the middle of the decade. In 1974 and 1975, for example, they utilized concerted action meetings to inform the labor-market partners about the domestic and international consequences of the first round of oil price increases in 1973 and to urge both groups to restrict wage increases as a necessary step to reduce inflationary pressure. Although the unions and employer associations in fact responded to government exhortations to exercise restraint during wage negotiations in 1974-75, labor officials became increasingly critical of concerted action as an informal policy-making arena. In part, they felt overwhelmed by a steady increase in the number of official participants (including representatives of additional federal ministries and the Council of Economic Advisers). In addition, union officials became resentful of joint government and employer pressure for them to exercise greater restraint than was apparently expected of West German business.[3] Accordingly, the move by a group of industrial firms and employer associations in 1977 to challenge the constitutionality of the 1976 law on extended rights of codetermination, recounted in the previous chapter, proved a convenient excuse for the DGB to declare its refusal to participate in further sessions. Thus, concerted action collapsed, partially reversing West Germany's evolution toward democratic corporatism.

Functional Equivalents and Economic Performance in the 1970s and 1980s

The demise of concerted action did not mean an end to corporatist policy linkages altogether. Instead, trilateralism has been replaced by intensified bilateral consultations, with federal government officials continuing to play the key policy initiating and coordinating role. The result is the emergence of a functional equivalent to area D (depicted in figure 6.1) in the form of so-called Bungalow discussions at the official residence of the federal chancellor in Bonn. The effectiveness of such consultations has varied, however, in relation to the composition of the government and economic conditions.

Former Chancellor Schmidt initiated bilateral private discussions with employer and union leaders following the cancellation of the 1977 concerted action session. According to informed observers, his intent was to inform the labor-market partners about government economic policy and to encourage them to cooperate in its implementation through mutual price and wage restraint.[4] An additional objective, especially from 1980 onward, was to consider appropriate measures to curtail West Germany's rapidly increasing rate of unemployment. Thus, Schmidt sought to maintain the spirit of concerted action but in a decidedly less formal and intimidating atmosphere than had characterized the earlier trilateral meetings.

Schmidt succeeded to the extent that the "objectivization" of economic issues, which proved an important indirect consequence of joint employer and labor participation in concerted action meetings from 1967 to 1977, facilitated federal government efforts to dampen inflationary responses to the second round of oil price increases in 1979. Thus, unions and employers negotiated moderate wage increases averaging less than 5 percent in 1979 and 1980. Wage and price restraint on the part of the labor-market partners enabled West Germany to post substantially lower levels of inflation in both years than was the case in other advanced industrial democracies: 4.1 and 5.5 percent, respectively, compared to 9.1 percent and 10.1 percent for the leading OECD countries as a group.[5]

Even the Bungalow discussions ultimately failed, however, to restore previous levels of economic expansion and low unemployment. For a combination of international, structural, and attitudinal reasons, the West German economy did not adequately respond to SPD-FDP attempts to maintain the declared objectives of the 1967 Law on Stability and Growth. West German exports slowed during the early 1980s as both industrial and Third World countries experienced prolonged stagflation. Simultaneously, a decline in domestic and foreign demand for steel, automobiles, chemicals, and other manufactured goods indicated the advent of an ongoing shift in the West German economy—comparable to parallel trends in the United States, Britain, and other advanced Western nations—from traditional "smokestack" industries to newer high-technology and service enterprises. An important consequence is that Germany's spiraling unemployment rate, which by 1983 had reached 9 percent, became increasingly structural in nature and therefore impervious to short-term fiscal or monetary measures designed to stimulate renewed growth.

Exacerbating the negative effects of structural change is the unwillingness of many West German entrepeneurs to follow the lead of their American and Japanese counterparts in investing venture capital in new growth industries such as computer software and services. Their conservatism has apparently been reinforced by a negative attitude toward financial risks on the part of private banks. As a German investment consultant lamented recently: "[The banks] invest in security. They first ask you about assets and real estate, not about your business plans or your product."[6]

Conflicting partisan strategies to cope with Germany's deepening economic crisis caused the coalition breach between the SPD and the FDP that presaged Chancellor Kohl's election in October 1982 and the CDU/CSU-FDP victory in March 1983. Members of the new Cabinet have subsequently continued Schmidt's strategy of informal bilateral policy consultations as a supplement to the government's own policy efforts to restore growth. Whether CDU/CSU-initiated discussions with employer groups and organized labor can ensure the survival of established patterns of democratic corporatism as they had evolved by the early 1980s, or whether alternative forms of policy making will eventually emerge in their place, will depend on West Germany's economic performance during the remainder of the 1980s and the early 1990s.

An End to the German Model?

The restoration of CDU/CSU leadership in 1982-83 did not result in fundamental departures in the federal government's economic policies, despite expectations to the contrary on the part of many domestic and foreign observers. Admittedly, the new government sought to curtail a growing budget deficit by cutting a variety of social services (see chapter 7). Similarly, the CDU/CSU-FDP coalition trimmed the cost of job-retraining programs in its efforts to reduce the rate of increase in public expenditures.[7] In 1988 the coalition partners also introduced modest reductions in individual income tax rates designed to stimulate increased private investment.[8] In general, however, the CDU/CSU-FDP Cabinet continued to rely on fiscal and monetary policies and selective interventionist measures similar to those of the previous Grand Coalition and SPD-FDP governments in seeking to engineer a controlled recovery from West Germany's economic doldrums. Its policy initiatives largely involved differences in priority and emphasis rather than kind.

Yet in the eyes of West Germany's principal policy actors, differences of degree matter. In the short run, the government's tilt toward relatively more deflationary policies exacerbated labor-management relations. An early expression of renewed labor-market conflict was a spate of warning strikes that union officials instigated during the spring of 1983 to press their demands for a shorter workweek as a preferred strategy, in their view, for reducing unemployment. Labor-management strife escalated during the spring of 1984 when metalworkers and printers walked off their jobs for 7 weeks to demand a 35-hour workweek. The conflict was resolved with a compromise on 38.5 hours a week.

A probable result of recurrent labor unrest in the future would be the refusal by DGB and member union officials to participate in any continuation of bilateral or trilateral policy consultations on behalf of economic stabilization. The upshot would be a definitive suspension of corporatist policy-making linkages—with unforeseen consequences for the maintenance of the "German model" as a viable mechanism of sociopolitical stability and economic prosperity.

Organized labor's response to the economic crisis of the late 1970s and early 1980s is potentially indicative of a radical alternative to the combination of budgetary austerity and selective intervention employed by both the Schmidt and Kohl governments. As a long-term strategy to manage structural change and maximize employment, DGB officials have dusted off early postwar demands by the labor movement to extend rights of parity codetermination from the factory level to macroeconomic policy making in the form of regional, Land, and national economic councils. The declared purpose of such councils is not to infringe on the lawmaking authority of elected officials but instead, in the words of an authoritative DGB spokesman, "to equalize the existing preeminence of private economic interests . . . in the preparliamentary stage of policy decisions."[9]

The DGB's current "initiative" to achieve macro-level *Mitbestimmung* in which representatives of organized labor would join with employer groups and elected political representatives in determining industrial, investment, regional, and other economic policies will hardly yield substantive results as long as its principal ally, the SPD, remains in opposition. Moreover, DGB prescriptions concerning the economic intent of such a reform are highly unclear. If organized labor were to exercise policy influence through new forms of institutionalized trilateral policy consultations to achieve government intervention on behalf of declining industries simply as a means to save jobs, the result would inevitably be a move toward protectionism and a likely decline in the nation's standard of living. Conversely, joint government-employer-labor subvention of what participants in the American debate on industrial policy have identified as export-oriented "sunrise industries" could reinvigorate West German corporatism on the basis of concerted action of a new, more dynamic sort.

Notes

1. Philippe Schmitter distinguishes between "societal" (voluntaristic) and "state" (coercive) corporatism in "Still the Century of Corporatism?" in *The New Corporatism*, ed. Frederick B. Pike and Thomas Stritch (Notre Dame, Ind.: University of Notre Dame Press, 1974). Reprinted in Schmitter and Gerhard Lehmbruch, eds., *Trends Toward Corporatist Intermediation* (Beverly Hills, Calif.: Sage, 1979).

2. A good summary of Imperial and Weimar organizational precedents and postwar moves to establish the BDA, the BDI, and the DIHT can be found in Gerard Braunthal, *The Federation of German Industry in Politics* (Ithaca, N.Y.: Cornell University Press, 1965).

3. Klaus von Beyme, *Gewerkschaften und Arbeitsbeziehungen in kapitalistischen Ländern* (Munich: R. Piper & Verlag, 1977), 255.

4. Interviews with the author, summer 1981.

5. These outcomes are explored in a comparative Japanese-German context in M. Donald Hancock and Haruo Shimada, "Wage Determination in Japan and West Germany: A Corporatist Interpretation," in *The Political Management of Economic Change in Japan and the Federal Republic of Germany,* ed. Peter H. Merkl and Haruhiro Fukui (forthcoming).

6. Quoted in "Risk Is a Dirty Word to West Germans," *Wall Street Journal,* 26 October 1983.

7. The average pay for job retraining was cut from 82 percent of a worker's previous income to 68 percent, making the former the equivalent of prevailing unemployment compensation.

8. The 1988 bill proved highly controversial even within coalition ranks, primarily because reductions in individual rates were largely offset by accompanying increases

in gasoline taxes and the introduction of a new tax on interest income.

9. Dieter Schuster, *Die deutsche Gewerkschaftsbewegung,* 6th ed. rev. (Düsseldorf: DGB-Bundesvorstand, 1980), 129. The 1981 program of the DGB explicitly advocates the formation of a network of economic and social advisory councils. Their members would represent workers and employers on a partiy basis. See DGB-Bundesvorstand, *Grundsatzprogramm des Deutschen Gewerkschaftsbundes* (Düsseldorf, 1981), 11.

7. Sociopolitical Outcomes: Achievements and Dissent

Alongside West Germany's relative economic success and distinctive corporatist policy-making linkages, various sociopolitical achievements stand out as additional components of the "German model" of advanced industrial society. Among them are a distinctive combination of postwar structural and attitudinal changes, the provision of an extensive array of social services, and the existence of a reasonably efficient and adaptive educational system. At the same time, dissidents on both the left and the right have repeatedly criticized alleged shortcomings of the established sociopolitical order and fundamental policy choices. Together, these dual themes of contemporary German politics — achievements and dissent — underscore renewed ambivalence concerning the future of the Federal Republic.

Structural and Cultural Transformation

Principal factors contributing to political stability in West Germany include, as noted, the simplification of the party system and the emergence of a largely consensual political culture. The rise of the Christian Democrats, the Social Democrats, and the Free Democrats to their current parliamentary preeminence contrasts sharply with the fragmentation of the party system that characterized the Weimar and Imperial eras. As shown in table 2.2 in chapter 2, popular support for antisystem, regional, and other splinter parties has fallen dramatically since 1949 in comparison with the opposite trend during the waning years of the Weimar Republic.

The decline of extremist political movements has reinforced the evolution of a mature civic culture in the Federal Republic. More legalistic and authoritarian in style and substance than prevailing political cultures in North America, the United Kingdom, and Scandinavia, West Germany's political culture nonetheless encompasses widely shared beliefs among policy elites and an overwhelming majority of citizens in constitutionalism, individual civil liberties, competitive elections, and socioeconomic pluralism. These beliefs have been effectively translated into high levels of electoral participation (which averaged 87 percent in the 11 national elections held from 1949 to 1987); the peaceful alternation of executive power between the CDU/CSU and the SPD in 1969 and 1982; and elite-mass tolerance for dissenting movements, such as citizen action groups during the 1970s and the Greens during the 1980s.[1]

A more diffuse cultural facet of contemporary Germany is the Germans' self-image. In successive opinion surveys, the West Germans have consistently considered their best qualities to include "industriousness," "efficiency," "ambition," "love of order," "dependability," and "thoroughness."[2] These self-images have been transformed into the quality workmanship that characterizes most West German technology and exports, and reinforce the sense of pride with which an overwhelming majority of citizens honor postwar Germany's economic and political achievements.

Social Services

Supportive attitudes also extend to the provision of state-sponsored social services, although in recent years an increasing number of Germans have come to question their mushrooming costs. Beginning with the passage of three major bills by the Imperial Reichstag during the 1880s that introduced insurance benefits for workers in case of illness and industrial accidents and on their retirement, Germany proceeded to establish the world's first (and still one of its most comprehensive) welfare states.[3] During the Weimar era national legislation extended welfare provisions to miners and unemployed persons and significantly improved general retirement benefits. As a result of these measures, virtually all adult Germans were brought under some form of statutory insurance coverage by the late 1920s.

Since the founding of the Federal Republic, successive legislative acts have substantially enhanced welfare provisions. Among them are the Law on the Equalization of (wartime) Burdens, enacted in 1952; the introduction of children's allowances in 1954; the extension of medical coverage to pensioners and nonmanual workers (1957, 1961, 1970); a sweeping reform of retirement pensions in 1957 that introduced supplementary benefits reflecting individual differences in wages; and various laws designed to encourage profit sharing and individual ownership (1959, 1961, 1963). The cumulative effect of these measures, as Gaston Remlinger observes, is to "give Germany a social security system geared to the potentialities of an advanced industrial economy and attuned to the country's conception of social justice."[4]

Employers and workers jointly contribute nearly two-thirds of the money required to finance retirement benefits, health and accident insurance benefits, and other social services, with the federal government, the Länder, and local government units providing the remaining funds through legislative appropriations. The provision of social services accounts for fully 47 percent of all public expenditures in the Federal Republic. Combined federal, state, and local expenditures for social services have risen from 29 billion marks in 1963 to 574.1 billion marks (1985). Social services rank as the most expensive item in the annual federal budget, claiming 32 percent of national outlays in 1985 (compared to 20 percent for defense, the second highest category).[5] Pensions are the most expensive item, followed in decreasing order by sickness benefits, employment promotion, social assistance, and accident insurance.[6]

Throughout most of the postwar period, Christian Democrats and Social Democrats have concurred for pragmatic as well as humane reasons on the necessity to maintain West Germany's comprehensive welfare system. The economic crisis of the late 1970s and early 1980s, however, provoked a deepening ideological split between the two major parties concerning the costs of the government's social programs. Whereas former Chancellor Schmidt and other SPD stalwarts asserted the need to maintain established social services despite the recent economic downturn, the Kohl government sought to restrict public expenditures in its efforts to restore economic growth through greater reliance on private initiative. Thus, similar to prior initiatives by the Thatcher and Reagan administrations in Britain and the United States, the CDU/CSU-FDP Cabinet implemented a series of reductions in social services, beginning in 1983-84. They included a six-month postponement in a planned increase in retirement benefits, an end to government grants to students, the introduction of maximum income limits for the receipt of children's allowances, and (most controversial) a reduction in unemployment benefits. Predictably, SPD and union spokesmen denounced the reductions as harmful to less-privileged members of society.

Educational Reform

Germany's educational system also combines traditional and adaptive elements. Structurally, public education in the Federal Republic is a synthesis of a historical pattern of rigid separation among different educational levels and postwar reform efforts designed to expand educational opportunities. All children between the ages of six and ten attend a compulsory primary school known as the *Grundschule.* Thereafter, students attend one of a variety of secondary schools, depending on their academic competence and vocational ambitions, for an additional period of eight years. Historically, the latter consisted of two basic types: vocationally oriented junior high schools *(Realschulen)* and college preparatory schools called *Gymnasien (Gymnasium* in the singular). Since the mid-1960s, however, traditional patterns of secondary education have become increasingly blurred as a result of multiple reforms, including the introduction of a new intermediate-level school known as the *Hauptschule* (or main school), an expansion of educational opportunities and study programs in the *Gymnasien,* and the introduction of some 230 experimental unitary schools known as *Gesamtschulen,* which are modeled loosely on American and Scandinavian precedents.

Higher education and most research activities remain the prerogative of West Germany's 48 liberal arts universities, which provide instruction in social and natural sciences, medicine, and law; 7 technical universities, which concentrate primarily in engineering; various teachers' colleges; and a number of specialized academies of religion, art, music, athletics, journalism, and television. In contrast to traditions of higher education in the United States, Canada, and Britain, German universities are considered equal in their quality of instruction and research. For historical and pedagogical reasons, however, several stand out as exceptional: Munich, Göttingen, Frankfurt, Hamburg, Bonn, Tübingen, and Cologne.

As is the case with secondary education, higher education has been subject to successive reform efforts, primarily at the instigation of the Social Democrats on the Land level. One instance is the creation of 22 new universities and colleges during the 1970s, most of them located in the highly populous state of North Rhine-Westphalia, to help meet West Germany's growing demand for skilled white-collar workers. A second, much more controversial change involved efforts from the late 1960s onward to open institutional decisions on faculty recruitment, research activities, curriculum reform, and related issues to participation by representatives of the junior faculty, students, and administrative staff. To curtail the administrative and curriculum diversity that resulted throughout West Germany, the Bundestag voted in 1975 to direct the Länder to implement common standards with respect to university self-governance, forms of student government, the length of university studies, and disciplinary codes. By 1980, all 10 Länder plus West Berlin had complied with the parliamentary directive, albeit not without considerable opposition by students and many faculty members to the prospect of imposed administrative conformity from above.

Educational reforms during the 1970s prompted "the strongest expansion ever in the history of the German educational system,"[7] as the number of students enrolled in elementary and secondary schools increased from 8.6 million in 1969 to a peak of just over 10 million in 1976. Even more dramatic, in relative terms, was a threefold jump in the number of university students from 386,000 in 1969 to over a million in 1980.

In quantitative terms, West Germany's educational explosion seems to have vindicated aspirations voiced by the cultural ministers of the various Länder in 1964 to achieve the "education of each individual to the highest level of his/her capability."[8] The number of *Gymnasium* graduates rose from 16,000 in 1969 to 22,000 by 1985, while the number of university graduates obtaining the equivalent of a master's degree increased from 16,000 to more than 52,000 during the same period. Simultaneously, the number of successful doctoral candidates increased from 9800 in 1972 to 12,585 in 1985.[9]

Similar to the postwar debate on the magnitude and costs of Germany's social programs, educational reforms have evoked widespread criticism. Numerous teachers, parents, and politicians (especially within ranks of the CDU/CSU and the FDP) have attacked the expansion of educational opportunities on the *Gymnasium* level and the implementation of the new unitary schools primarily because they allegedly dilute the traditional elitest quality of German secondary education. Ideological critics have also denounced SPD-led efforts to democratize the educational system on the grounds that schools should not serve as instruments of planned social change.

Neoconservative intellectuals and politicians have simultaneously criticized what they perceive to be potentially antidemocratic tendencies inherent in the educational reform movement. A noteworthy example is Helmut Schelsky, a sociologist at the University of Münster, who resigned his chair in 1973 at the University of Bielefeld in opposition to the extension of participatory rights in matters of university governance to junior faculty members and students (many of whom were admittedly avowed Marxists). Subsequently, Schelsky criticized the emergence of what he described as a "new class" of academics, journalists, intellectuals, and other so-called purveyors of "information, news, scientific discourse, and educational . . . knowledge." This "secular priesthood," as he terms it, has engaged the "producers of essential goods" (who include, in his view, both workers and capitalists) in a fateful struggle for political control in advanced industrial society.[10] Schelsky pessimistically concludes that the "new class" of experts in "meaning and salvation" will most likely succeed in establishing its dominion over education, the formation of social consciousness, and in time the productive process itself.[11]

More down-to-earth problems afflicting Germany's educational system include severe restrictions on admission to medical and other professional facilities, a scarcity of jobs awaiting nonmedical university graduates (a situation painfully familiar to many North American students), and, paradoxically, a recent decline in the number of secondary students. By the mid-1980s almost a million fewer students were enrolled in elementary and secondary schools than in 1976, a trend based in Germany's declining birthrate. An unanticipated consequence was the necessity to close or merge numerous *Gymnasien*. The response on the part of some teachers and parents was to launch advertising campaigns to attract additional pupils to the elementary schools.[12]

The German Model and Its Critics

More fundamental domestic criticism of *das Modell Deutschland* has been voiced by dissidents on both the left and the right, including radical socialists, terrorists, the Greens, conservatives, and feminists. Much of the criticism of these groups is based on traditional ideological norms, but some attacks reflect new forms of critical consciousness characteristic of "postmaterialist" values in the Federal Republic and other Western democracies.

Radical socialists reappeared as a potent force of social criticism during the late 1960s as both a partial cause and consequence of the student demonstrations and public debate over the Grand Coalition's proposed emergency legislation. Their spokesmen included disenchanted Young Socialists ("Jusos") and revisionist Marxist intellectuals such as Claus Offe and Jürgen Habermas, both of whom obtained prestigious academic appointments during West Germany's period of rapid educational expansion.[13] Common to both the Jusos and Germany's radical academicians is their ideological critique of "late capitalism" *(Spätkapitalismus)* and the alleged use of the West German "state" as a covert instrument of class rule by the bourgeoisie. According to Habermas and others, the internal contradictions of the industrial capitalist order have engendered a fundamental "crisis of legitimacy" in the Federal Republic and other capitalist societies—a crisis that, in their view, will lead to the ultimate demise of capitalism and its replacement by some form of socialism.[14]

Actively seeking to discredit the established democratic order and West Germany's alliance through NATO with the United States, Canada, and Britain are members of the underground Red Army Faction. After a temporary lull in armed attacks on public officials following the federal government's crackdown on terrorist activity in the late 1970s, Germany's "urban guerrillas" resumed a campaign of selective violence. In May 1981, terrorists murdered Hesse's economics minister and later bombed an American-NATO air force base in Ramstein and attempted to assassinate the American military commander in Europe. The terrorists are the least representative of domestic critics of the German model; nonetheless, they remain capable of launching debilitating attacks on the established sociopolitical order.

On the democratic radical left, environmentalists and citizen action groups successfully lobbied during the late 1970s to stop the construction of three nuclear sites and to postpone a decision by regional officials to store nuclear wastes in deep salt domes in Lower Saxony. The Greens subsequently coopted environ-mentalist and pacifist criticisms of Land and national policies, with their suc-cess in successive Landtag and national elections during the 1980s reflecting increased public apprehension concerning nuclear energy, the effects of acid rain, and security issues.

At the opposite ideological extreme, conservative politicians and employer representatives have repeatedly attacked SPD and DGB policy initiatives as al-leged harbingers of an eventual transformation of the existing economic system into socialism. Franz Josef Strauss, for one, condemned the SPD's advocacy of state investment controls in its long-range "economic and political orienta-tion framework" of 1975 as a first step toward economic collectivization. Equal-ly critical are business spokesmen who interpret established practices of codeter-mination and the DGB's current campaign to implement macro-level economic and social councils as threats to private ownership.

Alongside familiar left-right criticisms of established institutions and policies is yet another group of dissidents: Germany's feminists. A women's movement had appeared as early as the Imperial era in the form of organized efforts by Social Democrats and Liberals to achieve legal equality between the sexes. Feminist organizations remained active during the Weimar Republic but were suppressed under National Socialism.[15] A successor *Frauenbewegung* grad-ually emerged in the early 1970s in the wake of the student and other protests during the 1960s.

Unlike its predecessor organizations, the contemporary women's movement is not linked to particular parties or ideologies, although the Greens have made a determined effort to appeal to female voters.[16] Nor are its demands narrowly political. Instead, Germany's feminists—similar to many of their counterparts in the United States, Britain, and Scandinavia—are primarily intent on achiev-ing libertarian economic and social objectives. These entail, in part, the tradi-tional demand for "equal pay for equal work." At the same time, they encom-pass efforts to achieve greater respect for women as persons, enhanced career opportunities for women, and changes in childhood socialization patterns that are aimed at diminishing cultural differences in sex roles. To promote these objectives, West German feminists have concentrated much of their energy on consciousness-raising activities in urban clubs, private discussion groups, and popular publications.[17] To what extent these activities will actually change mass attitudes and behavior patterns remains to be seen, but their intent is nothing less than a radical transformation of the country's social system.

Toward an Uncertain Future

Recurrent criticism on both the left and the right, accompanied during the 1980s by the advent of slower economic growth and increased unemployment, underscore the potential for alternative patterns of economic and political change in the years ahead. Whether destabilizing socioeconomic tendencies and domestic ideological criticism will lead to the demise of the German model or, conversely, to its renewal through active system change is the central challenge confronting government and opposition leaders alike as the Federal Republic enters its fifth decade of existence.

Notes

1. David P. Conradt, "Changing German Political Culture," in *The Civic Culture Revisited*, ed. Gabriel A. Almond and Sidney Verba (Boston: Little, Brown, 1980).

2. Elisabeth Noelle and Erich Peter Neumann, *Jahrbuch der öffentlichen Meinung 1976* (Munich: Verlag Fritz Molden, 1976), 56.

3. Peter Flora and Arnold J. Heidenheimer, eds., *The Development of Welfare States in Europe and America* (New Brunswick: Transaction Books, 1981).

4. Gaston V. Rimlinger, *Welfare Policy and Industrialization in Europe, America and Russia* (New York: Wiley, 1971).

5. Statistiches Bundesamt, *Statistisches Jahrbuch 1986* (Stuttgart: Verlag W. Kohlhammer GmbH, 1986), 396-97, 418-19, 421.

6. Ibid., 396.

7. Christopher Führ, "Review of Ten Years of Educational Reform in the Federal Republic of Germany, or Was There an Educational Catastrophe?" *Western European Education* 6 (Winter 1974-75): 39.

8. Quoted in ibid.

9. *Statistisches Jahrbuch 1986*, 350-63.

10. Helmut Schelsky, *Die Arbeit tun die anderen. Klassenkampf und Priesterherrschaft der Intellektuellen* (Munich: Deutscher Taschenbuch Verlag, 1977), 17.

11. Ibid. A number of American intellectuals have joined the discussion of whether a comparable "new (ruling) class" has emerged in the United States as well. For brief statements on the concept by Daniel Bell, Michael Harrington, Seymour Martin Lipset, Jeane Kirkpatrick, and others, see "Is There a New Class?" in *Society* 16 (January/February 1979): 14-62.

12. "Mit Prämie um Schüler werben. Bundesdeutsche Schulen fürchten um ihre Existenz," *DAAD Letter. Hochschule und Ausland*, December 1983, 34.

13. Products of the so-called "Frankfurt School" of critical sociology, Offe and Habermas have contributed noteworthy, if inconclusive, revisions of Marxist theory. Offe, who was appointed professor of political science at the University of Bielefeld in 1974, has sought to combine Marxist analysis with systems analysis and thereby develop a critical theory of the state under "late capitalism." Habermas, a more abstract theorist than Offe, has sought to analyze the development of capitalist society and its ostensible "crisis of legitimacy." A useful summary and critique of Offe and Habermas can be found in Heide Gerstenberger, "Theory of the State. Special Features of the Dis-

cussion in the FGB," in *German Political Systems. Theory and Practice in the Two Germanies,* ed. Klaus von Beyme (Beverly Hills, Calif.: Sage, 1976), 69-92.

14. In August 1977 the Jusos issued a strategy paper characterizing the economic slowdown in the Federal Republic as "the deepest crisis" since the founding of the republic in 1949. Juso spokesmen attributed West Germany's economic doldrums to an international "crisis of capitalism," which government policies had allegedly abetted by "encouraging the concentration (of industry and capital), destroying jobs, and subsidizing private profit." Quoted in *Frankfurter Allgemeine Zeitung,* 9 August 1977, 2.

15. See Richard J. Evans, *The Feminist Movement in Germany 1894-1933* (Beverly Hills, Calif.: Sage, 1976).

16. In the November 1986 state election in Hamburg, for example, the Greens fielded an all-female slate of candidates. They won 10.4 percent of the popular vote, primarily at the expense of the SPD.

17. An illustrative publication containing both interviews and critical chapters on the contemporary status of women in West Germany is Alice Schwarzer's *Der 'kleine Unterschied' und seine grossen Folgen. Frauen über sich — Beginn einer Befreiung* (Frankfurt: Fischer Taschenbuch, 1977). Also see Peter H. Merkl, "The Women of West Germany," *Center Magazine* 7 (May/June 1974): 68-69.

8. Prospects

Germany's turbulent past has strongly tempered the response of West Germany's leaders and citizens to recurrent destabilizing international and domestic trends during the postwar period. As recounted in chapter 1, persisting conflicts among different groups and social classes over fundamental modernizing issues of national unity, authority, and citizen rights had proven a principal cause of Germany's domestic instability and external aggression from the mid-nineteenth century onward. In contrast, the capitulation of the Third Reich and comprehensive political and economic reforms during the occupation interlude accorded postwar elites an opportunity to achieve structural cohesion and system legitimation based on a combination of group cooperation and solid policy success. Their achievements can be measured by the institutionalization of the "German model" of largely stable modernity.

To maintain the established political order, as well as postwar prosperity, West German elites have acted in concert to defend fundamental system principles. Politically, the Christian Democrats and the Social Democrats forged the Grand Coalition in 1966 in response to the temporary resurgence of popular support for the neofascist NPD rather than dissipate their strength through elite disunity, as was the case with Weimar's democrats in 1930-33. Moreover, government officials from all three of the mainstream parties have studiously avoided policy measures that might undermine fiscal stability or unleash rampant inflation comparable to the traumatic experience of 1923. They have done so even at the expense of increased unemployment levels during the 1980s and, under CDU/CSU-FDP aegis, in defiance of U.S. government pressure to stimulate a faster rate of growth to facilitate increased American exports.[1] Thus, to answer a central question posed in the introduction to this volume, "Bonn is not Weimar" because West German leaders have resolved not to permit history to repeat itself.

The maintenance of *das Modell Deutschland* is not without its political and social costs. One external consequence is that efforts by leaders of the mainstream parties to ensure the survival of the Federal Republic through membership in the European Community and NATO effectively preclude German

reunification in the face of the DDR's parallel divergence as a "developed socialist society" allied with the Soviet Union.[2] Domestically, the *Berufsverbot* of
1972 and the antiterrorist legislation later in the decade, both of which were
implemented to protect the West German state and its citizens from ideological
assaults primarily from the left, have posed serious constitutional and philosophical questions about the limits of legitimate rights of dissent in modern
democratic society.[3] Continuing efforts by government officials and the police
to contain ideological criticism and terrorist activities have generated a dis-
cernibly more conformist public atmosphere in the Federal Republic today than
was true in the late 1960s and early 1970s—much to the consternation of liber-
tarians both in Germany and abroad.[4]

Yet the German model is by no means impervious to change. At strategic
postwar junctures, political leaders have introduced important innovations that
testify to institutional responsiveness and adaptability in the Federal Republic. A
leading example is the 1967 Law for Promoting Economic Stability and Growth,
which provided the statutory basis for the introduction of corporatist policy-
making linkages that facilitated Germany's economic expansion during the late
1960s and much of the 1970s. Equally significant, policy makers proved responsive to domestic sociopolitical critics when they implemented a variety of educational reforms during the 1960s and extended worker representation on company
boards with the adoption of the codetermination act of 1976. More recently,
electoral gains by the Greens have prompted the mainstream parties to become
more environmentally conscious and helped induce the federal government to
establish a new ministry of the environment in 1986, as noted in chapter 5.

Whether *das Modell Deutschland* can survive in the decades ahead will
depend on multiple factors. A minimum condition is the maintenance of stable
executive leadership. This requires in turn cohesive governing coalitions and
elite-public confidence in the competence of the chancellor and other key Cabinet officials. As long as a legislative majority in the form of a hypothetical SPD-
Green coalition remains elusive (and improbable), the FDP will continue to
play its crucial role in determining the political composition of the federal Cabinet. The Free Democrats will predictably continue to ally themselves nationally
with the Christian Democrats until at least the next scheduled Bundestag election in 1990, but changed political and/or economic conditions could conceivably prompt them to renew a coalition with the Social Democrats in the
more distant future. A possible harbinger of such a shift was the formation
of an SPD-FDP government in Hamburg in August 1987.

A second necessary condition for the future viability of the German model
is continued economic growth. Through the late 1980s, West Germany succeeded in maintaining a modest level of growth (averaging just over 2.0 percent

annually between 1986 and 1988) and an inflation rate of less than 0.1 percent. Whether growth will continue at a satisfactory rate through the 1990s is dependent, first, on the domestic and external effects of the attainment of a fully integrated European Community by the targeted year of 1992. A unified regional market offers the promise of industrial expansion to West German (and other European) firms, but lower labor costs in Spain, Portugal, and elsewhere on the EEC periphery may divert manufacturing away from the German heartland. The result would be even higher unemployment in the Federal Republic than the 9 percent level of the mid-1980s.

The prospect that unemployment will not only persist at unprecedented postwar levels but might even increase underscores the importance of labor-market conditions as a third factor pertaining to the survival of the German model. The mainstream parties, employer groups, and the DGB and its member unions jointly affirm a policy of maximum employment but, as recounted in chapters 5 and 6, they differ on basic strategies to achieve it. Whereas the CDU/CSU, the FDP, and employers favor a general market approach to economic renewal and employment growth, the SPD and the DGB advocate the need for greater government intervention to encourage industrial expansion and job security. The debate between these alternative strategies underlies much of the recent conflict in the labor market, notably the 1984 steelworkers' strike on behalf of a shorter workweek.

In the short run, the CDU/CSU-FDP's economic and social preferences have prevailed. To promote social peace under conditions of persisting high unemployment, Cabinet officials have continued the earlier SPD practice of informal consultations concerning general economic trends, prices, and wages with leaders of employment groups and unions. Whether such efforts can placate organized labor depends on the willingness of the federal government and employers to retain established codetermination rights and procedures. The longer-term expansion of informal democratic corporatist arrangements into the DGB's ideological vision of an institutionalized system of regional and national economic councils will require the return of the Social Democrats to executive power, backed by a firm parliamentary majority. Such a prospect depends in turn on the complex interplay of ideological, personality, and other factors that are the essence of democratic electoral competition.

Thus, West Germany stands at a critical political and economic crossroad. The alternatives that currently confront decision makers and citizens in the Federal Republic are not as fundamental as those of 1848, 1918, 1933, or 1945. They nonetheless underscore anew the importance of human resolve and policy choice as principal factors of system performance and change.

Notes

1. Norbert Walter, "West Germany's Economy. Origins, Problems, and Perspectives." *German Issues* 5 (Washington, D.C.: American Institute for Contemporary German Studies, 1987), 25.

2. System divergence is emphasized in the various contributions to Lyman H. Legters, ed., *The German Democratic Republic. A Developed Socialist Society* (Boulder, Colo.: Westview, 1978).

3. See Petra Shattuck, "The Impact of Nuclear Power on Civil Liberties: The West German Example," *First Principles. National Security and Civil Liberties* 5, no. 3 (November 1979): 1-5.

4. David Zane Mairowitz, "Scissors in the Head: West Germany's Extreme Reaction to Extremism," *Harper's,* May 1978, 28-31. See also the report on recent efforts by the CSU minister of the interior, Friedrich Zimmermann, to restrict protest demonstrations and increase official surveillance of dissidents in "A Right-Wing Face of Germany," *Economist,* 27 August 1983, 27-28.

Appendix:
The Basic Law*

Preamble

The German People . . .

Conscious of their responsibility before God and men,

Animated by the resolve to preserve their national and political unity and to serve the peace of the world as an equal partner in a united Europe,

Desiring to give a new order to political life for a transitional period,

Have enacted, by virtue of their constituent power, this Basic Law for the Federal Republic of Germany.

They have also acted on behalf of those Germans to whom participation was denied.

The entire German people are called upon to achieve in free self-determination the unity and freedom of Germany.

1. Basic Rights

ARTICLE 1 (PROTECTION OF HUMAN DIGNITY)

1. The dignity of man shall be inviolable. To respect and protect it shall be the duty of all state authority.

2. The German people therefore acknowledge inviolable and inalienable human rights as the basis of every community, of peace, and of justice in the world.

3. The following basic rights shall bind the legislature, the executive, and the judiciary as directly enforceable law.

ARTICLE 2 (RIGHTS OF LIBERTY)

1. Everyone shall have the right to the free development of his personality insofar as he does not violate the rights of others or offend against the con-

---

*Abridged and adapted from Press and Information Office, *The Basic Law of the Federal Republic of Germany* (Bonn, 1987).

stitutional order or the moral code.

2. Everyone shall have the right to life and to inviolability of his person. The liberty of the individual shall be inviolable. These rights may only be encroached upon pursuant to a law.

ARTICLE 3 (EQUALITY BEFORE THE LAW)

1. All persons shall be equal before the law.

2. Men and women shall have equal rights.

3. No one may be prejudiced or favored because of his sex, his parentage, his race, his language, his homeland and origin, his faith, or his religious or political opinions.

ARTICLE 4 (FREEDOM OF FAITH AND CREED)

1. Freedom of faith, of conscience, and freedom of creed, religious or ideological, shall be inviolable.

2. The undisturbed practice of religion is guaranteed.

3. No one may be compelled against his conscience to render war service involving the use of arms. . . .

ARTICLE 5 (FREEDOM OF EXPRESSION)

1. Everyone shall have the right freely to express and disseminate his opinion by speech, writing, and pictures and freely to inform himself from generally accessible sources. Freedom of the press and freedom of reporting by means of broadcasts and films are guaranteed. There shall be no censorship. . . .

3. Art and science, research and teaching, shall be free. Freedom of teaching shall not absolve from loyalty to the constitution.

ARTICLE 6 (MARRIAGE, FAMILY, ILLEGITIMATE CHILDREN)

1. Marriage and family shall enjoy the special protection of the state.

2. The care and upbringing of children are a natural right of, and a duty primarily incumbent on, the parents. . . .

4. Every mother shall be entitled to the protection and care of the community.

5. Illegitimate children shall be provided by legislation with the same opportunities for their physical and spiritual development and their place in society as are enjoyed by legitimate children.

ARTICLE 7 (EDUCATION)

1. The entire educational system shall be under the supervision of the state. . . .

3. Religious instruction shall form part of the ordinary curriculum in state and municipal schools. . . .

ARTICLE 8 (FREEDOM OF ASSEMBLY)

1. All Germans shall have the right to assemble peaceably and unarmed without prior notification or permission. . . .

ARTICLE 9 (FREEDOM OF ASSOCIATION)

1. All Germans shall have the right to form associations and societies.

2. Associations, the purposes or activities of which conflict with criminal laws or which are directed against the constitutional order or the concept of international understanding, are prohibited.

3. The right to form associations to safeguard and improve working and economic conditions is guaranteed to everyone and to all trades, occupations, and professions. . . .

ARTICLE 10 (PRIVACY OF POSTS AND TELECOMMUNICATIONS)

1. Privacy of posts and telecommunications shall be inviolable.

2. This right may be restricted only pursuant to a law. Such law may lay down that the person affected shall not be informed of any such restriction if it serves to protect the free democratic basic order or the existence or security of the Federation or a Land. . . .

ARTICLE 12 (RIGHT TO CHOOSE TRADE, OCCUPATION, OR PROFESSION)

1. All Germans shall have the right freely to choose their trade, occupation, or profession. . . .

ARTICLE 12A (LIABILITY TO MILITARY AND OTHER SERVICE)

1. Men who have attained the age of eighteen years may be required to serve in the armed forces, in the Federal Border Guard, or in a civil defense organization.

2. A person who refuses, on grounds of conscience, to render war service involving the use of arms may be required to render a substitute service. . . .

ARTICLE 13 (INVIOLABILITY OF THE HOME)

1. The home shall be inviolable.

2. Searches may be ordered only by a judge, or, in the event of danger in delay, by other organs as provided by law and may be carried out only in the form prescribed by law. . . .

ARTICLE 14 (PROPERTY, RIGHT OF INHERITANCE, EXPROPRIATION)

1. Property and the right of inheritance are guaranteed. . . .

3. Expropriation shall be permitted only in the public weal. It may be effected only by or pursuant to a law that shall provide for the nature and extent of the compensation. . . .

ARTICLE 15 (SOCIALIZATION)

Land, natural resources, and means of production may for the purpose of socialization be transferred to public ownership or other forms of publicly controlled economy by a law that shall provide for the nature and extent of compensation. . .

ARTICLE 19 (RESTRICTION OF BASIC RIGHTS)

1. Insofar as a basic right may, under this Basic Law, be restricted by or pursuant to a law, such law must apply generally and not solely to an individual case. . . .

2. The Federation and the Constituent States (Länder)

ARTICLE 20 (BASIC PRINCIPLES OF THE CONSTITUTION)

1. The Federal Republic of Germany is a democratic and social federal state.

2. All state authority emanates from the people. It shall be exercised by the people by means of elections and voting and by specific legislative, executive, and judicial organs.

3. Legislation shall be subject to the constitutional order; the executive and the judiciary shall be bound by law and justice.

4. All Germans shall have the right to resist any person or persons seeking to abolish that constitutional order, should no other remedy be possible.

ARTICLE 21 (POLITICAL PARTIES)

1. The political parties shall participate in the forming of the political will of the people. They may be freely established. Their internal organization must conform to democratic principles. . . .

2. Parties that, by reason of their aims or the behavior of their adherents, seek to impair or abolish the free democratic basic order or to endanger the existence of the Federal Republic of Germany, shall be unconstitutional. The Federal Constitutional Court shall decide on the question of unconstitutionality. . . .

ARTICLE 28 (FEDERAL GUARANTEE OF LÄNDER CONSTITUTIONS)

1. The constitutional order in the Länder must conform to the principles of republican, democratic, and social government based on the rule of law, within the meaning of this Basic Law. In each of the Länder, counties *(Kreise)*, and communes *(Gemeinden)*, the people must be represented by a body chosen in general, direct, free, equal, and secret elections. . . .

2. The communes must be guaranteed the right to regulate on their own responsibility all the affairs of the local community within the limits set by law. . . .

ARTICLE 30 (FUNCTIONS OF THE LÄNDER)

The exercise of governmental powers and the discharge of governmental functions shall be incumbent on the Länder insofar as this Basic Law does not otherwise prescribe or permit.

ARTICLE 31 (PRIORITY OF FEDERAL LAW)

Federal law shall override Land law. . . .

3. The Federal Parliament (Bundestag)

ARTICLE 38 (ELECTIONS)

1. The deputies to the German Bundestag shall be elected in general, direct, free, equal, and secret elections. They shall be representatives of the whole people, not bound by orders and instructions, and shall be subject only to their conscience. . . .

3. Details shall be regulated by a federal law.

ARTICLE 39 (ASSEMBLY AND LEGISLATIVE TERM)

1. The Bundestag shall be elected for a four-year term. . . .

ARTICLE 40 (PRESIDENT, RULES OF PROCEDURE)

1. The Bundestag shall elect its president, vice presidents, and secretaries. It shall draw up its rules of procedure. . . .

ARTICLE 43 (PRESENCE OF THE FEDERAL GOVERNMENT)

1. The Bundestag and its committees may demand the presence of any member of the federal government.

2. The members of the Bundesrat or of the federal government as well as persons commissioned by them shall have access to all meetings of the Bun-

destag and its committees. They must be heard at any time.

ARTICLE 44 (COMMITTEES OF INVESTIGATION)

1. The Bundestag shall have the right, and upon the motion of one-fourth of its members the duty, to set up a committee of investigation that shall take the requisite evidence at public hearings. The public may be excluded. . . .

ARTICLE 45B (DEFENSE COMMISSIONER OF THE BUNDESTAG)

A defense commissioner *(Wehrbeauftragter)* of the Bundestag shall be appointed to safeguard the basic rights and to assist the Bundestag in exercising parliamentary control. . . .

ARTICLE 45C (PETITIONS COMMITTEE)

1. The Bundestag shall appoint a petitions committee to deal with requests and complaints addressed to the Bundestag pursuant to Article 17. . . .

4. The Bundesrat

ARTICLE 50 (FUNCTION)

The Länder shall participate through the Bundesrat in the legislation and administration of the Federation.

ARTICLE 51 (COMPOSITION)

1. The Bundesrat shall consist of members of the Land governments that appoint and recall them. . . .

2. Each Land shall have at least three votes; Länder with more than 2 million inhabitants shall have 4, Länder with more than 6 million inhabitants five votes.

3. Each Land may delegate as many members as it has votes. The votes of each Land may be cast only as a block vote and only by members present or their substitutes. . . .

ARTICLE 53 (PARTICIPATION OF THE FEDERAL GOVERNMENT)

The members of the federal government shall have the right, and on demand the duty, to attend the meetings of the Bundesrat and of its committees. They must be heard at any time. The Bundesrat must be currently kept informed by the federal government of the conduct of affairs.

4a. The Joint Committee

ARTICLE 53A

1. Two-thirds of the members of the Joint Committee shall be deputies of the Bundestag and one-third shall be members of the Bundesrat. The Bundestag shall delegate its deputies in proportion to the sizes of its parliamentary groups; such deputies must not be members of the federal government. Each Land shall be represented by a Bundesrat member of its choice; these members shall not be bound by instructions. . . .

2. The federal government must inform the Joint Committee about its plans in respect of a state of defense. The rights of the Bundestag and its committees under paragraph 1 of Article 43 shall not be affected by the provision of this paragraph.

5. The Federal President

ARTICLE 54 (ELECTION BY THE FEDERAL ASSEMBLY)

1. The federal president shall be elected, without debate, by the Federal Assembly *(Bundesversammlung)*. . . .

2. The term of the office of the federal president shall be five years. Re-election for a consecutive term shall be permitted only once.

3. The Federal Assembly shall consist of the members of the Bundestag and an equal number of members elected by the diets of the Länder. . . .

ARTICLE 58 (COUNTERSIGNATURE)

Orders and decrees of the federal president shall require for their validity the countersignature of the federal chancellor or the appropriate federal minister. . . .

ARTICLE 59 (AUTHORITY TO REPRESENT THE FEDERATION IN INTERNATIONAL RELATIONS)

1. The federal president shall represent the Federation in its international relations. He shall conclude treaties with foreign states on behalf of the Federation. He shall accredit and receive envoys. . . .

ARTICLE 60 (APPOINTMENT OF FEDERAL CIVIL SERVANTS AND OFFICERS)

1. The federal president shall appoint and dismiss the federal judges, the federal civil servants, the officers and noncommissioned officers, unless otherwise provided for by law.

2. He shall exercise the right of pardon in individual cases on behalf of the Federation.

3. He may delegate these powers to other authorities. . .

ARTICLE 61 (IMPEACHMENT)

1. The Bundestag or the Bundesrat may impeach the federal president before the Federal Constitutional Court for willful violation of this Basic Law or any other federal law. The motion for impeachment must be brought forward by at least one-fourth of the members of the Bundestag or one-fourth of the votes of the Bundesrat. The decision to impeach shall require a majority of two thirds of the members of the Bundestag or of two-thirds of the votes of the Bundesrat. . . .

2. If the Federal Constitutional Court finds the federal president guilty of a willful violation of this Basic Law or of another federal law, it may declare him to have forfeited his office. . . .

6. The Federal Government

ARTICLE 62 (COMPOSITION)

The federal government shall consist of the federal chancellor and the federal ministers.

ARTICLE 63 (ELECTION OF THE FEDERAL CHANCELLOR—DISSOLUTION OF THE BUNDESTAG)

1. The federal chancellor shall be elected, without debate, by the Bundestag upon the proposal of the federal president.

2. The person obtaining the votes of the majority of the members of the Bundestag shall be elected. The person elected must be appointed by the federal president.

3. If the person proposed is not elected, the Bundestag may elect within 14 days of the ballot a federal chancellor by more than one-half of its members.

4. If no candidate has been elected within this period, a new ballot shall take place without delay, in which the person obtaining the largest number of votes shall be elected. If the person elected has obtained the votes of the majority of the members of the Bundestag, the federal president must appoint him within 7 days of the election. If the person elected did not obtain such a majority, the federal president must within 7 days either appoint him or dissolve the Bundestag.

ARTICLE 64 (APPOINTMENT OF FEDERAL MINISTERS)

1. The federal ministers shall be appointed and dismissed by the federal president upon the proposal of the federal chancellor. . . .

ARTICLE 65 (DISTRIBUTION OF RESPONSIBILITY)

1. The federal chancellor shall determine, and be responsible for, the general policy guidelines. Within the limits set by these guidelines, each federal minister shall conduct the affairs of his department autonomously and on his own responsibility. . . .

ARTICLE 65A (POWER OF COMMAND OVER ARMED FORCES)

Power of command in respect of the armed forces shall be vested in the federal minister of defense. . . .

ARTICLE 67 (VOTE OF NO-CONFIDENCE)

1. The Bundestag can express its lack of confidence in the federal chancellor only by electing a successor with the majority of its members and by requesting the federal president to dismiss the federal chancellor. The federal president must comply with the request and appoint the person elected. . . .

ARTICLE 68 (VOTE OF CONFIDENCE — DISSOLUTION OF THE BUNDESTAG)

1. If a motion of the federal chancellor for a vote of confidence is not assented to by the majority of the members of the Bundestag, the federal president may, upon the proposal of the federal chancellor, dissolve the Bundestag within 21 days. . . .

7. Legislative Powers of the Federation

ARTICLE 70 (LEGISLATION OF THE FEDERATION AND THE LÄNDER)

1. The Länder shall have the right to legislate insofar as this Basic Law does not confer legislative power on the Federation.

2. The division of competence between the Federation and the Länder shall be determined by the provision of this Basic Law concerning exclusive and concurrent legislative powers. . . .

ARTICLE 72 (CONCURRENT LEGISLATION OF THE FEDERATION, DEFINITION)

1. In matters within concurrent legislative powers the Länder shall have power to legislate as long as, and to the extent that, the Federation does not exercise its right to legislate.

2. The Federation shall have the right to legislate in these matters to the extent that a need for regulation by federal legislation exists because:

1. a matter cannot be effectively regulated by the legislation of individual Länder, or

2. the regulation of a matter by a Land law might prejudice the interests of other Länder or of the people as a whole, or

3. the maintenance of legal or economic unity, especially the maintenance of uniformity of living conditions beyond the territory of any one Land, necessitates such regulation.

ARTICLE 73 (EXCLUSIVE LEGISLATION)

The Federation shall have exclusive power to legislate in the following matters:

1. foreign affairs as well as defense including the protection of the civilian population;

2. citizenship in the Federation

3. freedom of movement, passport matters, immigration, emigration, and extradition;

4. currency, money and coinage, weights and measures, as well as the determination of standards of time;

5. the unity of the customs and commercial territory, treaties on commerce and on navigation, the freedom of movement of goods, and the exchanges of goods and payments with foreign countries, including customs and other frontier protection;

6. federal railroads and air transport;

7. postal and telecommunication services;

8. the legal status of persons employed by the Federation and by federal corporate bodies under public law;

9. industrial property rights, copyrights and publishers' rights;

10. cooperation of the Federation and the Länder in matters of

a. criminal police,

b. protection of the free democratic basic order, of the existence and security of the Federation or of a Land (protection of the constitution) and

c. protection against efforts in the federal territory that, by the use of force or actions in preparation for the use of force, endanger the foreign interests of the Federal Republic of Germany,

as well as the establishment of a Federal Criminal Police Office and the international control of crime. . . .

ARTICLE 74 (CONCURRENT LEGISLATION)

Concurrent legislative powers shall extend to the following matters:

1. civil law, criminal law, and execution of sentences, the organization and procedure of courts, the legal profession, notaries, and legal advice;

2. registration of births, deaths, and marriages;
3. the law of association and assembly;
4. the law relating to residence and establishment of aliens;
4a. the law relating to weapons and explosives;
5. the protection of German cultural treasures against removal abroad;
6. refugees and expellee matters;
7. public welfare;
8. citizenship in the Länder;
9. war damage and reparations;

10. benefits to war-disabled persons and to dependents of those killed in the war as well as assistance to former prisoners of war;

10a. war graves of soldiers, graves of other victims of war and of victims of despotism;

11. the law relating to economic matters (mining, industry, supply of power, crafts, trades, commerce, banking, stock exchanges, and private insurance);

11a. the production and utilization of nuclear energy for peaceful purposes, the construction and operation of installations serving such purposes, protection against hazards arising from the release of nuclear energy or from ionizing radiation, and the disposal of radioactive substances;

12. labor law, including the legal organization of enterprises, protection of workers, employment exchanges and agencies, as well as social insurance, including unemployment insurance;

13. the regulation of educational and training grants and the promotion of scientific research;

14. the law regarding expropriation. . . .

15. transfer of land, natural resources, and means of production to public ownership or other forms of publicly controlled economy;

16. prevention of the abuse of economic power;

17. promotion of agricultural and forest production. . . .

18. real estate transactions, land law and matters concerning agricultural leases, as well as housing, settlement, and homestead matters. . . .

19. measures against human and animal diseases that are communicable or otherwise endanger public health. . . .

22. road traffic, motor transport, construction and maintenance of long-distance highways. . . .

24. waste disposal, air purification, and noise abatement. . . .

ARTICLE 75 (GENERAL PROVISIONS OF THE FEDERATION)

Subject to the conditions laid down in Article 72, the Federation shall have the right to enact skeleton provision concerning:

1. the legal status of persons in the public service of the Länder, communes, or other corporate bodies under public law. . . .

1a. the general principles governing higher education; . . .

3. hunting, nature conservation, and landscape management.

4. land distribution, regional planning, and water regime;

5. matters relating to the registration of changes of residence or domicile. . . .

ARTICLE 76 (BILLS)

1. Bills shall be introduced in the Bundestag by the federal government or by members of the Bundestag or by the Bundesrat.

2. Bills of the federal government shall be submitted first to the Bundesrat. . . .

3. Bills of the Bundesrat shall be submitted to the Bundestag by the federal government within three months. In doing so, the federal government must state its own views.

ARTICLE 77 (PROCEDURE CONCERNING ADOPTED BILLS — OBJECTION OF THE BUNDESRAT)

1. Bills intended to become federal laws shall require adoption by the Bundestag. Upon their adoption they shall, without delay, be transmitted to the Bundesrat by the president of the Bundestag.

2. The Bundesrat may, within three weeks of the receipt of the adopted bill, demand that a committee for joint consideration of bills, composed of members of the Bundestag and members of the Bundesrat, be convened. . . . If the consent of the Bundesrat is required for a bill to become a law, the convening of this committee may also be demanded by the Bundestag or the federal government. . . .

3. Insofar as the consent of the Bundesrat is not required for a bill to become law, the Bundesrat may . . . enter an objection within two weeks against a bill adopted by the Bundestag. . . .

4. If the objection was adopted with the majority of the votes of the Bundesrat, it can be rejected by a decision of the majority of the members of the Bundestag. If the Bundesrat adopted the objection with a majority of at least two-thirds of its votes, its rejection by the Bundestag shall require a majority of two-thirds. . . .

ARTICLE 78 (CONDITION FOR PASSING OF FEDERAL LAWS)

A bill adopted by the Bundestag shall become a law if the Bundesrat consents to it, or fails to make a demand pursuant to paragraph 2 of Article 77, or fails to enter an objection, . . . or if the objection is overriden by the Bundestag.

ARTICLE 79 (AMENDMENT OF THE BASIC LAW)

1. This Basic Law can be amended only by laws that expressly amend or supplement the text thereof. . . .

2. Any such law shall require the affirmative vote of two-thirds of the mem-

bers of the Bundestag and two-thirds of the votes of the Bundesrat.

3. Amendments . . . affecting the division of the Federation into Länder, the participation on principle of the Länder in legislation, or the basic principles laid down in Articles 1 and 20 shall be inadmissible.

ARTICLE 80 (ISSUE OF ORDINANCES HAVING FORCE OF LAW)

1. The federal government, a federal minister, or the Land governments may be authorized by a law to issue ordinances having the force of law *(Rechtsverordnungen)*. . . .

2. The consent of the Bundesrat shall be required, unless otherwise provided by federal legislation, for ordinances having the force of law issued by the federal government or a federal minister concerning basic rules for the use of facilities of the federal railroads and of postal and telecommunication services. . . .

ARTICLE 80A (STATE OF TENSION)

1. Where this Basic Law or a federal law on defense, including the protection of the civilian population, stipulates that legal provisions may only be applied in accordance with this article, their application shall, except when a state of defense exists, be admissible only after the Bundestag has determined that a state of tension *(Spannungsfall)* exists or if it has specifically approved such application. . . . (Such) determination of a state of tension and such specific approval shall require a two-thirds majority of the votes cast.

2. Any measures taken by virtue of legal provisions enacted under paragraph 1 of this article shall be revoked whenever the Bundestag so requests.

3. In derogation of paragraph 1 of this article, the application of such legal provisions shall also be admissible by virtue of, and in accordance with, a decision taken with the consent of the federal government by an international organ within the framework of a treaty of alliance. Any measures taken pursuant to this paragraph shall be revoked whenever the Bundestag so requests with the majority of its members.

ARTICLE 81 (STATE OF LEGISLATIVE EMERGENCY)

1. Should, in the circumstances of Article 68, the Bundestag not be dissolved, the federal president may, at the request of the federal government and with the consent of the Bundesrat, declare a state of legislative emergency with respect to a bill, if the Bundestag rejects the bill although the federal government has declared it to be urgent. The same shall apply if a bill has been rejected although the federal chancellor had combined with it the motion under Article 68.

2. If, after a state of legislative emergency has been declared, the Bundestag again rejects the bill or adopts it in a version stated to be unacceptable to the federal government, the bill shall be deemed to have become a law to the extent that the Bundesrat consents to it. . . .

3. During the term of office of a federal chancellor, any other bill rejected by the Bundestag may become a law in accordance with paragraphs 1 and 2 of this Article within a period of six months after the first declaration of a state of legislative emergency. After the expiration of this period, a further declaration of a state of legislative emergency shall be inadmissable during the term of office of the same federal chancellor.

4. This Basic Law may not be amended nor repealed nor suspended in whole or in part by a law enacted pursuant to paragraph 2 of this Article. . . .

8. The Execution of Federal Laws and the Federal Administration

ARTICLE 83 (EXECUTION OF FEDERAL LAWS BY THE LÄNDER)
The Länder shall execute federal laws as matters of their own concern insofar as this Basic Law does not otherwise provide or permit. . . .

ARTICLE 85 (EXECUTION BY LÄNDER AS AGENTS OF THE FEDERATION)
1. Where the Länder execute federal laws as agents of the Federation, the establishment of the requisite authorities shall remain the concern of the Länder except insofar as federal laws consented to by the Bundesrat otherwise provide. . . .

ARTICLE 87 (MATTERS OF DIRECT FEDERAL ADMINISTRATION)
1. The foreign service, the federal finance administration, the federal railroads, the federal postal service, and . . . the administration of federal waterways and of shipping shall be conducted as matters of direct federal administration with their own administrative substructures. . . .

2. Social insurance institutions whose sphere of competence extends beyond the territory of one Land shall be administered as federal corporate bodies under public law. . . .

ARTICLE 87A (BUILD-UP, STRENGTH, AND FUNCTIONS OF THE ARMED FORCES)
1. The Federation shall build up armed forces for defense purposes. . . .

2. Apart from defense, the armed forces may be used only to the extent explicitly permitted by this Basic Law.

3. While a state of defense or a state of tension exists, the armed forces

shall have the power to protect civilian property and discharge functions of traffic control insofar as this is necessary for the performance of their defense mission. Moreover, the armed forces may, when a state of defense or a state of tension exists, be entrusted with the protection of civilian property in support of police measures. . . .

ARTICLE 88 (FEDERAL BANK)
The Federation shall establish a note-issuing and currency bank as the Federal Bank *(Bundesbank)*. . . .

8a. Joint Tasks

ARTICLE 91A (DEFINITION OF JOINT TASKS)
1. The Federation shall participate in the discharge of the following responsibilities of the Länder, provided that such responsibilities are important to society as a whole and that federal participation is necessary for the improvement of living conditions . . .:

> 1. extension and construction of institutions of higher education including university clinics;
> 2. improvement of regional economic structures;
> 3. improvement of the agrarian structure and of coast preservation.

2. Joint tasks shall be defined in detail by federal legislation requiring the consent of the Bundesrat. . . .

ARTICLE 91B (COOPERATION OF FEDERATION AND LÄNDER IN EDUCATIONAL PLANNING AND RESEARCH)
The Federation and the Länder may . . . cooperate in educational planning and in the promotion of institutions and projects of scientific research of supraregional importance. . . .

9. The Administration of Justice

ARTICLE 92 (COURT ORGANIZATION)
Judicial power shall be vested in the judges; it shall be exercised by the Federal Constitutional Court, by the federal courts provided for in this Basic Law, and by the courts of the Länder.

ARTICLE 93 (FEDERAL CONSTITUTIONAL COURT, COMPETENCY)
1. The Federal Constitutional Court shall decide:

1. on the interpretation of this Basic Law in the event of disputes concerning the extent of the rights and duties of a highest federal organ or of other parties concerned who have been vested with rights of their own by this Basic Law or by rules of procedure of a highest federal organ;
2. in case of differences of opinion or doubts on the formal and material compatibility of federal law or Land law with this Basic Law, or on the compatibility of Land law with other federal law, at the request of the federal government, of a Land government, or of one-third of the Bundestag members;
3. in case of differences of opinion on the rights and duties of the Federation and the Länder, particularly in the execution of federal law by the Länder and in the exercise of federal supervision;
4. on other disputes involving public law, between the Federation and the Länder, between different Länder or within a Land, unless recourse to another court exists;
4a. on complaints of unconstitutionality, which may be entered by any person who claims that one of his basic rights . . . has been violated by public authority;
4b. on complaints of unconstitutionality, entered by communes or associations of communes on the ground that their right to self-government under Article 28 has been violated by a law other than a Land law open to complaint to the respective Land constitutional court;
5. in the other cases provided for in this Basic Law.

2. The Federal Constitutional Court shall also act in such other cases as are assigned to it by federal legislation.

ARTICLE 94 (FEDERAL CONSTITUTIONAL COURT, COMPOSITION)
1. The Federal Constitutional Court shall consist of federal judges and other members. Half of the members . . . shall be elected by the Bundestag and half by the Bundesrat. . . .

ARTICLE 95 (HIGHEST COURTS OF JUSTICE)
1. For the purposes of ordinary, administrative, fiscal, labor, and social jurisdiction, the Federation shall establish as highest courts of justice the Federal Court of Justice, the Federal Administrative Court, the Federal Fiscal Court, the Federal Labor Court, and the Federal Social Court. . . .
2. The judges of each of these courts shall be selected jointly by the competent federal minister and a committee for the selection of judges consisting of the competent Land ministers and an equal number of members elected by the Bundestag. . . .

ARTICLE 97 (INDEPENDENCE OF THE JUDGES)

    1. The judges shall be independent and subject only to the law. . . .

10. Finance

ARTICLE 104A (APPORTIONMENT OF EXPENDITURES)

    1. The Federation and the Länder shall meet separately the expenditures resulting from the discharge of their respective tasks insofar as this Basic Law does not provide otherwise.

    2. Where the Länder act as agents of the Federation, the Federation shall meet the resulting expenditures. . . .

    4. The Federation may grant the Länder financial assistance for particularly important investments by the Länder or communes or associations of communes, provided that such investments are necessary to avert a disturbance of the overall economic equilibrium or to equalize differences of economic capacities within the federal territory or to promote economic growth. . . .

ARTICLE 106 (APPORTIONMENT OF TAX REVENUES)

    1. The yield of fiscal monopolies and the revenues from the following taxes shall accrue to the Federation:

    1. customs duties,
    2. excise taxes insofar as they do not accrue to the Länder. . . or jointly to the Federation and the Länder . . . or to the communes. . . . .
    3. the road freight tax,
    4. the capital transfer taxes, the insurance tax, and the tax on drafts and bills of exchange,
    5. nonrecurrent levies on property, . . .
    6. income and corporation surtaxes,
    7. charges imposed within the framework of the European Communities.

    2. Revenues from the following taxes shall accrue to the Länder:

    1. property (net worth) tax,
    2. inheritance tax,
    3. motor-vehicle tax,
    4. such taxes on transactions as do not accrue to the Federation pursuant to paragraph 1 of this article or jointly to the Federation and the Länder pursuant to paragraph 3 of this article,
    5. beer tax,
    6. taxes on gambling establishments.

3. Revenues from income taxes, corporation taxes, and turnover taxes shall accrue jointly to the Federation and the Länder (joint taxes) to the extent that the revenues from income tax are not allocated to the communes pursuant to paragraph 5 of this article. The Federation and the Länder shall share equally the revenues from income taxes and corporation taxes. . . .

5. A share of the revenues from income tax shall accrue to the communes, to be passed on by the Länder to their communes on the basis of income taxes paid by the inhabitants of the latter. . . .

6. Revenues from taxes on real property and businesses shall accrue to the communes; revenues from local excise taxes shall accrue to the communes. . . . Communes shall be authorized to assess the communal percentages of taxes on real property and businesses within the framework of existing laws. . . .

7. An overall percentage, to be determined by Land legislation, of the Land share of total revenues from joint taxes shall accrue to the communes and associations of communes. . . .

ARTICLE 107 (FINANCIAL EQUALIZATION)

1. Revenues from Land taxes and the Land share of revenues from income and corporation taxes shall accrue to the individual Länder to the extent that such taxes are collected by revenue authorities within their respective territories (local revenues). . . .

2. Federal legislation shall ensure a reasonable equalization between financially strong and financially weak Länder. . . . Such legislation may also provide for grants to be made by the Federation from federal funds to financially weak Länder. . . .

ARTICLE 110 (BUDGET OF THE FEDERATION)

1. All revenues and expenditures of the Federation shall be included in the budget. . . . The budget must be balanced. . . .

2. The budget shall be established by means of a law covering one year or several fiscal years separately before the beginning of the first of those fiscal years. . . .

3. Bills within the meaning of the first sentence of paragraph 2 of this article as well as bills to amend the budget law and the budget shall be submitted simultaneously to the Bundesrat and to the Bundestag. . . .

ARTICLE 112 (EXPENDITURES IN EXCESS OF BUDGETARY ESTIMATES)

Expenditures in excess of budgetary appropriations and extrabudgetary expenditures shall require the consent of the federal minister of finance. Such consent may be given only in the case of an unforeseen and compelling necessity. . . .

10a. State of Defense

ARTICLE 115A (DETERMINATION OF A STATE OF DEFENSE)

1. The determination that the federal territory is being attacked by armed force or that such an attack is directly imminent (state of defense) shall be made by the Bundestag with the consent of the Bundesrat. Such determination shall be made at the request of the federal government and shall require a two-thirds majority of the votes cast. . . .

2. If the situation imperatively calls for immediate action and if insurmountable obstacles prevent the timely meeting of the Bundestag, or if there is no quorum in the Bundestag, the Joint Committee shall make this determination with a two-thirds majority of the votes cast. . . .

3. The determination shall be promulgated in the *Bundesgesetzblatt* (Federal Law Gazette) by the federal president. . . . If this cannot be done in time, the promulgation shall be effected in another manner. . . .

4. If the federal territory is being attacked by armed force and if the competent organs of the Federation are not in a position at once to make the determination provided for in the first sentence of paragraph 1 of this article, such determination shall be deemed to have been made and promulgated at the time the attack began. The federal president shall announce such time as soon as circumstances permit.

5. When the determination of the existence of a state of defense has been promulgated and if the federal territory is being attacked by armed force, the federal president may, with the consent of the Bundestag, issue internationally valid declarations regarding the existence of such state of defense. Subject to the conditions mentioned in paragraph 2 of this article, the Joint Committee shall thereupon deputize for the Bundestag.

ARTICLE 115B (POWER OF COMMAND DURING STATE OF DEFENSE)

Upon the promulgation of a state of defense, the power of command over the armed forces shall pass to the federal chancellor.

ARTICLE 115C (LEGISLATIVE COMPETENCE OF THE FEDERATION DURING STATE OF DEFENSE)

1. The Federation shall have the right to exercise concurrent jurisdiction even in matters belonging to the legislative competence of the Länder by enacting laws to be applicable upon the occurrence of a state of defense. Such laws shall require the consent of the Bundesrat.

2. Federal legislation to be applicable upon the occurrence of a state of defense . . . may make provision for:

1. preliminary compensation to be made in the event of expropriations, . . .
2. deprivations of liberty for a period not exceeding four days, if no judge has been able to act within the period applying in normal times. . . .

3. Federal legislation to be applicable upon the occurrence of a state of defense to the extent required for averting an existing or directly imminent attack, may, subject to the consent of the Bundesrat, regulate the administration and the fiscal system of the Federation and the Länder in divergence from sections 8, 8a, and 10, provided that the viability of the Länder, communes, and associations of communes is safeguarded, particularly in fiscal matters. . . .

ARTICLE 115D (SHORTENED PROCEDURE IN THE CASE OF URGENT BILLS DURING STATE OF DEFENSE)

1. While a state of defense exists, the provisions of paragraphs 2 and 3 of this article shall apply in respect of federal legislation. . . .
2. Bills submitted as urgent by the federal government shall be forwarded to the Bundesrat at the same time as they are submitted to the Bundestag. The Bundestag and the Bundesrat shall debate such bills in common without delay. Insofar as the consent of the Bundesrat is necessary, the majority of its votes shall be required for any such bill to become a law. . . .
3. The second sentence of paragraph 3 of Article 115a shall apply mutatis mutandis in respect of the promulgation of such laws.

ARTICLE 115E (STATUS AND FUNCTIONS OF THE JOINT COMMITTEE)

1. If, while a state of defense exists, the Joint Committee determines with a two-thirds majority of the votes cast, . . . that insurmountable obstacles prevent the timely meeting of the Bundestag, or that there is no quorum in the Bundestag, the Joint Committee shall have the status of both the Bundestag and the Bundesrat and shall exercise their rights as one body.
2. The Joint Committee may not enact any law to amend this Basic Law or to deprive it of effect or application either in whole or in part. . . .

ARTICLE 115F (EXTRAORDINARY POWERS OF THE FEDERATION DURING STATE OF DEFENSE)

1. While a state of defense exists, the federal government may to the extent necessitated by circumstances:

1. commit the federal Border Guard throughout the federal territory;
2. issue instructions not only to federal administrative authorities but also to Land governments and, if it deems the matter urgent, to Land authorities, and may delegate this power to members of Land governments to be designated by it.

2. The Bundestag, the Bundesrat, and the Joint Committee shall be informed without delay of the measures taken in accordance with paragraph 1 of this article.

ARTICLE 115G (STATUS AND FUNCTIONS OF THE FEDERAL CONSTITUTIONAL COURT DURING STATE OF DEFENSE)

The constitutional status and the exercise of the constitutional functions of the Federal Constitutional Court and its judges must not be impaired. The law on the Federal Constitutional Court may not be amended by a law enacted by the Joint Committee except insofar as such amendment is required, also in the opinion of the Federal Constitutional Court, to maintain the capability of the court to function. Pending the enactment of such a law, the Federal Constitutional Court may take such measures as are necessary to maintain the capability of the Court to carry out its work. Any decisions by the Federal Constitutional Court in pursuance of the second and third sentences of this article shall require a two-thirds majority of the judges present.

ARTICLE 115H (LEGISLATIVE TERMS AND TERMS OF OFFICE DURING STATE OF DEFENSE)

1. Any legislative terms of the Bundestag or of Land diets due to expire while a state of defense exists shall end six months after the termination of such state of defense. A term of office of the federal president due to expire while a state of defense exists . . . shall end nine months after the termination of such state of defense. The term of office of a member of the Federal Constitutional Court due to expire while a state of defense exists shall end six months after the termination of such state of defense.

2. Should the necessity arise for the Joint Committee to elect a new federal chancellor, the committee shall do so with the majority of its members; the federal president shall propose a candidate to the Joint Committee. The Joint Committee can express its lack of confidence in the federal chancellor only by electing a successor with a two-thirds majority of its members.

3. The Bundestag shall not be dissolved while a state of defense exists. . . .

ARTICLE 115L (REPEALING OF EXTRAORDINARY LAWS, TERMINATION OF STATE OF DEFENSE, CONCLUSION OF PEACE)

1. The Bundestag, with the consent of the Bundesrat, may at any time repeal laws enacted by the Joint Committee. The Bundesrat may request the Bundestag to make a decision in any such matter. Any measures taken by the Joint Committee or the federal government shall be revoked if the Bundestag and the Bundesrat so decide.

2. The Bundestag, with the consent of the Bundesrat, may at any time declare the state of defense terminated by a decision to be promulgated by the federal president. The Bundestag may request the Bundesrat to make a decision in any such matter. The state of defense must be declared terminated without delay when the prerequisites for the determination thereof no longer exist.

3. The conclusion of peace shall be the subject of a federal law.

11. Transitional and Concluding Provisions

ARTICLE 146 (DURATION OF VALIDITY OF THE BASIC LAW)
This Basic Law shall cease to be in force on the day on which a constitution adopted by a free decision of the German people comes into force.

For Further Reading

ABERBACH, JOEL; PUTNAM, ROBERT D.; and ROCKMAN, BERT A. *Bureaucrats and Politics in Western Democracies.* Cambridge: Harvard University Press, 1981.

ADENAUER, KONRAD. *Erinnerungen 1955-1959.* Stuttgart: Deutsche Verlags-Anstalt, 1967.

_____. *Memoirs 1945-53.* Chicago: Regnery, 1955.

BAKER, KENDALL L.; DALTON, RUSSELL J.; and HILDEBRANDT, KAI. *Germany Transformed: Political Culture and the New Politics.* Cambridge: Harvard University Press, 1981.

BEYME, KLAUS VON. *Gewerkschaften und Arbeitsbeziehungen in kapitalistischen Ländern.* Munich: Piper, 1977.

_____. *Die politische Elite in der Bundesrepublik Deutschland.* Munich: Piper, 1977.

_____. *The Political System of the Federal Republic of Germany.* New York: St. Martin's Press, 1983.

BRACHER, KARL DIETRICH. *Die Auflösung der Weimarer Republik.* Stuttgart: Ring, 1977.

_____. *The German Dictatorship.* New York: Praeger, 1970.

_____; SAUER, WOLFGANG; and SCHULZ, GERHARD. *Die nationalsozialistische Machtergreifung.* Cologne: Westdeutscher Verlag, 1960.

BRANDT, WILLY. *In Exile. Essays, Reflections and Letters 1933-1947.* Philadelphia: University of Pennsylvania Press, 1971.

BRAUNTHAL, GERARD. *The Federation of German Industry in Politics.* Ithaca, N.Y.: Cornell University Press, 1965.

_____. *The West German Legislative Process.* Ithaca, N.Y.: Cornell University Press, 1972.

_____. *The West German Social Democrats, 1969-1982.* Boulder: Westview Press, 1983.

BROWN, BERNARD E., ed. *Eurocommunism and Eurosocialism: The Left Confronts Modernity.* New York: Cyrco Press, 1979.

BULLOCK, ALAN. *Hitler: A Study in Tyranny.* Rev. ed. New York: Harper & Row, 1963.

CAMERON, DAVID R. "The Expansion of the Public Economy: A Comparative Analysis." *American Political Science Review* 62, no. 4 (December 1978): 1243-61.

CERNY, KARL H., ed. *West Germany at the Polls*. Washington, D.C.: American Enterprise Institute, 1978.

CONRADT, DAVID P. "Changing German Political Culture." In *The Civic Culture Revisited*, edited by Gabriel A. Almond and Sidney Verba. Boston: Little, Brown, 1980.

————. *The German Polity*. 3d ed. White Plains, N.Y.: Longman, 1986.

COONEY, JAMES A.; CRAIG, GORDON; SCHWARTZ, HANS PETER; and STERN, FRITZ, eds. *Federal Republic of Germany and the United States: Changing Political, Social, and Economic Relations*. Boulder: Westview Press, 1984.

CRAIG, GORDON A. *Germany, 1866-1945*. New York: Oxford University Press, 1967.

————. *The Politics of the Prussian Army, 1640-1945*. New York: Oxford University Press, 1956.

DAHRENDORF, RALF. *Society and Democracy in Germany*. Garden City, N.Y.: Doubleday, 1967.

DALTON, RUSSELL J. *Citizen Politics in Western Democracies: Public Opinion and Political Parties in the United States, Great Britain, West Germany, and France*. Chatham, N.J.: Chatham House, 1988.

DAVISON, W. PHILLIPS. *The Berlin Blockade: A Study in Cold War Politics*. Princeton: Princeton University Press, 1958.

EDINGER, LEWIS J. *Kurt Schumacher: A Study in Personality and Political Behavior*. Stanford: Stanford University Press, 1965.

FEST, JOACHIM. *Hitler*. New York: Random House, 1975.

FLORA, PETER, and HEIDENHEIMER, ARNOLD J., eds. *The Development of the Welfare State in Europe and America*. New Brunswick: Transaction Books, 1981.

FRIED, ROBERT C. "Party and Policy in West German Cities." *American Political Science Review* 70, no. 1 (January 1976): 11-24.

GAY, PETER. *Weimar Culture. The Outsider as Insider*. New York: Harper & Row, 1970.

GREBING, HELGA. *The History of the German Labour Movement*. London: Oswald Wolff, 1969.

GROSSER, ALFRED. *Germany in Our Time. A Political History of the Postwar Years*. New York: Praeger, 1970.

GUNLICKS, ARTHUR B. "The German Federal System Today: National, State, and Local Relations in an Era of Cooperative Federalism." In *Subnational*

Politics in the 1980s, edited by Louis A. Picard and Raphael Zariski. New York: Praeger, 1987.

HANCOCK, M. DONALD. *The Bundeswehr and the National Peoples Army: A Comparative Study of German Civil-Military Polity.* Denver: University of Denver, 1973.

_____. "Productivity, Welfare, and Participation in Sweden and West Germany." *Comparative Politics* 11 (1978): 4-23.

HANRIEDER, WOLFRAM F. *The Stable Crisis.* New York: Harper & Row, 1970.

_____. *West German Foreign Policy: 1949-1979.* Boulder: Westview Press, 1980.

HARRISON, REGINALD J. *Pluralism and Corporatism.* London: Allen & Unwin, 1980.

HEIDENHEIMER, ARNOLD J. *Adenauer and the CDU.* The Hague: Martinus Nijhoff, 1960.

HIBBS, DOUGLAS A., JR. "Political Parties and Macroeconomic Policy." *American Political Science Review* 5, no. 4 (December 1977): 1467-87.

HISCOCKS, RICHARD. *The Adenauer Era.* Philadelphia: Lippincott, 1966.

INGLEHART, RONALD. *The Silent Revolution.* Princeton: Princeton University Press, 1977.

IRVING, R.E.M. *The Christian Democratic Parties of Western Europe.* London: Allen & Unwin, 1979.

JACOBSEN, HANS-ADOLF. *Nationalsozialistische Aussenpolitik 1933-1938.* Frankfurt: Metzner, 1968.

KATZENSTEIN, PETER J., ed. *Between Power and Plenty: Foreign Economic Policies of Advanced Industrial States.* Madison: University of Wisconsin Press, 1978.

_____. *Policy and Politics in West Germany. The Growth of a Semisovereign State.* Philadelphia: Temple University Press, 1987.

KENDALL, WALTER. *The Labour Movement in Europe.* London: Allen Lane, 1975.

KOLINSKY, EVA, ed. *Opposition in Western Europe.* London: Croom Helm, 1987.

_____. *Parties, Opposition, and Society in West Germany.* New York: St. Martin's Press, 1984.

KOMMERS, DONALD P. *Judicial Politics in West Germany.* Beverly Hills, Calif.: Sage, 1976.

LEHMBRUCH, GERHARD, and SCHMITTER, PHILIPPE C., eds. *Patterns of Corporatist Policy-Making.* Beverly Hills, Calif.: Sage, 1982.

LIJPHART, AREND. *Democracies: Patterns of Majoritarian and Consensus Government in Twenty-One Countries.* New Haven: Yale University Press, 1984.

LOEWENBERG, GERHARD. *Parliament in the German Political System*. Ithaca, N.Y.: Cornell University Press, 1966.

MANN, GOLO. *The History of Germany Since 1789*. New York: Praeger, 1968.

MARKOVITS, ANDREI S., ed. *The Political Economy of West Germany*. New York: Praeger, 1982.

_____. *The Politics of the West German Trade Unions*. New York: Cambridge University Press, 1986.

MAYNTZ, RENATE, and SCHARPF, FRITZ W. *Policy-Making in the German Federal Bureaucracy*. New York: Elsevier, 1975.

MERKL, PETER. *German Foreign Policies, East and West*. Santa Barbara, Calif.: ABC-Clio Press, 1977.

_____. *The Origin of the West German Republic*. New York: Oxford University Press, 1965.

_____, ed. *Western European Party Systems*. New York: Free Press, 1980.

_____. "West German Women: A Long Way from Kinder, Küche, Kirche." In *Women in the World: 1975-1985, the Women's Decade*, edited by Lynne G. Iglitzin and Ruth Ross. Santa Barbara, Calif.: ABC-Clio Press, 1986.

MERRITT, RICHARD L., and MERRITT, ANNA J., eds. *Living with the Wall: West Berlin, 1961-1985*. Durham, N.C.: Duke University Press, 1985.

MOORE, BARRINGTON, JR. *Social Origins of Dictatorship and Democracy*. Boston: Beacon Press, 1966.

NEUMANN, FRANZ. *Behemoth: The Structure and Practice of National Socialism, 1933-1944*. New York: Octagon Books, 1963.

PIKE, FREDERICK, and STRITCH, THOMAS, eds. *The New Corporatism*. Notre Dame, Ind.: Notre Dame University Press, 1974.

SCHMITTER, PHILIPPE C., and LEHMBRUCH, GERHARD, eds. *Trends Toward Corporatist Intermediation*. Beverly Hills, Calif.: Sage, 1979.

SCHORSKE, CARL E. *German Social Democracy, 1905-1917*. New York: Wiley, 1955.

TURNER, HENRY ASHBY, JR. *Stresemann and the Politics of the Weimar Republic*. Princeton: Princeton University Press, 1963.

VERBA, SIDNEY. "The Remaking of Political Culture." In *Political Culture and Political Development*, ed. Lucian Pye and Sidney Verba. Princeton: Princeton University Press, 1965.

WALLACH, H.G. PETER, and ROMOSER, GEORGE K., eds. *West German Politics in the Mid-Eighties*. New York: Praeger, 1985.

WALLICH, HENRY C. *Mainsprings of German Revival*. New Haven: Yale University Press, 1955.

WILDENMANN, RUDOLF. *Partei und Fraktion*. Meisenheim/Glan: Verlag Anton Hain, 1955.

Index